RECONNOITRING CENTRAL ASIA

THE TRANSCASPIAN RAILWAY—THE NOMAD AND THE LOCOMOTIVE. [*Frontispiece.*

RECONNOITRING CENTRAL ASIA

PIONEERING ADVENTURES IN THE REGION LYING BETWEEN RUSSIA AND INDIA

BY

CHARLES MARVIN

Aurthor of "The Russians at Merv and Herat," "The Disastrous Russian Campaign against the Turcomans," "The Russian Advance towards India," "Merv, the Queen of the World," "Grodekoff's Ride to Herat," "The Russian Railway to India," "Our Public Offices," etc.

"I am a great advocate for reconnoitring on all occasions, not only in war, but in peace also."—General Sir Charles MacGregor.

GYAN

Published by

GYAN

Gyan Publishing House
5, Ansari Road
Daryaganj, New Delhi-110002
Phone: 011-47034999, 9811692060
E-mail: books@gyanbooks.com

Distribution Network
gyanbooks.com
India, USA, Canada, UK, Australia, France

ISBN : 978-81-212-3941-7 (PB)
First Published, 1886

2nd Impression 2020

Printed at: Gyan Press, Delhi.

Reconnoitring Central Asia
Author: Charles Marvin

TO

R. RUDDOCK, ESQ.,

EDITOR OF THE "NEWCASTLE DAILY CHRONICLE,"

This work is inscribed

AS A MARK OF PRIVATE ESTEEM AND
PUBLIC RECOGNITION OF THE BROAD AND PATRIOTIC
VIEWS HE HAS ALWAYS ADVOCATED IN REGARD
TO THE POLICY OF ENGLAND IN
THE EAST.

PREFACE.

In the following pages I have attempted to give a popular account of the principal pioneering exploits in the region lying between the Caspian and India. It would have been easy to have extended the series, so as to have included the very large band of explorers who have laid bare the geographical secrets of Kashgaria and the region adjacent. A moment's reflection, however, served to convince me that I should make it unwieldy by doing this, and that further I should distract the reader by calling away his attention from time to time to a part of Central Asia, having nothing in common with that extending from the Caspian Sea to the river Indus. Besides, Kashgaria possesses little interest for the English public, while the area embracing Askabad and Merv, Bokhara and Meshed, Candahar, Cabul, and Herat, will continue to attract notice for many years to come, until at length the Central Asian Question solves itself by the junction of the frontiers of the two rival empires.

Many of the explorers, Russian as well as English, I know personally; but this is a circumstance which I have not allowed for one moment to influence my opinions to the detriment of those with whom I am not acquainted. In my writings on Central Asia I try to arbitrate impartially between Russia and England, Liberal and Conservative, Russophobe and Russophile, and if I have failed on this occasion to deal with equal fairness, and with equal freedom from carping, ungenerous criticism, in treating of the achievements of the various Russian and English explorers, the fault is neither due to personal bias nor to narrow views of patriotism.

My generalizations are not hasty ones. For

some years past I have had to deal almost daily with the books mentioned in this volume, in writing for the press and preparing my works on Central Asia. It was impossible, under such conditions, not to be continually instituting comparisons between the exploits of the explorers and the effect of them upon contemporary politics; while constant reference to their books for purposes of information could not but provoke closer criticism than is possible from a single reading for a chance review.

Some of the chapters originally appeared in a skeleton form in the columns of the *Newcastle Weekly Chronicle*, and the work was completed after my return from the Tsar's coronation. While yet engaged revising it I was called away on a journey to the Caucasus and Caspian region, and when I came back the work had the benefit of a second revision, bringing all its information down to date.

Grosvenor House,
Plumstead Common, Kent.

CONTENTS.

CHAPTER I.

ARMINIUS VÁMBÉRY'S JOURNEY IN DISGUISE TO THE KHANATES OF CENTRAL ASIA.

CHAPTER II.

CAPTAIN MARSH'S RIDE FROM THE CASPIAN TO INDIA.

CHAPTER III.

COLONEL VALENTINE BAKER'S VISIT TO THE PERSO-TURCOMAN FRONTIER.

CHAPTER IV.

J. A. MACGAHAN'S CHASE OF GENERAL KAUFMANN'S ARMY.

CHAPTER V.

CAPTAIN NAPIER'S SECRET MISSION.

CHAPTER VI.

COLONEL C. M. MACGREGOR'S SURVEY OF KHORASSAN.

CHAPTER VII.

CAPTAIN BURNABY'S RIDE TO KHIVA.

CHAPTER VIII.

GENERAL PETRUSEVITCH AND THE TURCOMANS.

CHAPTER IX.

CAPTAIN BUTLER, THE SECRET ENGLISH AGENT.

CHAPTER X.

PASHINO, THE SECRET RUSSIAN AGENT.

CHAPTER XI.

GRODEKOFF'S RIDE TO HERAT.

CHAPTER XII.

O'DONOVAN'S DASH TO MERV.

CHAPTER XIV.

LIEUTENANT ALIKHANOFF'S JOURNEY WITH A RUSSIAN CARAVAN TO MERV.

CHAPTER XV.

LESSAR'S DISCOVERY OF THE EASY ROAD TO INDIA.

CHAPTER XVI.

THE PAST AND FUTURE OF PIONEERING IN CENTRAL ASIA.

CHAPTER I.

ARMINIUS VÁMBÉRY'S JOURNEY IN DISGUISE TO THE KHANATES OF CENTRAL ASIA.

Commencement of the forward movement of Russia in Central Asia—Condition of the region—Early life of Arminius Vámbéry—Career in Turkey—Difficulty of assuming successfully a disguise among Asiatics—Conolly's advice on the subject—How Vámbéry orientalized himself—Anecdotes of the experiences that befell him—The great task Vámbéry set himself to achieve—His feelings on quitting Europe for the wilds of Central Asia—The horrors of the slave trade—A terrible spectacle—His journey to Khiva across the desert—Reception at Khiva—Denounced as a Frenghi—Blesses the fanatic Khan—Is made to gorge himself by devotees till he wishes himself back in the desert—Gouging out the eyes of Turcomans—Nearly perishes in the desert journey to Bokhara—Boldly confronts the Emir—Makes his way to Afghanistan—Enters Herat a beggar—His interview with Yakoob Khan—"By G——. I swear you are an Englishman!"—Makes his way home viâ Meshed—His subsequent career in Europe—His "Travels in Central Asia," and his services to England.

"The sight of a map with blank spaces on it produces in me a feeling of mingled shame and restlessness. Of course it is not any particular fault of mine that maps have blank spaces on them, but I always feel the glaring whiteness of the blanks looking reproachfully at me. Judging from my own feelings, I think it would be a good plan if the Geographical Society were to have all unexplored tracts painted on their maps some conspicuous colour, say scarlet, as the sight of these burning spots, thus prominently brought to their notice, would, I feel sure, rouse much of the latent energy of young Britons, and perhaps divert a good deal of it from mooning about the Row to more useful wanderings to unknown regions."—GENERAL SIR CHARLES MACGREGOR (*Wanderings in Balochistan*, page 2).

IN 1863, the public in England were greatly excited at the aggressive operations of the Russians in Central Asia. Three years previous had commenced afresh the forward movement towards India that had marked the reign of the Emperor Nicholas, but which had been suspended during and immediately after the Crimean War. In 1860, the Russians had taken the Khokandese fortresses of Tokmak and Pishpek; Kolpakovsky had routed 20,000 Khokandese at Uzun-Agatch; and the Orenburg authorities had established a naval station at Kazala, on the river Syr Daria. The following year the fortress of Yani Kurgan had been taken, and a post established at Julek. In 1862, the Khokandese had again experienced several defeats, and Russia was known to be organizing an expedition at Orenburg to renew the war the following spring. At this juncture, when the eyes of England were fixed upon the menaced khanates of Khokand, Bokhara, and Khiva, a lame Hungarian took upon himself the task of trudging in disguise across the deserts of Central Asia, to ascertain for this country what the Russians were doing in the mysterious region beyond.

For nearly twenty years the expanse lying between Russia and India had been left unvisited by European travellers. Previous to this nearly every portion of Central Asia had been overrun by explorers, of whom the names of Baillie Fraser, Arthur Conolly, Alexander Burnes, Wolff, Abbott, Shakespear, Taylour Thomson, and the Frenchman Ferrier, rise readily to the lips. But the collapse of the English expedition to Afghanistan, and the cruel murder of Stoddart and Conolly in Bokhara, had given Central Asia an evil reputation. Travellers had avoided it. By degrees mists had gathered over the khanates, and the public of Europe had come to regard Central Asia as an uncanny region, a prey to anarchy and murder, in which no Frenghi could show himself without risking a cruel and lingering death, or what was perhaps worse, lifelong slavery among thousands of other unfortunates in Khiva and Bokhara. Only in 1860 the Turcomans of Merv had conquered and captured a Persian army, 20,000 strong, to a man, and after storing its cannon in their fortress—where they exist to this day—had sent nearly the whole of the captives to be sold as slaves in Central Asia. Such was the dread which, acts like these inspired, that no Englishman dared venture beyond the Persian frontier to see what the Russians were doing on the Aral, and it is a question whether even the intrepid Arminius Vámbéry would have undertaken his dangerous journey but for being able to perform it in disguise.

Arminius Vámbéry was born in 1832, at Duna Gzerdahely, situated on one of the largest islands in the Danube. "Impelled," he says, "by a particular inclination to linguistic studies," he had in "early youth occupied himself with several languages of Europe and Asia." This led him later on to proceed to Constantinople, where several years' residence in the Turkish houses, and frequent visits to Islamitic schools and libraries, soon transformed him into a Turk, if not an Efendi. For six years he acted as translator in the Turkish Foreign Office, all the while increasing his mastery of the Oriental philology and acquiring a minute knowledge of the language and religion of the Eastern countries he meant some day to explore. In 1862, he left Constantinople for Persia, where he spent nearly a year, patiently familiarising himself with the people and country before taking in hand the enterprise, on which would be staked his liberty and life. At length he felt himself fit for the disguise he intended to assume—that of a dervish, which would enable him to travel to Central Asia in company with one of the bands of holy mendicants that were constantly passing between Khiva and Mecca.

Of the difficulty of sustaining a disguise among Asiatics, the explorer Conolly, who tried the *rôle* of desert trader in the Turcoman region, himself bears witness:—"If I were to travel again in such countries in the disguise of a native, I would take the character of a poor one; but I think that a European can hardly hope to escape detection, for, though he may be conversant with the idioms, his mode of delivery, his manner even of sitting, walking, or riding—in short, his *tout ensemble*, is different from that of an Asiatic, and the very care he takes not to betray himself gives him an air that causes him to be noticed. A man may, I think, get on best in the character of a French or Italian doctor. These itinerant gentry are sometimes met with, and as their country is supposed to be somewhere about the antipodes, they are not viewed with distrust. Among people so ignorant a Sangrado may pass for a great hakeem; the simplest medicines will cure their ailments, and you may tell those beyond your skill that it is not their *nusseeb* (fortune) to be cured. No character will gain you such good treatment, and it has this great advantage—that it does not oblige you to conceal your religion, or, what is worse, to affect the Mahomedan. Few will question you, and you may make free use of the names of their most esteemed hakeems—Solerat and Bokrat, Sokman and Aboo Allee Seine; but if you should happen to meet a man of as great pretensions as yourself, and he should begin to try you with queries, ask him whether a shivering fever is a cold or hot disease."

The task the lame man Vámbéry set himself to achieve was no easy one. It was simple enough to assume the rags and dirt of a dervish, to wear a felt jacket and patchwork robe, to twine strips of ragged linen round his feet, and fix on his head an immense turban, "serving as a parasol by day and a pillow by night"; but when it came to associating with the holy beggars, he found it a most anxious task to suppress his European habits, for, as he says, "we Occidentals eat, drink, sleep, sit, and stand, nay, I feel inclined to say, laugh, weep, sigh, and gesticulate, otherwise than Eastern people. I shudder even now when I think back of the fatigue I underwent during the first few days, and how much I suffered from the wet and cold, the uncleanliness—which makes one's hair stand on end—and the never-ending, harassing worry with the fanatic Sheeahs during our long and tedious daily marches in the Persian province of Mazenderan. Sometimes it rained from early in the morning until late in the evening, and, whilst not a thread of my tattered garments remained dry, I was obliged to wade for hours knee-deep in mud. Being conscious of my habit of gesticulating with my hands when speaking—a habit peculiar to many Europeans, but strictly forbidden in

Central Asia—and fearing lest I should commit this mistake, I adopted a coercive remedy. I pretended to suffer from pains in the arms, and strapping them down to the body, they soon lost the habit of involuntary movement. In like manner I seldom ventured to make a hearty meal late in the evening, for fear of being troubled with heavy dreams, which might cause me to speak some foreign language. I bore in mind the words of one of my companions, who observed one morning with great *naïveté* that my snoring sounded different from that of the Turkestanis, whereupon another interpreter informed him: 'Yes, thus people snore in Constantinople.'"

In one of his works he tells us of a droll incident, fraught with danger of discovery, which occurred to him in Bokhara. "As is well known, the difference in the washing of the arm produces apparent consequences on this part of the body. Among the Sunnis, in consequence of ablutions five times a day from earliest youth, the points of the hair incline towards the palms of the hands. Among the Sheeahs, on the contrary, they incline towards the elbow; and hence, from the appearance of the hairs, the religious sect of the individual may be inferred. The astonishment of some Bokhariots may be imagined when they discovered that my hairs neither inclined upwards nor downwards, but grew all round my arm. 'A remarkable Mussulman that!' they said; 'an unknown race.' And I am certainly regarded by many, even at the present day, as an abortion in the Islam growth of hair."

Setting out from Teheran March 28th, 1863, with a party of twenty-three hadjis, Vámbéry travelled along the Caspian littoral to the bay of Astrabad, making himself on the way good friends with his fellow-pilgrims, who were as savoury a set of mortals as one might pick out from the dirtiest dens of Seven Dials, and earning their respect and esteem by assiduous attention to his devotions. It was not without a certain amount of remorse and anxiety that he left Teheran behind. His enterprise was one that might have daunted the boldest heart. Central Asia at that period was a dark and mysterious region, peopled by cruel and fanatical Mussulmans, who held in bondage tens of thousands of miserable captives torn from their border homes in Persia, Afghanistan, and even Russia. The rulers of these Mussulmans were despotic sovereigns, habitually practising all the cruelties of Bashi Bazouks, and having at the moment a bitter hatred in their hearts against all Europeans, in consequence of the successes which the White Faces of the West had gained over their dusky troops on the shores of the Sea of Aral.

Apart from the ordinary perils of the journey, Vámbéry was conscious of exposing himself to four great risks. To reach the khanates of Central Asia he had to traverse the terrible and almost unknown desert between the Caspian and the Oxus, which in after-years became the grave of the greater part of General Markozoff's expedition against the Khivans. In making his way to this desert, and in passing across it, he had to slip through bands of roving Tekké Turcomans, people who had no respect for pilgrims, and would have made him a slave for life had they caught him on his journey. Having reached the khanates, an agonizing death awaited him if it was discovered he was a European, and there was a possibility, nearly realized in the case of Khiva, that the ruler might forcibly compel him to take up permanent residence with his people. Finally, he was conscious that at any moment on the road it might be discovered that he was a false Mussulman, in which case even his warmest friends among the hadjis would consider themselves bound to put him to death.

Hence, one can well understand the feelings that disquieted him at intervals after his severance from civilization and humanity at Teheran. "During the greater part of the day, society, occupation, and events of varied interest prevented the intrusion of these suspicions; but at night," he says, "when everything around was hushed in silence, and I sat alone in a solitary corner of my tent, or in the waste and barren desert, I became absorbed in thought. Fear appeared before me in its blackest guise and most terrible aspect; nor would it leave me for a long, long time, however much I attempted to dispel it by sophistry or light-heartedness. Oh, this terrible Megæra! How she tormented me, how she tortured me, at those very moments when, seeking repose, I was about to lose myself in contemplation of the grandeur of nature and the wonderful constitution of man! In the long struggle between us, fear was finally subdued; but it is this very struggle which I now blush to remember, for it is marvellous what efforts are required to grow familiar with the constant and visible prospect of death."

Travelling for a week, Vámbéry and his companions reached the bay of Astrabad, at the south-east corner of the Caspian. Here his secret was nearly discovered by a keen-eyed Russian, who remarked as the party touched at the naval station at Ashurada, in traversing the bay in a lugger—"Smotrite kakoi bieloï etot hadji!"—"See how white this hadji is!" From the island of Ashurada the Russians maintained a sort of police supervision over the south-east shores of the Caspian, the Turcoman inhabitants of which were accustomed to make piratical descents on the Persian coast and carry off people into perpetual slavery in the khanates of Central Asia.

Respecting Russia's right to conquer Central Asia, and England's wisdom in opposing her, much argument may be expended, and many opinions expressed; but there is one fact that stands out clear from all controversy—the conquest of Central Asia has been a blessing not only for Central Asia itself, but for all the nations abutting upon it. Cruel as have been some of the acts marking the conquest, and in spite of the defects of Russian administration, it is impossible for any man possessing the ordinary feelings of humanity to read the terrible accounts of the slave trade in Central Asia, prevailing up to the annexation of the region by Russia, without feeling thankful that the whole of the khanates have passed under the sway of the White Tsar.

In 1841, when Major Abbott visited the khanate of Khiva, out of a population of 2,468,500 people, 700,000, or about one in every three, were slaves. In the city of Khiva alone were 12,000 Heratis and 30,000 Persians, the rest of the slaves being scattered about the khanate as tillers of the soil. Writing of the same period, Wolff, the traveller, calculated that out of the two and a half million people composing the population of Bokhara, 200,000 were in a state of bondage. Burnes observed of a Bokharan village near the Oxus, in 1832, that, "though not boasting of more than twenty houses, there were yet seven or eight Persian slaves; and these unfortunate men appear to be distributed in a like proportion throughout the country."*

When Vámbéry reached the pirate coast of the Caspian in 1863, the tide of Russian conquest was commencing to roll, which was destined in little more than ten years to sweep away the atrocious institution of slavery from nearly every corner of Central Asia, and restore thousands of captives to their long-lost homes.

At Gömüch Tepé, the Turcoman fishing village where Vámbéry landed after crossing the bay of Astrabad, and where he was treated with the greatest kindness by the natives, "not a night passed," he says, "without a shot echoing from the sea-shore to announce the arrival of some piratical vessel laden with booty. In the morning my heart bled at the horrid sight of the poor Persians in the first moments of their misfortune."

How heart-rending these sights were, may be gathered from his description of one of them in

* For a full account of the horrors of the Central Asian slave trade, see "Merv, the Queen of the World, and the Scourge of the Man-stealing Turcomans." By Charles Marvin. London: W. H. Allen and Co., 1880.

his "Sketches of Central Asia" :—"I entered the tent of Khandjan after the morning prayer and found a noble company listening with the greatest attention to the narrative of a young Turcoman, who was covered with dust and dirt, and whose face bore evident traces of excitement and severe hardship. He was describing in a low voice, but in lively colours, a marauding excursion against the Persians of the evening before, in which he had taken part. Whilst he was speaking, the women, servants, and slaves (what must have been the thoughts of these latter!), squatted down round the circle of listeners, and many a curse was hurled at the slaves, the clanking of the chains on their feet interrupting for a time the general quiet. It struck me as remarkable that in proportion as the speaker warmed in describing the obstinate resistance of the unfortunate people who were fallen on unawares, the indignation of the audience increased at the audacity of the Persians not to have at once quietly submitted to being plundered.

"No sooner was the narration of this great feat of arms at an end, when all arose to their feet to have a look at the spoils, the sight of which excites in the Turcoman's breast a mingled feeling of envy and pleasure. I followed them likewise, and a terrible picture presented itself to my eyes. Lying down in the middle of the tent were two Persians, looking deadly pale and covered with clotted blood, dirt, and dust. A man was busily engaged putting their broken limbs into fetters, when one of them gave a loud, wild shriek, the rings of the chains being too small for him. The cruel Turcoman was about to fasten them forcibly round his ankles. In a corner sat two young children on the ground, pale and trembling, and looking with sorrowful eyes towards the tortured Persian. The unhappy man was their father; they longed to weep, but dared not: one look of the robber, at whom they stole a glance now and again, with their teeth chattering, was sufficient to suppress their tears. In another corner a girl, from fifteen to sixteen years old, was crouching, her hair dishevelled and in confusion, her garments torn and almost entirely covered with blood. She groaned and sobbed, covering her face with her hands. Some Turcoman woman, moved either by compassion or curiosity, asked her what ailed her, and where she was wounded. 'I am not wounded,' she exclaimed, in a plaintive voice, deeply touching. 'This blood is the blood of my mother, my only one, and the best and kindest of mothers. Oh! *ana djan, ana djan* (dear mother)!' Thus she lamented, striking her head against the trellised woodwork of the tent, so that it almost tumbled down. They offered her a draught of water, and her tongue became loosened, and she told them how she (of course a valuable prize) had been lifted into the saddle beside the robber, but that her mother, tied to the stirrups, had been obliged to run along on foot. After an hour's running in this manner, she grew so tired that she sank down exhausted every moment. The Turcoman tried to increase her strength by lashing her with his whip, but this was of no avail; and as he did not want to remain behind, away from his troop, he grew in a rage, drew his sword, and in a second struck off her head. The blood spurting up, had covered the daughter, horseman, and horse; and, looking at the red spots upon her clothes the poor girl wept loudly and bitterly.

"Whilst this was going on in the interior of the tent, outside, the various members of the robber's family were busy inspecting the booty he had brought home. The elder women seized greedily upon one or another utensil for domestic use, whilst the children, who were jumping about merrily, were trying on the different garments, now one, now another, and producing shouts of laughter.

"Here was all triumph and merriment, not far from it a picture of the deepest grief and misery. And yet no one is struck by the contrast; every one thinks it very natural that the Turcoman should enrich himself with robbery and pillage."

After a prolonged stay among the pirates and robbers of Gömüch Tepé, Vámbéry and the pilgrims set off on their long and dangerous journey across the desert to Khiva. Before starting Vámbéry was exposed to some danger by the suspicions of a malevolent Afghan, a native of Candahar, who had been expelled that city during its occupation by the English in 1842 for a crime he had committed, and who recognised the traveller as a European by his features. Vámbéry had a deal of trouble with this man, but he played his part of dervish with such firmness and audacity that the rest of the pilgrims grew indignant at the Afghan's tittle-tattle, and made him hold his tongue.

Crossing the river Atrek, Vámbéry passed close by the spot destined in after-years to be the site of the Russian camp of Tchikishlar, the subsequent starting point of several expeditions against the Turcomans, and trudging due north across the steppes lying between the Atrek and the Caspian, emerged into the great desert of Kara Kum, not far from the present terminal point of the Transcaspian railway, Kizil Arvat. Nowadays one can go by train and steamer all the way from Charing Cross to Kizil Arvat, the journey occupying little more than a week; but in Vámbéry's time the region was almost *terra incognita*, distant months of tedious and perilous journey even from Russia, and known only to the world by a short excursion which the brave explorer Lieutenant Arthur Conolly had made to the verge of the desert during his overland trip to India in 1829.

Both Vámbéry and Conolly traversed the country between the Caspian and Atrek during the warm season of the year, when its scorched aspect inspired the belief that the character of the soil did not differ materially from the wilder waste of the Kara Kum. But since the Russians occupied the country it has been found that heavy rains clothe the steppes with grass in the autumn, and that wherever the water is stored, magnificent crops of wheat and melons can be raised in the summer. In course of time the region no doubt will be colonized by Cossacks and other Russian peoples engaged in pastoral pursuits, and roaming grounds will be formed for the huge flocks and herds which are now disappearing from South Russia with the growth of agriculture. In the meanwhile, in the northern part of the region, between Krasnovodsk and Kizil Arvat, Frenchmen and Russians are developing the naphtha deposits among the Little Balkan hills. One of these hills, known as the Naphtha Hill, consists almost entirely of a huge mass of naphtha and mineral wax, valued at £35,000,000 sterling. The district is called the "Black California," and promises to become in time an important industrial centre, from which will be sent fuel and oil to the cities and tents of Central Asia,

KIZIL ARVAT.

[To face page 20.

throughout which region both these necessaries are dear and scarce.

In 1869 the Russians had no footing at all on the east Caspian coast between Fort Alexandrovsky, founded by Perovsky in 1834, and the island of Ashurada, occupied a few years later. It was not until six years after Vámbéry's journey that Krasnovodsk was seized; and thus, in proceeding from Gömüch Tepé to the fringe of the Kara Kum desert, the traveller had to pass between the littoral Yomood Turcomans on the one hand and the Goklan and Tekké Turcomans of the higher Atrek and Akhal oasis on the other. These tribes were professional slave-catchers, kidnapping every unfortunate they could lay their hands on, and selling them into captivity at Khiva or Bokhara. But fortune befriended Vámbéry. The desert was attained without attack, and after several days' hardships under which a traveller of less indomitable will would have sunk, the burning sands were left behind, and the Hungarian cast his rapturous gaze on the outlying settlements of the oasis of Khiva. Ten years later, a Russian column, marching to invade Khiva in almost the same direction as the pilgrims, collapsed miserably when half-way across the desert, and had to retreat, leaving half its numbers dead behind.

Khiva had been visited by several English and Russian travellers a generation earlier, and thus its characteristics were well known to geographers. But for many years no European had penetrated to the oasis, and English statesmen were consequently ignorant of the recent political and economic changes of a country, which was daily assuming greater importance by reason of the Russian advance. At that time so much was thought of Khiva as an outpost of India, that there were many able Englishmen seriously in favour of fighting Russia if she occupied the country.

To one coming from the sandy desert, the green pasture lands and cool tents of the Yomood Turcomans living on the edge of the oasis were inexpressibly refreshing. These warlike subjects of the Khan greeted the dervishes with the same simple hearty welcome they in after-years displayed to the Russian troops, despatched to perpetrate the shameful "Yomood massacre." Travelling a couple of days through their camps, the pilgrims reached the Uzbeg villages, on the outskirts of Khiva, the vegetation becoming more and more luxuriant the further they advanced, and the evidences greater of comfort and prosperity.

At the very entrance of the gate of the city they were met by several pious Khivans, who handed up to them bread and dried fruit as they sat upon their camels. For years so numerous a troop of hadjis had not arrived in Khiva. All stared at them in astonishment, and the exclamations "Aman eszen geldin ghiz!" ("Welcome!"), "Ha shah bazim! Ha Arszlanim!" ("Ah, my falcon, my lion!"), resounded on all sides in their ears. "On entering the bazaar, Hadji Bilal," says Vámbéry, "intoned a telkin. My voice was heard above them all, and I felt real emotion when the people impressed their kisses upon my hands and feet, yes, upon the very rags which hung from me. In accordance with the custom of the country, we dismounted at the caravanserai. Scarcely had the head of this, the Mehrem (a sort of chamberlain and confidant of the Khan), addressed the ordinary questions to our caravan leader, when the Afghan pressed forward and called aloud, 'We have brought to Khiva three interesting quadrupeds and a no less interesting biped.' The first part of this pleasantry was of course applied to the buffaloes, animals not before seen in Khiva; but as the second part was pointed at me, it was no wonder that many eyes were immediately turned upon me, and amidst the whispers it was not difficult to distinguish the words 'Djansiz' (spy), 'Frenghi,' and 'Urus' (Russian). I made an effort to prevent the blood rising to my cheeks, and was upon the point of withdrawing, when the Mehrem ordered me to remain, using exceedingly uncivil expressions. I was about to reply, when Hadji Salih, whose exterior inspired respect, came in, and entirely ignorant of what had passed, represented me in the most flattering colours to my inquisitor, who, surprised, told me, smiling as he did so, to take a seat by his side."

Hadji Salih made a sign to Vámbéry to accept the invitation, but assuming the air of one highly offended, and throwing an angry look upon the Mehrem, he retired and made his way to the house of a distinguished Khivan, whom he had heard had once lived at Constantinople. This personage was delighted to see a Turkish

Efendi, who could tell him the latest news of the many acquaintances he had left behind at Stamboul, and when the traveller returned to the caravanserai it was with the consciousness that he had at least one friend to support him in any troubles at Khiva. To add to his satisfaction, he found that in his absence the irritated Afghan had been driven off with curses and reproaches by the Khivans, for his impiety in casting doubts on the sacred character of a dervish.

The next day the traveller was summoned to appear before the Khan. As the dervish approached the reception room the crowd gave way on all sides, and he was glad to hear the women exclaiming to one another, "Behold the dervish from Constantinople, who is to give his blessing to our Khan. May God give ear to his words!"

After the customary greeting with the Mehter, or Minister of Home Affairs, a pause elapsed to allow every arrangement to be made to impress the arrival from Stamboul, and then a curtain was rolled up, and Vámbéry saw before him Said Mahommed, Padishahi Kharezm, or, as he would be called in ordinary prose, Khan of Khiva, sitting on a dais with his left arm supported upon a round silk velvet pillow, and his right holding a short golden sceptre.

Respecting his feelings at this critical moment Vámbéry says, "No European can realize to himself what it was to stand, a disguised Frenghi (this word of terror to the Orientals !), face to face with such a tyrant as the Khivan khan, and to have to bestow upon him the customary benediction. If this man were to discover the dangerous trick, this man with the sallow face and sinister look, as he sits there surrounded by his satellites—such an idea is only endurable to the mind steeled to the highest pitch of resolution." Had he been discovered, the penalty would have been to have had his eyes gouged out, or to have been buried up to his chin in earth and then pelted to death with clay pellets, or to have been murdered in some other miserable and agonizing manner.

With a firm step and a bold gesture, the false dervish raised his hands, being imitated by the Khan and the people present, and recited a short *Sura* from the Koran, then two *Alla-*

humu Sella, and a usual prayer beginning with the words *Allahumu Rabbena*, and finally concluded with a loud amen and prolonged stroking of the beard. Whilst the Khan was still stroking his beard, each of the rest exclaimed, "Kabul bolgay!" ("May my prayer be heard!"). The dervish afterwards approached the Khan, who extended his hands to him, and when both had duly executed the Musafeha, or greeting prescribed by the Koran, accompanied by the reciprocal extension of the open hands, he retired a few paces, and the religious ceremonial was at an end.

The Khan now questioned him respecting the object of his journey and the impressions made upon him by the desert, the Turcomans, and Khiva. Vámbéry replied that he had suffered much, but that his sufferings were now richly rewarded by the sight of the *hazrets djemel* (beauty of his majesty). When asked how long he meant to stay, the dervish replied that he wished first to visit the saints who reposed in the soil of the khanate, and that he should then proceed further on. With respect to the money the Khan offered him, he added, "We dervishes do not trouble ourselves with such trifles. The holy *nefes* (breath) which my *pir* (chief of my order) has imparted to me for my journey can support me four or five days without any nourishment, and I have no other wish than that God will permit his Majesty to live a hundred and twenty years!" The twenty ducats the Khan offered him he refused, on the grounds that it was a sin for a dervish to keep money, but he accepted a white ass to facilitate his pilgrimage. Blessing then the Khan, the traveller withdrew, and hurried home through the crowded forecourt and bazaar. When he found himself again alone within the four walls of his cell, "he drew," he says, "a long breath, not a little pleased to find that the Khan, who in appearance was so fearfully dissolute, and who presented in every feature of his countenance the real picture of an enervated, imbecile, and savage tyrant, had behaved to me in a manner so unexceptionable; and that, so long as my time permitted, I could now traverse the khanate in all directions unmolested. During the whole evening I had floating before me the picture of the Khan with his deep-set eyes, with his chin thinly covered with hair, his white lips, and trembling voice. 'What a happy fatality,' I repeated to myself, 'that gloomy superstition often imposes limits to the might and bloodthirstiness of such tyrants!'"

After this he had to pay the usual penalty of court success by suffering from the excessive honour paid him by the *élite* of the city. "Directly it was known that I shared the favour of royalty, everybody wanted to have me as guest, and with me all the other hadjis. What a torture this was to me to have daily to accept six, seven, or eight invitations, and to comply with the usage by taking something in every house! My hair stands on end at the recollection how often I was forced to seat myself, between three and four o'clock in the morning, before sunrise, opposite a colossal dish of rice swimming in the fat of the sheep-tail, which I was to assail as if my stomach was empty. How, upon such occasions, I again longed for the dry unleavened bread of the desert, and how willingly I would have exchanged this deadly luxury for wholesome poverty!

"In Central Asia it is the practice, even on the occasion of an ordinary visit, to set before you the *desturkhan* (a napkin of coarse linen and of a variety of colours, for the most part dirty). In this enough bread is generally placed for two persons, and the guest is to eat some pieces of this. 'To be able to eat no more' is an expression regarded by the Central Asiatic as incredible, or, at least, as indicating low breeding. My pilgrim brethren always gave brilliant proofs of their *bon ton.* My only wonder is that they could support the heavy pillow, for upon one occasion I reckoned that each of them had devoured one pound of fat from the tail of the sheep, two pounds of rice, without taking any account of bread, carrots, turnips, and radishes, and all this washed down, without any exaggeration, by from fifteen to twenty large soup plates full of green tea. In such heroic feats I was naturally a coward; and it was the astonishment of every one that I, so well versed in books, should have acquired only a half-acquaintance with the requisites of polite breeding!"

But it was not all "pleasure" at Khiva. Besides having to foil palace plots to ruin him, and evade a scheme of the Khan to marry him to an Uzbeg woman and settle him for life in the oasis, he had to witness scenes of cruelty which still haunt him in his dreams. One day, on quitting the palace, he found in the outer court about three hundred Tchaudor Turcomans, prisoners of war, covered with rags, who had been captured in retaliation for the plundering of a Khivan caravan by their tribe. "These were so tormented by the dread of their approaching fate, and by the hunger which they had endured several days, that they looked as if they had just risen from the grave. They were separated into two divisions, namely, such as had not yet reached their fortieth year, and were to be sold as slaves, and such as from their rank or age were regarded as *aksakals* (grey beards), or leaders, and who were to suffer the punishment imposed by the Khan. The former, chained together by their iron collars in numbers of from ten to fifteen, were led away; the latter submissively awaited the punishment awarded. They looked like lambs in the hands of their executioners. Whilst several were led to the gallows or the block, I saw how, at a sign from the executioner, eight aged men placed themselves down on their backs upon the earth. They were then bound hand and foot, and the executioner gouged out their eyes in turn, kneeling to do so on the breast of each poor wretch; and after every operation he wiped his knife, dripping with blood, upon the white beard of the hoary unfortunate. Ah, cruel spectacle! As each fearful act was completed, the victim, liberated from his bonds, groping around with his hands, sought to gain his feet! Some fell against each other, head against head; others sank powerless to the earth again, uttering low groans, the memory of which will make me shudder as long as I live."

In those days men were hanged for casting a look upon a thickly veiled female. Women suspected of intrigues were buried up to the breast and pelted to death. As in Khiva there are no stones, hard pellets of earth were used. At the third discharge the poor victim was completely covered with dust, and the body, dripping with blood, was horribly disfigured; death alone put an end to her torture. Such scenes were varied by the arrival of horsemen with slaves and the heads of the Khan's enemies. The former were handed over as presents to the Khan, or some other great personage, and the latter tumbled out by the sackful on the ground in front of the Treasurer. "As the bearded or beardless heads rolled out of the sack like potatoes, the Treasurer kicked them together with his foot until a large heap was formed, consisting of several hundreds. Each hero had a receipt given him for the number of heads delivered, and a few days later came the day of payment."

The Cossack, according to English ideas, is a stern ruler, but nobody who has lived in Russia and knows life in Central Asia can seriously pretend that the world in general, and Turkestan in particular, is the worse for the conquest of the khanates. The imposition of English or of Russian administration over the wild countries of Central Asia appears to me such a blessing, that whatever territory is unessential to the security of India, and the control of which we do not desire, I would freely allow Russia to annex.

It is not pleasant to reflect that if Russia had listened to English advice, remonstrances, entreaties, and threats, Khiva would have still been lawlessly independent, and that during the years that have elapsed since its conquest thousands of wretched beings would have been tortured and killed with all those refinements of cruelty practised in Vámbéry's time.

In spite of these barbarous usages, it was in Khiva Vámbéry says he passed the most agreeable days of his whole journey. The people were exceedingly kind to him. "I had only to appear in public, when passers-by, without any begging on my part, absolutely pelted me with many articles of attire and other presents. I took care never to accept considerable sums. I shared the articles of attire amongst my less fortunate brethren, always yielding to them what was best and handsomest, and reserving for myself, as became a dervish, what was poorest and least pretending. Notwithstanding this, a great change had taken place in my position, and to avow it openly, I saw with joy that I was now well furnished with a strong ass, with money, clothing, and provisions, and that I was perfectly equipped to continue my journey."

This lay further east, to the khanate of Bokhara, which is separated from it by a desert, split in two parts by the river Oxus, the northern, known as the Kizil Kum, the home of the Kirghiz tribes, and the southern, the Kara

Kum, roamed over by the Turcomans. To get to Khiva, Vámbéry and his fellow-pilgrims had to traverse the desert, keeping in their course as close to the river Oxus as they could.

"It was on a Monday, late in the afternoon, when we suspended the functions of conferrers of blessings, and extricated ourselves from the embraces that seemed as if they would never end, and quitted Khiva. Many, whose zeal was transcendental, ran for half a league after us; their feeling of devotion forced tears from their eyes, and full of despair, we heard them exclaim, 'Who knows when Khiva will again have the great good-fortune to harbour in her walls so many pious men!'"

The eight days' journey from Khiva to Bokhara was marked with more physical suffering than perhaps Vámbéry anywhere else experienced during his travels. In traversing the desert, the pilgrims' water supply fell short, and they suffered terribly the pangs of thirst. "Two of our poorer companions, forced to tramp on foot by the side of their feeble beasts, fell so sick that we were forced to bind them at full length upon the camels, as they were perfectly incapable of riding or sitting. We covered them over, and as long as they were able to articulate they kept exclaiming, 'Water! water!' the only words that escaped their lips. Alas! even their best friends denied them the life-dispensing draught; and when we, on the fourth day, reached Medemin Bulag, one of them was freed by death from the dreadful torments of thirst. It was one of the three brothers who had lost their father at Mecca. I was present when the unfortunate man drew his last breath. His tongue was quite black, the roof of his mouth of a greyish white; in other respects his features were not much disfigured, except that his lips were shrivelled, the teeth exposed, and the mouth open. I doubt much whether, in these extreme sufferings, water would have been of service; but who was there to give it to him? It is a horrible sight to see the father hide his store of water from the son, and brother from brother; each drop is life, and when men feel the torture of thirst, there is not, as in the other dangers of life, any spirit of self-sacrifice, or any feeling of generosity."

Nearly smothered by a scorching sand storm, the exhausted band trudged on, Vámbéry experiencing such sufferings that he felt that "no death could be more painful." At last, on the outskirts of the desert, when all hope of surviving had nearly disappeared, the pilgrims came upon some Persian slaves, who assisted them to reach Bokhara.

It strikes one as odd that in these remote and barbarous regions, as in more civilized Europe, the travellers' first acquaintance with a country should commence with custom-house officers. On reaching the Bokharan border town, the pilgrims were stopped, and their luggage examined with the same vexatious formalities practised at the frontier of every European state.

The pilgrims thought their sacred character would gain them exemption from examination, but piety has no place in protective tariffs, and every article belonging to them was rigorously inspected and written down. Vámbéry was left to the last, "when the official, looking in my face, laughed and told me to show my trunk, 'for that we (meaning, probably, Europeans, as he took me for one) had always fine things with us.' I happened to be in an excellent humour, and had on my dervish or fool's cap. I interrupted the cunning Bokharan, saying that I had, in effect, some beautiful things, which he would see himself when he came to examine my property, movable and immovable. As he insisted upon seeing everything, I ran into the court, fetched my ass, and led it to him up the stairs and over the carpet; and after having introduced it, amid the loud laughter of my companions, I lost no time in opening my knapsack, and then showed him the few rags and old books which I had collected in Khiva."

Liberated from the custom-house officers, the pilgrims made their way to the city of Bokhara, where Vámbéry donned the native dress and lived for three weeks among priests and abbots. The metropolis of the most powerful khanate of Central Asia, Bokhara contained within its walls all manner of Asiatic comforts and luxuries to compensate the traveller for his hardships in the desert, and to refresh him while pursuing his investigations among the ruins of palaces, mosques, and tombs. Wherever he went he was surrounded by a crowd of inquisitive persons. "Ah! how they shook me by the hands, and how they embraced me! how they wearied me to death! An immense turban crowned my head; a large Koran hung suspended from my neck; I had assumed the exterior of an ishan or sheikh, and was obliged to submit to the *corvée* which I had so provoked. Still I had reason to be contented, for the sanctity of my character protected me from secular interrogation, and I heard how the people about questioned my friends, or whispered their criticisms to each other. 'What extreme piety,' said one, 'to come all the way from Constantinople alone in order to visit our saint Bahaeddin!'"

Suspecting he was a Frenghi, the Emir's officials did all they could by means of spies to penetrate his secret, but he baffled them. When they then invited him to a feast that they might entrap him in conversation, he started a theological discussion, and setting one Bokharan against the other, as one might do bigoted Churchmen and Dissenters in England, slipped quietly out of the snare. After this they left him in peace.

Having seen enough of the city of Bokhara, he travelled with the few remaining members of the pilgrim band to Samarcand, a journey of six days. Shortly after his arrival the Emir Mozaffar Eddin entered in state on his return from a victorious war against the Khokandese, and the following day Vámbéry was summoned to see him alone. The suspicions the Bokharan officials entertained of the dervish had been transmitted to the Emir.

Mozaffar Eddin was quite a different personage from the Khan of Khiva. He was in his forty-second year, of middle height, and somewhat corpulent. He had a very pleasing countenance, fine black eyes, and a thin beard. When Vámbéry was shown into the audience chamber, the Emir was sitting on a mattress or ottoman of red cloth, surrounded by writings and books.

With great presence of mind, the dervish recited a short Sura, with the usual prayer for the welfare of the sovereign, and after the Amen, to which Mozaffar himself responded, Vámbéry took his seat, without permission, quite close to his royal person. "The boldness of my proceeding—quite, however, in accordance with the character which I had assumed—seemed not displeasing to him. I had long forgotten the art of blushing, and so was able to sustain the look which he now directed full in my face, with the intention, probably, of disconcerting me. 'Hadji, thou comest, I hear, from Roum, to visit the tombs of Bahaeddin and the saints of Turkestan.'

"'Yes, Sire, but also to quicken myself by the contemplation of thy sacred beauty,'" according to the forms of conversation usual on these occasions.

"'Strange! and thou hadst no other motive in coming hither from so distant a land?'

"'No, Sire, it had always been my warmest desire to behold the noble Bokahra, and the enchanting Samarcand, upon whose sacred soil, as was remarked by Sheikh Djelal, one should rather walk on one's head than on one's feet. But I have, besides, no other business in life, and have long been moving about everywhere as a *djihangeste* (world-pilgrim).

"'What, thou, with thy lame foot, a *djihangeste!* That is really astonishing.'

"'I would be thy victim!' (an expression equivalent to 'Pardon me'). 'Sire, thy glorious ancestor (peace be with him!) had certainly same infirmity, and he was even *djihanghir'* " (conqueror of the world).*

This reply was agreeable to the Emir, who put questions to him respecting the impressions produced on him by Bokhara and Samarcand, and was so pleased with the Persian sentences and Koran verses with which he embellished his replies, that he presented him with a dress and thirty pieces of silver. After this scene the traveller was advised by his friends to quit Samarcand in all speed, not to make any stay even at Karshi, but to gain as rapidly as possible the further bank of the Oxus, where, amongst the hospitable Ersari Turcomans, he might await the arrival of the caravan for Herat.

The departure involved a final parting from the pilgrims, to some of whom Vámbéry had become really attached during his six months' adventures and sufferings with them. "My pen," he says, "is too feeble to convey any adequate idea of the distressing scene that took

* Timour, whom the Emirs of Bokhara erroneously claim as their ancestor, was, as is well known, lame; hence his enemies called him Timur Lenk (Tamerlane, the *lame Timour*).

place between us; on both sides we were equally moved. Separation was in our case equivalent to death, for how could it be otherwise in those countries where there was positively not a hope of seeing each other again? When we parted outside the city gate I wept like a child. My friends were all bathed in tears, and long did I see them—I see them now—standing there in the same place, with their hands raised to heaven, imploring Allah's blessing upon my far journey. I turned round many times to look back. At last they disappeared, and I found I was only gazing upon the domes of Samarcand, illuminated by the faint light of the rising moon."

Five days' journeying with a small caravan brought the traveller to the fortress of Kerki, on the Oxus, bordering Afghanistan. From here Vámbéry made excursions in various directions, notably one of four days' duration to Mazar-i-Sherif, near Balkh, a place of no great importance then, except as a shrine, but which has since developed into the capital of the Afghan possessions north of the Hindoo Koosh, and has become historical as the town where the Stolietoff mission stayed some time before proceeding to Cabul, and where Shere Ali breathed his last after the promises of the Russian envoy had involved him in ruin.

Recent events have rendered Vámbéry's wanderings in the region between the Oxus and Herat of great importance to England. With the exception of Grodekoff, he is the only modern traveller who has visited Afghan Turkestan and the outposts of the Hindoo Koosh—Balkh, Andkhoi, Maimene, etc.—which Russia covets, and which some of her writers have declared can never be allowed to remain permanently in Afghan or English hands. Vámbéry saw the country when it consisted of a number of small independent states, or khanates, constantly at war with each other, and the victims from time to time of invasions from the Bokharans, the Afghans, and the Turcomans. Grodekoff, on the other hand, traversed the region after Shere Ali had conquered it and imposed Afghan rule—a cruel and odious despotism—throughout the length and breadth of the land.

In passing through these khanates, Vámbéry was so fleeced by the custom-house officers and local officials, that he entered Herat at the close of his six weeks' journey literally a pauper.* The European writer who perhaps more than any other publicist has urged the necessity of safeguarding Herat, and who has more powerfully than any other person pleaded the cause of the inhabitants against their usurping rulers and conquerors, the Afghans, was condemned to wander about the streets and bazaars begging for broken victuals and pence to keep himself from starvation. The gloomy character of his position was only relieved by the fidelity of a young Tartar, named Mollah Ishak, who refused to leave his side, and cheerfully undertook the hardest part of the begging.

Herat had only two months earlier been taken by storm after a long siege by the Afghans, and still bore traces of the ruin wrought by the bombardment and the assault. The insolence and cruelty of the Afghans were beyond bounds, and the inhabitants openly expressed their earnest desire that the English would come and deliver them from their rapacious conquerors.

* The journey from Bokhara is usually performed by caravans in twenty days, but owing to local tumults and other causes, Vámbéry's caravan was six weeks on the road.

To obtain some money to enable him to proceed to Meshed, Vámbéry resolved he would pay a visit to the Governor-General of Herat, Yakoob Khan. This prince, who succeeded Shere Ali, and was deported to India for conniving at the massacre of Major Cavagnari at Cabul, was then in his sixteenth year, and had been left in charge of Herat while the Ameer proceeded to quell some disturbances in another part of his dominions.

Every day it was customary for Yakoob Khan to grant a public audience to anybody wishing to see him, and to vary the monotony of this, the prince used to sit in an arm-chair by the window and amuse himself with watching the drill of the troops outside. "He seemed highly delighted with the wheeling of the columns, and the thundering word of command of the officer passing them in review, who, besides, pronounced the 'Right shoulder forward! Left shoulder forward!' with a genuine English accent."

When Vámbéry reached the palace court the drill was at its most interesting point. The men had a very military bearing, far better than the Ottoman army, that was drilled in the same manner forty years ago. They might, indeed, have been taken for European troops had not most of them worn on their stockingless feet the pointed Cabuli shoe, and short trousers so tightly stretched by their straps that they threatened every moment to burst and fly up above the knee.

"After watching the exercises a short time," says Vámbéry, "I went to the door of the reception-hall, which was filled by a number of servants, soldiers, and petitioners. If all made room for me, and allowed me undisturbed to enter the saloon, I had to thank the large turban I had assumed (my companion Mollah Ishak had assumed a similar one), as well as the anchorite appearance which my wearisome journey had imparted. I saw the prince on the chair; on his right hand sat his vizier, and next to him there were ranged against the wall other officers, Mollahs and Heratis. Before the prince stood his keeper of the seal, and four or five other servants. True to my dervish character, on appearing I made the usual salutation, and occasioned no surprise to the company when I stepped, even as I did it, right up to the prince, and seated myself between him and the vizier, after having required the latter, a corpulent Afghan, to make room for me by a push with the foot. This action of mine occasioned some laughing, but it did not put me out of countenance. I raised my hands to repeat the usual prayer, and whilst I repeated it Yakoob Khan looked me full in the face. I saw his look of astonishment, and when I was repeating the Amen, and all present were keeping time with me in stroking their beards, the prince half rose from his chair, and, pointing with his finger to me, called out, half laughing and half bewildered, 'Vallahi, billahi shuma, Inghiliz hestid!' ('By G——, I swear you are an Englishman!').

"A ringing peal of laughter followed the sudden fancy of the Ameer's son, but he did not suffer it to divert him from the idea; he sprang down from his seat, placed himself right before me, and, clapping both his hands like a child who has made some lucky discovery, he called out, 'Hadji, *kurbunet*' ('I would be thy victim'); 'tell me, you are an Englishman in disguise, are you not?'

"His action was so naïve, that I was really

sorry I could not leave the boy in his illusion. I had cause to dread the wild fanaticism of the Afghans, and, assuming a manner as if the jest had gone too far, I said, 'Sahib, makun' ('Have done'); 'you know the Prophet's saying, "He who takes even in sport the believer for an unbeliever is himself an unbeliever." Give me rather something for my *fatiha*, that I may proceed further on my journey.'

"My serious look, and the *hadis* which I recited, quite disconcerted the young man; he sat down half ashamed, and excusing himself on the ground of the resemblance of my features, said that he had never seen a hadji from Bokhara with such a physiognomy. I replied that I was not a Bokhariot, but a Stambuli, and when I showed him my Turkish passport, and spoke to him of his cousin, the son of Akbar Khan, who was at Constantinople in 1860 and met with a distinguished reception from the Sultan, his manner quite changed. My passport went the round of the company, and met with approbation. The prince gave me some krans, and dismissed me with the order that I should often visit him during my stay, which I accordingly did.

"However fortunate the issue of this amusing proceeding, it had still some consequences not very agreeable, as far as my continued stay in Herat was concerned. Following the prince's example, every one wanted to detect in me the Englishman. Persians, Afghans, and Heratis came to me with the express purpose of convincing themselves and verifying their suspicions. But what was most droll, they thought they saw in me a man *à la* Eldred Pottinger, who made his first entry into Herat disguised as a horse-dealer, and became later its master. They insisted that I had a credit here for hundreds, even thousands, of ducats, and yet no one would give me a few krans to purchase bread."

On the fifteenth of November, having scraped enough together to journey in a mendicant fashion to Meshed, Vámbéry set out with a caravan of two thousand persons, half of whom were pilgrims bound for the tomb of Imam Riza. Proceeding along the fruitful valley of the Hari Rud, the Persian frontier was reached on the second day, and ten days later, after many alarms in traversing a region ravaged by the Turcoman man-stealers, the caravan arrived at the capital of Khorassan. On the way, Vámbéry began to throw off his mask, and when he entered Meshed he no longer denied that he was a European.

Half-an-hour after his arrival he paid a visit to Colonel Dolmage, an English officer in the Persian service, with whom he was acquainted. He was attached to the prince-governor of Khorassan, and filled many important posts. When his servants summoned him he was still engaged at his official place of business. They announced Vámbéry as "a singular dervish from Bokhara." Colonel Dolmage hastened home, "regarded me fixedly for a long time, and only when I began to speak did he recognise me, and then his warm and tearful eye told me that I had found not only a European, but a friend. The gallant Englishman offered me his house, which I did not reject, and I have to thank his hospitality that I so far recovered from the hardships of my journey as to be able, in spite of the winter, in a month's time to continue my journey to Teheran."

The highway between Meshed and Teheran is so well known and so regularly traversed that

Vámbéry's uneventful journey along it needs no description, although it occupied him twenty-four days. At the Shah's capital he stayed another couple of months, the guest of the Turkish embassy, and then the fame of his exploits already spread about far ahead of him, and gaining him admiration and respect wherever he went, he started homewards, quitting Teheran for Europe on the 28th of March, 1864, the anniversary of the very day, a year earlier, he had commenced his journey to Central Asia.

No sooner was the safe termination of his travels known, than overtures were made to him to place his services at the disposition of the Russian Government. Had he accepted the offer, a lucrative appointment would have been his reward, and Russia on her part would have secured the most powerful pen in the subsequent Central Asian controversy. But Vámbéry did not approve of Russia's policy in Asia. His sympathies rested more with England. He therefore proceeded to London, where a hearty welcome was accorded by the public to the survivor of so many terrible dangers, and the graphic describer of them.

Returning later on to Buda-Pest, he accepted the professorship of Oriental languages at the university, and settled quietly down—strange as it may seem after such a display of adventurous spirit—to scientific studies, from which he has only allowed himself to be withdrawn from time to time to indicate in the European and English press the bearings of the Russian advance in the region traversed by him. His articles on the subject have given him a reputation as a political writer which throws into the shade somewhat the renown he enjoys among *savants* as an expert in the Tartar group of languages. As a linguist, he has few equals, speaking fluently twelve languages and writing in six. How remarkable his power over English is may be gathered from a perusal of his "Travels in Central Asia," which for graphic description and forcible diction has few equals in our literature of exploration.

CHAPTER II.

CAPTAIN MARSH'S RIDE FROM THE CASPIAN TO INDIA.

Russian progress in Central Asia after Vámbéry's return—English policy—Captain Marsh sets out to ride to India—Remarkable growth of Baku—A new Russia developing in the Caucasus—The three Russian descents on the East Caspian coast—Seizure of Ashurada and Krasnovodsk—The railway between London and Teheran—Apathy of the British mission at Teheran—England without influence in Persia—Character of Marsh's ride through Islam—The raids of the Turcoman man-stealers—Crucifixion of Turcomans at Meshed—Journey from Meshed to Herat—Experiences of an English officer at Herat—Yakoob Khan and Captain Marsh—Ride from Herat to Candahar and India—Results of the journey—Sir Charles MacGregor on *chupper*-riding in Persia.

"The possession of Herat by Russia means the possession of the one line by which India can be invaded. The possession of Herat by England means the annihilation of all the Russian hopes of an invasion of India."—COLONEL MALLESON, 1880 (*Herat*, page 877).

"If the English were to establish a commercial and political preponderance at Herat, we should hardly be able to hold our own in Northern Khorassan and Merv."—COLONEL M. VENUKOFF, 1883 (*Russian Thought*, May, 1883).

AFTER Arminius Vámbéry's return to Europe in 1864, there was a lull in Central Asian travel for nearly eight years. During that time the Russians were incessantly fighting and advancing. In 1865, General Tchernayeff took Tashkent; in 1866, Romanovsky beat 40,000 Bokharans at Irdjar, and stormed the fortress of Khodjent; in 1867, the Russian province of Turkestan was formed, and Kaufmann appointed governor-general; in 1868, the Russians captured Samarcand, and completely crushed the power of the Emir of Bokhara; in 1869, Krasnovodsk, on the Caspian, was occupied, and a second base of operations against India established; in 1870, General Abramoff defeated the rebellious subjects of the Emir of Bokhara at the Kulikahan Heights, and rendered that sovereign still more the vassal of the White Tsar; in the same year, Michailovsk, the present starting-point of the Transcaspian railway, was founded; in 1871, the Chinese territory of Kuldja was occupied on one side of Central Asia, and the Turcoman region from the mouth of the Atrek to Kizil Arvat annexed on the other side; finally, in 1872, preparations were commenced on a large scale for the conquest of Khiva. All this while England fumed and protested and took part in endless discussions, but, as is usual with her in such cases, did nothing. The louder the talk, the less the action—such is a maxim Russian statesmen have learned to apply to this country; and never was it better exemplified than during the period extending from Vámbéry's return from Khiva to the departure of the second European pioneer for Central Asia. This pioneer was Captain Hippisley Cunliffe Marsh, of the 18th Bengal Cavalry, who rode in 1872 from Enzeli, on the Caspian, to Jacobadad, near the river Indus, *viâ* Meshed, Herat, and Candahar.

Marsh arrived at Poti, the principal Black Sea port of the Caucasus, on the 1st of September, 1872, and found the Russians busily engaged constructing the railway to Tiflis, whence it has been recently extended to Baku, on the Caspian. The journey between the two seas, travelling rapidly the whole time and allowing a day or two's rest at Tiflis, occupied him nearly a fortnight. It can now be achieved in thirty-six hours, and might be in twenty-four. Baku he found to be a quiet little town, deriving its importance more from being the dockyard of the Caspian than the seat of the petroleum industry of the Caucasus. Since then vast alterations have taken place. Investigations have elicited that Baku contains more oil than Pennsylvania; millions of capital have been sunk in developing the industry; and scores of steamers—many 200 feet long—have been added to the Caspian marine to carry away the oil to the Volga, where several thousand oil trucks have been placed on the Russian railways to convey it to St. Petersburg, Warsaw, and Odessa. Instead of the "one wooden jetty" of Captain Marsh's time, twenty-five large piers now exist, and 7,000 vessels enter and clear Baku every year.

When Russia was conquering the Caucasus there were plenty of English politicians who advocated a policy of non-intervention and indifference, on the grounds that the conquest would prove a barren one. The rocks, they said, would only yield warlike hill tribes, whose marauding habits would provoke a drain on the Russian exchequer for generations to come. The Caucasus is now thoroughly subdued, brigandage is suppressed, and nearly every part of it, by means of railways and military roads, has been rendered accessible to the traveller and the trader. Instead of proving a useless annexation, the Caucasus region has become a great field of colonization for the surplus population of the middle Russian provinces, and the magnificent plains to the north of the Caucasus and the lovely valleys to the south of it are now attracting an ever-increasing stream of Russian emigrants. Side by side with the agricultural development of the country, the rockiest district of it has been found to possess sufficient petroleum to supply the whole world. Thanks to the corn of Stavropol and the oil of Baku, a new Russia is growing up astride the Caucasus. The present outposts of this lusty state are Kars, Erivan, and Askabad. If Russia's progress in Asia continues at the rate it has maintained since the Crimean war, the outposts before the end of the century will be Constantinople, Teheran, and Herat.

Leaving Baku in a steamer, Captain Marsh proceeded to the island of Ashurada, in Astrabad Bay, where the Russian sailor had nearly penetrated the secret of Vámbéry's disguise by noting the whiteness of his skin. Here he saw a number of vessels on their way to Tchikishlar and Krasnovodsk, with stores for the projected expedition to Khiva.

Everybody is familiar with the fierce and protracted struggle attending Russia's conquest of the west or Caucasian side of the Caspian. Successive wars had to be waged with Persia and Turkey, generations of conflicts fought out with native states and hill tribes, before the Caucasian region was finally subdued. On the eastern side of the Caspian, the conquest of the coast has been wholly unaccompanied by any such terrible expenditure of blood and money. The East Caspian littoral may be said to have been won by three swoops of the Russian eagle.

The first was in 1834, when General Perovsky descended upon the northern extremity of the coast opposite the mouth of the Volga, and established Fort Alexandrovsky among the Kirghiz nomads. The second was in 1841, in which year the war brig *Araxes,* without any previous warning, sailed into Astrabad Bay and seized the island of Ashurada, lying at the southernmost extremity of the coast. Finally, in 1869, Colonel Stolietoff—afterwards famous as the envoy at Cabul—with equal suddenness descended upon the coast at Krasnovodsk, midway between Alexandrovsky and Ashurada, and completed the seizure of the East Caspian littoral.

When Ashurada was occupied, Russia meant the little island to have served as a stepping-stone to greater conquests inland. Her idea was to pass from it in course of time to Astrabad, the first of the four great cities—Astrabad, Meshed, Herat, and Candahar—stretching along the historical highway of invasion of India. The fierce opposition, however, raised by England and Persia to any further extension of territory inland checked this design, and Russia was compelled, after waiting many years in the hope of taking Astrabad by a direct attack in front, to shift her base of operations and approach it *viâ* Krasnovodsk and Kizil Arvat on the flank. When Captain Marsh arrived at Ashurada the game was in full swing, and many Russian officers, coming on board the steamer, told him, "while chatting over wine and cigars, that they hoped one day to take India from us, as it was their destiny to be paramount in Asia!"

Returning westward along the southern Caspian coast, belonging to Persia, Marsh landed at Enzeli, the port for Teheran, on the morning of the 20th of September, 1872, and four days later set out on his "Ride through Islam" to India.

Six mules conveyed the traveller, a companion, their servants, and the baggage to Kasvin, where they obtained ponies and pushed on with these to Teheran, which they reached after seven days' continuous ride. French engineers are now engaged constructing a railway from Enzeli to Teheran, and before long it will be possible to do the distance between the Caspian and the Shah's capital in a few hours. Direct railway communication will then exist between London and Teheran, and the journey will be feasible in little more than a week.

At Teheran Captain Marsh found that the British Legation knew nothing about what was going on at Meshed and Herat, although England paid the officials amply enough to have rendered them less remiss in discharging their duties. Further, he not only got no help and no information about the road from them, but attempts were even made to dissuade him from undertaking his journey. It is the characteristic of Russian officials in such matters as these to do their utmost to promote the interests of the state. Judging from the experience of Marsh and many other pioneers, whose acquaintance we shall make directly, it would appear to be the settled policy of the Foreign Office and India Office at home, and the legations abroad, to treat with disdain or indifference, or even to go out of their way to openly thwart, any explorer, not a Government agent, who seeks to perpetrate the dreadful crime of doing something for the good of his country.

Holding such inverted views of patriotism, it is not surprising to learn that the British Legation exercised in 1872 no influence whatever over the Shah, and that the sovereign of Persia was drifting into a course which has since completely rendered him the puppet of Russia.

Luckily, Captain Marsh was not a man to be turned aside from his enterprise by the indifference and opposition of those who ought to have assisted him. Completing his preparations without extraneous aid, he rode out of Teheran on the seventeenth of October, bound for India, with his servant behind shouting "Hosh" and "Kabardar" ("Have a care") to clear the way. All his baggage consisted of a few clothes, a kettle, sugar and tea, etc., stuffed into four small saddle bags, of which two were carried by his servant's horse and two by his own. Before him lay a journey of 1,480 miles, of which half would be through Persia and the remainder through Afghanistan. The first day sixty-four miles were traversed, and the traveller put up at Ahoowon for the night. The next day he rode forty, and on the third arrived at the city of Shahrood, forty-five miles south-east of Astrabad, glad to get some regular food after subsisting up till then on bread and milk. Beyond here the road was exposed to Turcoman raids, and Marsh had intended travelling with a caravan; but, finding it waiting for the arrival of a lady of high birth from Teheran to accompany it, he pushed on without an escort to Meshed, and safely reached the city, unhindered by any adventures on the way. Hitherto Marsh had travelled *chupper*, or post, and in European dress; he now assumed the disguise of a Persian and purchased a Turcoman horse, on which he travelled the remaining 900 miles to India.

As stated in the last chapter, Meshed is the

capital of Khorassan, and is governed by a governor-general, who exercises despotic sway over the territory lying between the Caspian and the Afghan frontier near Herat. In Marsh's time the entire road from the Caspian to Herat was open to the raids of the Turcomans, who used to murder travellers and villagers, or carry them off into slavery in Central Asia. In Khiva alone at that period there were more than 40,000 slaves. When Vámbéry penetrated to Central Asia eight years earlier, Khiva and Bokhara had been the two principal slave-holding states. In the interval Russia had conquered Bokhara and suppressed slavery there, and was now preparing, in defiance of England's threats and protests, to march upon Khiva and extinguish the execrable slave trade in that khanate also. Restricted now to one market, the slave-catching Turcomans could not dispose of the whole of their captives, and were adopting a new system of either holding their prisoners until they were ransomed, or keeping them as labourers in their own Akhal and Merv settlements.

So great was the fear entertained by the

pusillanimous Persians of the warlike Turcomans, that the mere sight of a few horsemen hovering in the distance would put a whole caravan in a panic. Conscious of the terror he inspired, a Turcoman would not hesitate to attack half-a-dozen Persians, and would often succeed in making most of them prisoners. A Turcoman told Vámbéry that "the Persians, struck with a panic, often throw away their arms, demand the cords, and bind each other mutually. We have no occasion to dismount, except for the purpose of fastening the last of them."

As is always the case with cowards, the Persians inflicted fearful cruelties upon their courageous enemies whenever they fell into their hands. "On my way home from my visit to the prince-governor I saw a dreadful sight," says Marsh, in his account of Meshed. "On a dead wall, at the end of a lane, were three men crucified; they had large wooden tent-pegs driven through the hands and feet, and one through the back, with their faces to the wall. It made me shudder, one glance being sufficient. These unfortunates were three Turcomans the governor had lately caught red-handed in a raid on some village in the neighbourhood. These wretches are the terror of the country, and richly deserve death, but not such a dreadful one, for, to prolong the torture, the peg through the back was left in. Had it been extracted, they would have died at once. Some caught before had been flayed alive, and left to die by inches. They told me that eighty chiefs of the Turcomans had been invited to a conference at Meshed, and had been treacherously seized. So much for the civilization of Persia! This was by the order of one of the most accomplished men of the time."

After a few days' stay at Meshed, Captain Marsh set out for Herat with an escort of forty sowars provided by the prince-governor, "a lot of wild-looking men, armed and booted for the road, with letters from the prince to the different places on the way." This escort was exchanged for another and smaller one at the first stage, and the greater part of the distance to the Afghan frontier was done with only two or three men. The week's ride was not a very eventful one, and although the Turcomans were out in every direction, none of them came across the travellers. At Kafir Kaleh, an old ruined fort on the Perso-Afghan frontier, Marsh was deserted by the Persian escort, and had to push on to Kusan, the first Afghan post, ten or eleven miles beyond and in the full track of the Turcoman raids, without any protection whatever. Kusan is the most advanced outpost of Herat in this direction, and is situated sixty-eight miles from it. The place is small and ruinous, and could be captured at any time by a sotnya of Cossacks from Askabad. The Afghans treated the traveller well, and their attentions towards him increased every step during his three days' ride along the Hari Rud valley to Herat, which was reached on the 19th of November. There Captain Marsh was received with great distinction by the Eeshaghasi or Chamberlain, and "mobbed on all sides with salutations" from Yakoob Khan's officers. A suite of apartments was placed at his disposal, a guard was posted at the gate to keep off intruders, servants were sent to wait upon him, and, in short, Yakoob Khan did everything to minister to the comfort of his English guest.

Eight years had elapsed since the ragged

dervish Vámbéry had arrived in a poverty-stricken condition at Herat, and had nearly had his disguise penetrated by the youthful Afghan prince. In the interval the lad of eighteen had developed into a man of twenty-six, "well bred, with a pleasant, intelligent face, and a good voice." When he received Marsh—who donned his English uniform again—he conversed with him frankly in broken English about his affairs, and manifested the strongest sympathy for England. It is melancholy to reflect that a prince of such bravery and promise should have been converted by his long imprisonment by his father at Cabul into the weak and vacillating Ameer, who treacherously connived at the murder of Major Cavagnari. During the whole time of Marsh's stay at Herat, Yakoob Khan treated him as no other Englishman has ever been treated since in Afghanistan, and the people were so friendly that the officer was able to stroll about the streets freely in his uniform unattended, without any fear of insult or attack.

The ride of four hundred miles from Herat to Candahar was uneventful, and Marsh reached the latter city the second week in December, without experiencing any adventure, or any trouble, from the tribes the whole way. No European had visited Candahar since the Lumsden Mission in 1857-58, but the traveller was well treated by the officials, and the only cause of complaint he had was a refusal on the part of Shere Ali to allow him to proceed to Cabul. The hot-and-cold policy of the Indian Government had already, even at that period, laid the seeds of the Afghan war; Shere Ali distrusted the presence of any European in his dominions. In consequence of the Ameer's refusal, Captain Marsh had no alternative but to ride on to India, *viâ* Quetta and the Bolan Pass. Quetta then had not been occupied by England, and was garrisoned by the troops of the Khan of Khelat. The Khan himself was at Bagh, on the Indian side of the Bolan, into which Marsh rode early in January, after a troublesome journey through the pass, and, for the first time since leaving Teheran, met a fellow-countryman again, Major Harrison, the political agent. Here he rested a couple of days, and then rode on to the frontier station of Jacobabad, where he was hospitably treated by the officers of the Scinde Horse. Finally, after a day or two, he made his way to Sukkur, on the Indus. At this point, on the 10th of January, 1873, his 1,480 miles' ride from Teheran came to an end, the journey, including stoppages, having occupied him eighty-five days.

Geographically, very little was added to our stock of knowledge by this ride, and the work Marsh afterwards published, "A Ride through Islam," cannot be said to have given us an adequate account of the region traversed, being extremely thin and meagre. Perhaps this latter defect was due to the fact that he rode *chupper*, that is, he posted full speed through the country along the main roads, making scarcely any halts, and consequently merely glanced at it, as one might do from the windows of a railway carriage. "There are only two ways of travelling in Persia," says Sir Charles MacGregor: "one is to march with either hired or purchased cattle, the other to ride *chupper* right through the country and try and beat every one who has ever gone before you. By the latter means you will cover a great deal of ground, take in very little of the country, see nothing of the people, and arrive at your destination in a condition something between a skinned eel and a boiled lobster."

But if Marsh did not add anything of particular value to geographical literature, he certainly brought home with him military and political information of the highest importance. The Legation which had sought to prevent his journey was afterwards glad to use the data collected by him *en route*, and a Government which never rewarded him for his exploit found his ride to Herat and Candahar of immense value when it had to invade Afghanistan in that direction, and negotiate with the very prince who had received the English officer so hospitably during his journey.

The next time Marsh saw Afghanistan was in 1879, when the 18th Bengal Regiment—formerly the 2nd Mahratta Horse—was moved up to the frontier to take part in the Afghan war. In the interval, Marsh had risen to the rank of major, and a fellow-officer, Major the Hon. G. C. Napier, son of Lord Napier of Magdala, had also added to the renown of the regiment by his surveys of the Turcoman frontier to the north of Meshed. At present

Marsh and his troopers are located at Peshawur, the former ready to ride off pioneering in Central Asia again at a moment's notice, the latter to give a good account of the Russians should they ever attempt to show themselves openly at all at Cabul.

CHAPTER III.

COLONEL VALENTINE BAKER'S VISIT TO THE PERSO-TURCOMAN FRONTIER.

The Russians on the Atrek—Our lack of knowledge of their operations—Need of an Intelligence Office—The unexplored Perso-Turcoman border—Task undertaken by Colonel Baker, Lieutenant Gill, and Captain Clayton—A ton of luggage—Kindness of the Russian officials in the Caucasus—Arrival at Teheran and journey to Shahrood and Meshed—Baker hindered from going to Herat—Important results that might have attended his journey to that city—Proceeds to Kelat-i-Nadiri—His remarks on Nadir Shah's invasion of India—Growth of Russia's power east of the Caspian—Marvels of her advance—What our policy ought to be—Baker prevents a Persian raid upon the Turcomans—His account of the new Russian border—England negotiates with old maps, Russia with new ones—Baker prevented from going to Merv—His "Clouds in the East"—Value of his survey to England.

'We talk, and do nothing; 'tis shame for us all."—
SHAKESPEARE (*Henry V.*).

CAPTAIN MARSH, in riding through Islam, from Teheran to the Indus, in 1872-73, had seen nothing of the Russian operations in Central

Asia, and hence, on his arrival in India in the January of the latter year, had nothing to say about them. But, in the meantime, quite a panic had raged in England over the projected expedition to Khiva. A Russian column under Markozoff had operated during the winter of 1872 within a few miles of Astrabad—the Persian city at the south-east corner of the Caspian, which Napoleon and leading Russian and English strategists had declared to be the best base for any grand expedition against India. The scanty knowledge we possessed of the Atrek region, and the gross lack of statesmanship on the part of the English Government in maintaining no agents in Khorassan, afforded a favourable field for alarming conjectures and terroristic generalizations. It was said that the Atrek, which the Russians had only recently forced Persia to treat as the boundary, was a river rising near Merv; that a long line of Russian forts stretched up its course, and would eventually be extended to Merv itself; and, finally, that once at Merv, a mere raid would be sufficient for Kaufmann's Cossacks to obtain possession of Herat, the "key of India."

For the prevalence of this alarm England was herself quite as much to blame as Russia. It was not the duty of the Russian Government to report to England every movement it made in Central Asia, while, on the other hand, it was clearly the duty of the English Government to have kept itself informed by agents of what was going on east of the Caspian. But we had no intelligence branch at the Horse Guards, and none at the Foreign Office. At Teheran, where nothing of importance was occurring, we maintained a mission at a cost in salaries alone of £9,000. At Meshed, the point whence we derived all our knowledge of what was transpiring at Merv, Herat, and on the Atrek, we were represented by a native *vakeel*, or news writer, Abbas Khan, receiving £18 per annum! If the money wasted on the Legation at Teheran had been spent in maintaining a line of consuls from Astrabad to Khaf, along the Perso-Turcoman and Perso-Afghan frontiers, there would have been less alarm over vague rumours in England, the true bearings of the Russian movement would have been better known, and there would no doubt have been a sounder policy pursued in regard to Afghanistan. Lastly, there would have been no occasion for Valentine Baker and other officers to go pioneering in Central Asia, performing duties that lay within the province of accredited agents of the State.

Colonel Valentine Baker had commanded the 10th Hussars for a period of thirteen years when he decided upon setting out for the East to explore in a lateral direction the little-known region lying between the Caspian and Sarakhs. Numerous travellers had traversed the flanks of this region during the pioneering epoch of 1830-40, but they had journeyed chiefly north and south—no one had thoroughly passed across it from west to east, along the natural Perso-Turcoman border formed by the highlands of Khorassan. What we knew of the country was mainly of a hearsay character, derived from explorers like Fraser, who had penetrated parts of the southern outskirts of it, like Burnes and Wolff, who had flanked it on the east in passing from Bokhara to Meshed *viâ* Merv, or, again, like Conolly and Vámbéry, who had flanked it on the west in journeying from Astrabad in the direction of Khiva. The long narrow oases of Akhal and Atak—the former the scene afterwards of many desperate Russo-Turcoman conflicts, culminating in the crowning struggle of Geok Tepé—were both unknown to the European geographer, although the reconnoitring expeditions of Stolietoff in 1871, and Markozoff in 1872, had enabled Russia to map the topographical features with tolerable accuracy.

Valentine Baker left Charing Cross on the 20th of April, 1873, a little more than three months after the safe arrival of the preceding pioneer, Captain Marsh, in India, and about a month after the starting of the Russian expedition against Khiva. He was accompanied by Lieutenant Gill, R.E.—the Gill whose cruel murder by the Bedouins is still fresh in the reader's memory—and by Captain Clayton, of the 9th Lancers, who was afterwards killed during a polo match at Delhi. Vámbéry had set out for Central Asia in rags; Marsh's equipment had consisted of very little more than a clean shirt and a kettle; these three officers took with them, however, nearly a ton of luggage! But this luggage was not made up exclusively of "comforts." The officers meant to make a regular scientific survey of the Atrek region, besides enjoying a bit of sport, so that in excess of an armoury of weapons, and a number of presents for the border chiefs, they had with them a "large and ponderous box of surveying instruments." Nineteen mules were required for this and the effects of the servants they hired on reaching the Caspian region, so that the cavalcade formed quite an expeditionary column.

Journeying through Vienna, the travellers made their way down the Danube, and along the Black Sea to Constantinople, whence they proceeded in a steamer to Poti. By this time the Poti-Tiflis railway was finished; and they were able to traverse the distance to the Caucasian capital by train instead of by diligence, as had been the lot of Captain Marsh.

Letters of recommendation from the Prince of Wales to the Tsar's brother, the Grand Duke Michael, secured Baker a warm welcome at Tiflis. There was no enmity, no secrecy, no desire to frustrate their survey—orders were issued to show the officers everything. Baker had brought with him "secret and confidential"

War Office maps of the region to be explored, but he found a few days after his arrival at Tiflis that the War Office, as is its wont, had been hoarding up rubbish. Only a few months previous Colonel Stebnitzsky, whose personal topographical knowledge of Central Asia altogether exceeds that of any other expert, English or Russian, had been on a survey to the Perso-Turcoman frontier, and the Tiflis authorities freely and spontaneously gave Baker copies of his maps. When he reached the Caspian, the naval station at Ashurada was thrown open to his inspection, and a letter from the Viceroy enabled him to pay a visit to Tchikishlar, at the mouth of the Atrek, which subsequently served as the base of General Lazareff's disastrous expedition against the Tekké Turcomans in 1879. There, instead of a Russian fortress, respecting which innumerable alarmist articles were being written at the time, he found only a few sand heaps without a single soldier, "and saw at once the absurdity of the fuss which had been made in England about the place." Baker rightly guessed that Tchikishlar would never possess much strategical importance, and now that Krasnovodsk and Michailovsk have been made the principal ports of the Transcaspian region, it is very unlikely the place will be heard of any more.

At Astrabad he put up at the Russian consul's. Gospodin Bakoulin, "a very intelligent and well-informed man," did his utmost to render the travellers comfortable. He made no secret of Russia's territorial claims to the Atrek region, and Baker saw at a glance how urgently we needed some one on the spot to sustain the local Persian officials against the intrigues and the pecuniary pressure of Russia. At Teheran, where no interests were suffering, we had half-a-dozen Englishmen idling at the Legation; at Astrabad, where only one was wanted, we had none at all.

From Astrabad the explorers made their way by land to Teheran, which they reached about the time the Shah arrived in London on his well-known visit. Resting a few days at the Persian capital, they started eastward again. They had not gone far, when Captain Clayton was attacked by fever, and had to return to Teheran, leaving Baker and Gill to continue the journey alone, along the desert skirt of the Elburz range, to Shahrood.

On their way the travellers had plenty of sport and a brush or two with robbers, and enjoyed themselves exceedingly. From Shahrood they travelled with a caravan, protected by a large escort, and underwent the usual vexations and annoyances of caravan travel in proceeding to Meshed. As none of the rumoured Turcoman raiding parties showed themselves at all on the way, they might have followed Marsh's plan and pushed on alone, although they would have incurred greater danger than he did, since, owing to their extensive baggage train, they did not enjoy the facility of movement possessed by that luggageless *chupper* rider the previous year.

From Meshed, Baker meant to have gone on to Herat, and thence *viâ* the Murghab river to Merv, following the course a Russian army would pursue in advancing upon the key of India from Turkestan in that direction. Instead of dropping in uninvited upon Yakoob Khan, however, as Captain Marsh had wisely done, Baker wrote to him from Meshed to announce his coming, and in this manner brought about the frustration of his enterprise.

In reply to his letter, Yakoob Khan sent an

agent to inquire whether he was the bearer of good tidings, his father, the Ameer Shere Ali at Cabul, having provoked him into an attitude of revolt by disinheriting him—the true heir to the throne—in favour of his youngest son Abdullah, the offspring of a favourite wife. When he found Baker had no mission, he wrote a civil letter that he would have liked to see him, but that he had most positive instructions from the Indian Government not to receive any English officers, unless they came with an order from the British Government.

It is difficult to understand why such an order should have been given, as more good than harm was to be apprehended from the commingling of Englishmen and Afghans. Baker says of this :—"I have always deeply regretted that the order of our Government prevented our going to Herat. I feel sure that the influence we might have exerted would have prevented the serious outbreak which occurred between Yakoob Khan and his father, and which ended in Yakoob being treacherously imprisoned at Cabul." It was the shilly-shally policy of the Gladstone Government of this period which laid the foundations of the Afghan war.

Foiled in proceeding to Herat and Merv, Colonel Baker thought of making his way to Sarakhs, a great strategical point belonging to Persia, barring a Russian advance upon Herat, by way of the Caspian and the Akhal oasis. Unluckily, the prince-governor of Khorassan decided at the last moment not to pay his intended visit of inspection to the fortress, and the traveller did not consider himself justified in attempting the journey alone. He, therefore, struck due north, in the direction of the frontier at Kelat-i-Nadiri, through country less open to Turcoman raids than that intervening between Meshed and Sarakhs. A prostrating fever threatened for a time to prevent even the realization of this narrowed programme, but on quitting Meshed, Valentine Baker soon recovered his health, and was able to effect an excellent survey of the border region.

Kelat-i-Nadiri is a natural rock fortress, garrisoned by 700 or 800 Persian troops, overlooking the narrow fertile track—the Atak oasis—along which the Russians must march if ever they advance from Askabad to Sarakhs. It is situated only a few days' journey from Askabad, and as Baker explored the Persian country lying between the two places and reconnoitred a part of the Turcoman oasis also, it will be seen that his military survey afterwards became, by the growth of events, of the highest importance. While at Kelat, Baker took an excursion to Nadir Kala, the ruined stronghold of the great warrior who, to use Baker's words, "at a time when the fortunes of Persia appeared utterly desperate, by dint of sheer genius and determination of will, and within a few short years, cleansed his country of foreign enemies, conquered Afghanistan, forced that barrier of mountains which now guards our Indian frontier, and which we are so wont to consider impregnable, and with only 80,000 men crushed those monarchies which it took us centuries to subjugate, and, finally marching through the heart of Hindostan, conquered Delhi! To those who know the Persian character, and remember that these events only occurred a hundred and thirty-six years ago, the warlike genius of Nadir Shah appears astounding."

The Russians are now posted a few marches from Nadir Shah's castle, and they have the locomotive at Kizil Arvat, a few more marches to their rear. To that terminal station can be conveyed in two days bodies of troops from the Caucasus, where in time of war 350,000 men are maintained, and in five days reinforcements from Russia proper, with its army of 864,219 men on a peace footing and 2,300,000 men when mobilized for hostilities. The chieftains along the Persian frontier had much to say to Baker of the ease with which Russia could penetrate from Kizil Arvat to India. Their opinions fell upon deaf ears in England at the time, for it was imagined that deserts and mountains of colossal magnitude intervened between the furthest point the Russians had then attained and our Eastern empire. But events have proved the chieftains to have been right. Lessar has discovered the existence of one of the easiest roads in the world running from Askabad to Herat, and from Herat we know cruelly from Burrows's disaster at Maiwand how feasible it is to march an army to Candahar, whence no difficulty is experienced in attaining Quetta and India. Events move so rapidly in Central Asia that what is unknown and unapproachable to-day is surveyed and settled upon to-morrow. When

Vámbéry penetrated to the edge of the Kara Kum desert in 1863 anybody could have made a reputation by pushing east of his track to Kizil Arvat, that then inaccessible Tekké stronghold. One can now book through from Charing Cross to Moscow, and from Moscow take a railway ticket to Kizil Arvat station. In 1879, it was open to anybody to make a name for himself by penetrating to the unvisited fortresses Geok Tepé and Askabad; the Russians then holding Kizil Arvat. Geok Tepé and Askabad are now within the limits of the Postal Union, and I receive letters from both places for seven copecks, or twopence-halfpenny! A few more years, and the postman will be at Merv and the engine driver at Herat, and after a little while mails and passengers will be running through Afghanistan from Europe to India.

Yet there are English statesmen who fancy that Russia and India will be kept apart for another century. They are blind to the evidences of Russian progress afforded by the history of the last twenty years. The notion of Russia absorbing any part of Afghanistan, or forcing us to co-operate to break down the

Afghan barrier the Gladstone Government erected on evacuating Candahar in 1881, is treated as chimerical. The notion of a Russian railway to Herat and thence to India is ridiculed. Yet there is no certainty so certain as the junction of the Russian and English empires in Asia in the immediate future, and the establishment of direct commercial intercourse between Europe and India by way of the Caspian and Herat. It is inevitable that the Russians should sooner or later get to India. Rather than waste our energies in useless recrimination over the advances in the past, and in vague alarms at the dangers that may arise from the junction in the future, we should accommodate ourselves quietly to what we cannot prevent, and take care that the approximation of the two empires be attended with the selection of the best possible frontier line for the outer defence of India.

On the Khorassan frontier the clearness of the air is such that observations can be taken at incredible distances. From Nadir Shah's stronghold Baker could see distinctly Sarakhs, sixty miles to the south-east, and the river Tejend, lying in the steppe forty miles north of

Kelat. This Tejend is the river that washes Herat. After passing Sarakhs it twists round to the west and flows into the Turcoman steppe, or desert, where it forms the Tejend oasis, lying between the Khorassan frontier and Merv. The Russians have a project for turning the water from the desert marshes into some old channels that would cause it to flow still further west to within sight of Askabad. They would then possess a watercourse running direct from Herat, and could advance along its banks at any time with the assurance of finding forage and water the whole distance.

From Kelat, Baker went to Deregez, a little Kurd khanate on the Persian border, lying close to Askabad. The governor, Alayar Khan, residing at the chief town, Mahomedabad, received Baker well, and enabled him to forward a letter to the leader of the Merv Tekkés, Kaushid Khan, asking permission to visit Merv. In the interval he went hunting with Alayar Khan in the Turcoman country, killing boars and pheasants on the banks of the Tejend and reconnoitring the outlying settlements of Askabad. The chief of the escort, to amuse Colonel Baker, wanted to make a raid on the Tekké Turcoman settlement of Annau, now a Russian possession, just to show him what a foray was like, but the traveller disappointed him with a refusal. "Firm as a rock, I said that if anything of the sort were attempted, I would send a letter to Alayar Khan, who would be very angry. The project was reluctantly abandoned, and below us, looking as peaceful as if war and rapine were unknown, lay the unsuspecting village—the men and boys lazily tending their herds, the women weaving carpets in the tents, and the children basking in the sun, never dreaming that their savage enemies were plotting murder and destruction just above them, and that a few short minutes would have sealed their fate. Little thought they that the Frenghi was whispering words of mercy on their behalf, and saving them from captivity and death."

Of the present Russo-Persian border beyond the Caspian Baker wrote:—"Only those who have travelled long and far in Persia can imagine how refreshing it is to come across a plentiful supply of good water at every few miles; and this is the character of the entire northern slope of the Kuren" (and Kopet)

"Dagh range" (now being absorbed by Russia).

"What a splendid country this would be under settled rule! But Persia seems to take no trouble in maintaining her frontier. Unless some action is taken, it appears likely soon to lapse into Russian hands, and will thus give them a perfectly level, rich, and well-watered highway from the Caspian to Herat, with forts that only want occupying along the entire line. Yet we seem ready to allow this part of Persia to pass away from her without a remonstrance; and so defective is our topographical knowledge" (thanks to the English Government, always thwarting military explorers) "that we scarcely realize that this *is* Persia, and arguments upon the point are common in the daily papers between disputants on Central Asian affairs. No European foot had ever before passed along this route, and no Russian had ever penetrated here. There is an intense pleasure in feeling that you have got to entirely new ground. This pleasure was greatly enhanced when we hurried to our maps that we had brought from England—the very latest productions of the Topographical Department, supposed to be secret treasures, and upon which our diplomatic arrangements with the Russian Government were being made—and found that they were utterly useless, giving no idea whatever of the geographical features of the country. So entirely incorrect were they, that we threw them on one side. They gave us no guidance whatever, and were simply misleading at every step. And yet we wonder that we have boundary questions constantly to refer to arbitration, which are invariably decided against us."

At length the letter from Merv arrived. "Kaushid Khan wrote most civilly; he begged us on no account to come there, as it would give rise to great trouble with his people, and he could not be answerable for our safety." While Baker had been journeying through Persia, Khiva had fallen to the Russian arms, and the Tekkés of Merv, anticipating a march upon their oasis, had constructed under Kaushid Khan's supervision an immense fortress, capable of containing the whole population. Had Baker been supported in any way by the English Government, he thinks the Khan would undoubtedly have received him, but the Ministry of the day refused to recognise the traveller or assist him in any way.

Disappointed, then, in penetrating to Merv, Baker started on his way home, still continuing *en route* the survey of the Perso-Turcoman frontier. Kuchan, Shirvan, Budjnurd, and other points now lying alongside the new Russian border line, were visited in succession, and everywhere the traveller found the people dissatisfied with Persian rule, dismayed at the possibility of annexation by Russia, and desirous of passing under an English protectorate. The sources of the river Atrek were then explored, and afterwards the traveller journeyed on, *viâ* Shahrood, to Teheran, whence he proceeded through Russia to St. Petersburg; arriving there shortly before Christmas, 1873. Here he met Mr. Schuyler and Mr. Ashton Dilke (late M.P. for Newcastle, and brother of Sir Charles Dilke), who had just arrived from a journey to Bokhara. Schuyler had travelled part of the way with MacGahan, who left him at Fort Perovsky, and riding across the desert, carrying his life in his hand, reached General Kaufmann's army a few days before the fall of Khiva. An account of that ride deserves a chapter to itself.

Returning home, Colonel Baker published his "Clouds in the East," which contains at the end perhaps the best political and strategical report on Central Asia that has ever been published. At that time the eyes of England were fixed upon the Russian advance from the Turkestan base. Baker was the first to insist on the greater importance of the looming advance up the Atrek, along the Akhal oasis, and so to Herat and India—a movement that has since progressed in the form foreshadowed by him, and will probably continue until the frontiers of the two Asiatic empires become conterminous. Of the unhappy event that led to Colonel Valentine Baker's severance from the army nothing need be said here. Public opinion long ago arrived at the conclusion that the Colonel had retrieved his reputation by his gallantry and his generalship in Turkey—the only redeeming feature of the Russo-Turkish war—and few will begrudge the wish that he may render his country still greater service in Egypt, where England could not make a better reparation for the cowardly and inhuman policy of the Gladstone Cabinet in sacrificing Sinkat, than by giving a high post in the Egyptian army to the general who so bravely attempted its relief. Should English interests again become imperilled throughout the East, it is a satisfaction to know that we have at least one man on the spot willing to sacrifice himself for his country, and capable of taking a prominent part in the hour of danger. "You have one good general in your army," said Skobeleff to the writer a few months before his death. "He is Valentine Baker."

CHAPTER IV.

J. A. MACGAHAN'S CHASE OF GENERAL KAUFMANN'S ARMY.

The Russian expedition against Khiva—Three Englishmen go to the southern side of Central Asia, three Americans to the north of it—A special correspondent of the *Daily Telegraph* tries to get to Khiva and fails—Schuyler and MacGahan set out for the Aral region—Finding the Russians already gone from Kazala, MacGahan decides to chase them across the desert—Captain Verestchagin puts his veto on the undertaking—MacGahan succeeds in starting from Fort Perovsky—How he travelled as a man of peace—Experiences in the Kizil Kum—Fearful character of the desert—The five hundred miles' ride to Khala-ata—Kaufmann gone—Arrested by Colonel Weimarn; escapes the camp and pushes on—Exciting adventures in stalking the Russian army—Slipping through the Turcomans, he arrives at the Russian camp at the moment of victory—The capture of Khiva—The Turcoman campaign—MacGahan's thirty days' ride as a journalistic achievement—The failure of Robert Ker; his concoction of correspondence—Schuyler's journey and his book on Turkestan—MacGahan's after-career—His friendship with Skobeleff.

"MacGahan was universally esteemed throughout the whole Russian army, throughout the leng.h and breadth of which his name was as familiar as a household word by reason of his exploits in Central Asia. He came in from camp to Constantinople to nurse me when I was ill of the typhoid fever. Two days later he fell ill himself, the disease taking the form of typhus with spots; it attacked his brain, which was the most vulnerable part of him by reason of long-protracted mental strain, and he died of convulsions at the end of a week."—LIEUTENANT GREENE, U.S.A. (*Sketches of Army Life in Russia*, page 162).

WHEN, in the spring of 1873, three columns set out to invade the oasis of Khiva, the fear was general in England that the Russians would push their conquests further afield, and that before the war was over they would be at Merv or some other point in proximity to Herat. Perhaps it was with the idea of arresting this movement that the three English officers—Colonel Baker, Captain Clayton, and Lieutenant Gill—made their way to the southern side of Central Asia. It is certain that if the fears of England had been realized, the presence of two good cavalry officers and one of the engineers on the spot would have been exceedingly opportune, and Baker and his companions might have made as grand a stand against the Russians, at the head of the natives, as Butler, Nasmyth, and Ballard had done on the Danube in the summer of '54. In that case, too, a rencontre might have occurred at Merv as striking as any portrayed by the imaginative skill of Jules Verne. The three Englishmen, making their way to Merv from the south of Central Asia, might have met there three Americans—or rather two and a *quasi* one—arriving with the Russians from the north. Those three were J. A. MacGahan, correspondent of the *New York Herald*, Eugene Schuyler, First Secretary to the United States Legation at St. Petersburg, and David Ker, correspondent of the *Daily Telegraph*. The former two were Americans; the latter was an English subject, but travelling with a passport as a United States citizen, so as to evade the regulation framed by the Russian Government prohibiting Englishmen from entering the newly conquered territories in Central Asia.

It does not say much for the boasted enterprise of the English press that only one newspaper—the *Daily Telegraph*—should have sent a "special" to report the operations of the Russian army against Khiva, considering the stir and excitement its movements were occasioning in England in 1873. The Russian columns set out on their desert campaign early in March, and on the 8th of the month—the

7

day Markozoff started with the Krasnovodsk detachment that was doomed to come to grief in the Kara Kum sands—David Ker left London for Central Asia. At St. Petersburg he found Mr. MacGahan preparing to reach the operating army *viâ* Orenburg, but the obstacles likely to arrest the course of a "special" in that direction seemed to Mr. Ker so insuperable that he decided to attach himself to one of the two columns operating from the Caspian. These columns were composed of troops from the Caucasus, the commanders were not led away by the animus against England that was supposed to dominate the Russians in Turkestan, and the regulations enforced by Kaufmann on the Orenburg side of Central Asia did not apply to the region abutting upon the Caspian. Hence the assumption was fair that a "special" would stand a better chance of getting to Khiva with Lomakin or Markozoff than with the generals in Turkestan. But there was one circumstance that upset all these calculations. Both the columns had started before David Ker actually left London, so that when he got to Tiflis he found he had no chance of reaching Khiva from the Caspian, and must after all enter Central Asia by the forbidding portal of Orenburg. The time lost in journeying to the Caucasus, and making a long detour thence to get to Orenburg, operated fatally on the success of his undertaking, and he would have seen nothing of the campaign even if he had not been detained six weeks by the inexorable Captain Verestchagin at Kazala, close to the eastern shore of the Sea of Aral.

That same officer nearly destroyed the prospects also of Mr. MacGahan, who had arrived at Kazala a few weeks in advance of Ker, and had only by a remarkable display of tact, enterprise, and audacity succeeded in bolting across the desert to Khiva, and witnessing the closing scenes of the Russian campaign.

J. A. MacGahan had been accompanied from St. Petersburg to Kazala by his fellow-countryman Schuyler, one of the best living authorities on Russia, who was desirous of making a study on the spot of the Russian position in Central Asia. The "special" of the *New York Herald* was already, even at that time, famous for his dash and energy, and his employers knew that if it was possible at all to get to Khiva, MacGahan would allow no obstacle to deter him. When he left St. Petersburg with Schuyler, the belief of both was that they would be able to reach Kazala before the departure thence of the column led by the Grand Duke Nicholas Constantinovitch, but on their arrival they found 300 miles of desert to be intervening between them and the expeditionary force. The only course open to the correspondent, therefore, was to set out alone with swift horses and a good guide, and trust by following the trail of the Kazala detachment to reach the river Oxus in seven or eight days, before Kaufmann had passed it. The enterprise was full of danger. The Kirghiz of the Kizil Kum desert were said to be hostile to the Russians, and had the reputation of being marauders; and even if the correspondent passed safely through their camps, and escaped death from thirst, he would have to penetrate the cloud of Turcoman cavalry hovering about the rear of the Russian army. Nevertheless, to cross the desert was the only plan open to MacGahan. As he himself puts it, "Remaining at Kazala or going on to Tashkent was equivalent to staying at St. Petersburg. I had already spent so much of the *New York Herald's* money that I felt morally obliged to push forward; and I was very certain that anything less than an entry into Khiva would not be a satisfactory conclusion of my undertaking. The position of a correspondent is often a very embarrassing one. He embarks, perhaps, on an enterprise without fully counting the cost or foreseeing or appreciating half the difficulties to be encountered in its accomplishment, and then feels obliged to put on a brave face and carry it out at whatever risk, when in his inmost self he knows that if he were a free agent, he would be among the very last to undertake it. In this way he often gets a reputation for foolhardiness, or pluck, or perseverance, or cheek, which he really does not merit."

But it was easier to resolve upon this course than to carry it out. MacGahan was casting about for horses and a guide, with which to perform the journey, when Captain Verestchagin, the commandant, called upon him and said he could not take the responsibility of allowing him to proceed on so dangerous a journey without the sanction of the Governor-General.

From this decision he would not swerve, in

spite of all MacGahan's arguments, and as Kaufmann was in the heart of the Kizil Kum, nobody knew where, and it might take weeks to communicate with him, this determination was really an insurmountable barrier to carrying out his plan. A moment's reflection served to convince the "special" that a half-formed design he had conceived of escaping across the river Syr in the night was impracticable. Besides the difficulty of crossing the river, there was the necessity of buying horses, finding a guide, and making other needful preparations, which could not be done in a small place like Kazala, under the watchful eyes of Captain Verestchagin, without his finding it out. MacGahan therefore decided to carry out his desert ride from Fort Perovsky or some other point. Captain Verestchagin did not oppose his going on to Tashkent, and there was chance of finding an officer on the road who would prove more accommodating.

Verestchagin—no connection of the painter—was polite enough, however, to send a courier to Kaufmann with a letter from MacGahan, and that general readily sent back a permission, accompanied by a map and instructions for the road. But had MacGahan waited at Kazala for this answer, he would not have reached Khiva until a week after the fall of the place.

Four days' journey along the Tashkent post road brought MacGahan and Schuyler to Fort Perovsky, where several days were wasted by their interpreter, Ak Mamatoff—who did not relish the desert ride—in obtaining horses and a guide. The latter would not quit Perovsky without a passport ; hence, after all, the intended enterprise had to be made known to the authorities. Colonel Rodionoff, the district governor, however, proved as accommodating as Verestchagin had been the reverse. He not only readily gave the guide a pass, but rendered the American every assistance in his power.

Preparations being complete, MacGahan stepped into the ferry boat at Perovsky at three o'clock in the afternoon of April 30th, 1873, and bidding Schuyler and the Russians good-bye, set off on his adventurous journey. The party consisted of himself, Ak Mamatoff, Mustruf the guide, and a young Kirghiz whom he had hired to look after the six horses, carrying the riders and their baggage, food, and water.

Believing his journey would not last more than a week, and wishing to join the Russian army with as little delay as possible, MacGahan refused to take any camels, and thus had to leave behind such comforts as a tent, carpets, clothing, and extra provisions, which would have rendered his sojourn in the desert comparatively pleasant. "Had I known," he says, "how long I was doomed to wander about the desert, I would never have undertaken the journey with horses only."

Being a man of peace, MacGahan went lightly armed. "A heavy double-barrelled English hunting rifle, a double-barrelled shot gun, both of which pieces were breechloading, an eighteen-shooter Winchester rifle, three heavy revolvers, and one ordinary muzzle-loading shot gun, throwing slugs, besides a few knives and sabres, formed a light and unpretentious equipment. Nothing was farther from my thoughts than fighting. I only encumbered myself with these things in order to be able to discuss with becoming dignity questions relating to the rights of way and of property with the inhabitants of the desert, whose opinions on these subjects are somewhat peculiar."

The route adopted was the course of the Yani Daria, a small stream which flows out of the Syr to a point a third of the way across the Kizil Kum sands to Khiva. Four days ride brought the party to the extremity of this stream, where the Russians had built a small fort and dubbed it Blagoveschtschensk. The first two days of the journey passed off tolerably well, and the nights were pleasantly spent in Kirghiz tents, MacGahan's account of which makes one almost long for an opportunity of spending a holiday among the most hospitable of the Kizil Kum nomads. He always found them, he affirms, "kind, hospitable, and honest. I spent a whole month amongst them, travelling with them, eating with them, and sleeping in their tents. And I had along with me all this time horses, arms, and equipments which would be to them a prize of considerable value. Yet never did I meet anything but kindness, I never lost a pin's worth, and often a Kirghiz has galloped four or five miles after me to restore some little thing I had left behind. Why talk of the necessity of civilizing such people? The Kirghiz possesses to a remarkable degree the qualities of honesty, virtue, and hospitality—virtues which our civilization seems to have a remarkable power of extinguishing among primitive people. I should be sorry indeed ever to see these simple people inoculated with our civilization and its attendant vices."

Of course, a traveller's treatment by natives very largely depends upon the demeanour of the traveller himself. Good-natured, genial, and frank, MacGahan rendered himself welcome wherever he went. Having made up his mind that the best policy for him to pursue was to trust the Kirghiz rather than make them fear him in his passage across the desert, his first act on arriving at a tent was to hand the owner his rifle to take care of, and the second to romp with the children, if any were about. Such behaviour won over at once the nomads, and he left behind as good an impression of himself in the desert as he carried away with him of the natives.

But the third and the fourth days in the Kizil Kum were not so pleasant as the preceding ones. A storm arose in the evening; no friendly *aoul* or camp could be found, and the party had to pass a wretched night in the open,

KIRGHIZ HUNTING THE WOLF WITH WHIPS.

[*To face page* 106.

wrapped in their sheepskin overcoats, while a hurricane roared around them. The next day their water gave out. The long hot march in the sun completely prostrated MacGahan. His throat seemed to be on fire; his eyes grew inflamed and unsteady; he began to feel as though he were about to be attacked with brain fever. At length, after hours of intense suffering, the party struck again the road they had lost in the morning, and found a pit of slimy water, alongside which they passed the night. In the morning a few hours' ride brought them to Irkibai, or Fort Blagovestschensk, which he reached almost simultaneously with a Khivan ambassador that had left Kazala thirteen days previous, in advance of himself.

The Kazala detachment had left Irkibai a fortnight before MacGahan's arrival, and nothing was known of its whereabouts. The Russians at the desert fort, who treated the correspondent remarkably well, urged him to accompany the Khivan ambassador beyond Irkibai, the latter having an escort of twenty-five Cossacks besides his own followers. MacGahan, however, declined. Had he done so, he would not have reached Khiva until several days after its capitulation.

The worst part of the desert lay between Irkibai and the Oxus. The first well, Kizil Kak, was sixty miles distant from Irkibai; and that was sixty feet deep. Between the two places there was not a drop of water. The face of the country was fair. "Gentle elevations roll off in every direction, covered with masses of verdure of a dark rich green, that rival in exuberance the luxuriant carpet of an American prairie, and the sun, shining down from an unclouded sky, turns the spots of yellow sand, seen here and there, into patches of glorious golden light. But all this beauty is deceptive. These gentle hills are only sand, and the verdure which clothes them hides horrors as great as those covered by the roses that twine themselves over sepulchres. Blossoms shoot up, ripen, die, and rot in the course of a few days. The verdure consists of but a rank soft weed that breaks out into an eruptive kind of flower, which, dropping off at the slightest touch, emits a most offensive odour. Beneath the broad leaves lurk scorpions, tarantulas, immense lizards, often five or six feet long, turtles and serpents, and the putrefying bodies of dead camels. Once lost in this desert ocean, without guide or water, you may wander for days, until you and your horse sink exhausted to die of thirst, with the noxious weed for bed, winding-sheet, and grave."

Travelling the whole night, and, excluding a hurried nap, the whole of the next day, the party traversed the scorching sands, and reached late in the afternoon the well of Kizil Kak. Here they rested an hour or two with some Kirghiz, and then pushed on again, meeting not far off a caravan, the leader of which told them that he had seen the army ten days previous at Tamdy. As Tamdy was a hundred and sixty miles as the crow flies from Kizil Kak, the chances of catching up with Kaufmann seemed more remote than ever, especially as the army appeared to have taken a different route from the one originally intended. However, MacGahan was not to be daunted. For nine days he continued his ride across the desert, the hardships of travel, heat, and thirst relieved only by the good treatment he experienced whenever he was lucky enough to encounter a Kirghiz camp. At length, on the 16th of May, seventeen days from the time he had quitted Perovsky, he saw before him in the distance tents shining white in the morning sunlight, white masses of soldiers, and the glitter of bayonets. Surely it was Kaufmann this time!

But MacGahan was disappointed. He had ridden five hundred miles to Khala-ata only to find that Kaufmann had been gone five days, leaving a small detachment at that point to guard the line of communications. To make matters worse, the officer in command of the troops, Colonel Weimarn, treated him with the greatest rudeness, refusing to look at his papers, to give him fodder for his starving horses, or to allow him to go forward. Luckily, the Russian officers made amends for the bad behaviour of the German despot, and during his five days' compulsory detention at Khala-ata, MacGahan received all manner of kindnesses at their hands, and was hospitably lodged in the tent of the gallant Colonel Ivanoff, who, after the fall of Khiva, was made commandant of the Russian fortress of Petro-Alexandrovsk, and for his success in conducting several expeditions against the Turcomans, was eventually promoted to the post of governor of Samarcand.

On the evening of the fifth day, Colonel Weimarn, being uneasy at the non-arrival of news from Kaufmann, gave orders for a body of troops to move forward. MacGahan had been in the interval maturing his plans for escape, and took advantage of the confusion when the column marched at midnight to slip out of the camp and get ahead of the force by a long detour. Riding all night, and resting a bit in the morning, the correspondent made for the caravan route again in the afternoon, trusting to reach the wells of Adam Kurulgan before Weimarn's soldiery. What was his amazement, when he reached a hill overlooking the spot, to find the place in the possession of the Cossacks, who, he was informed by some Kirghiz horsemen riding near the place, had arrived there that very morning!

This was what Dick Swiveller would have called a "stunner." For the moment MacGahan was crushed. His horses were done up, and he did not know of the existence of any wells between those in the hands of the

Cossacks and the Oxus, some seventy miles distant. Without water the journey could not be done, and to get it without being captured afresh seemed an impossibility. At last he remembered overhearing a scrap of conversation, while at Khala-ata, in which mention was made of another well somewhere between Adam Kurulgan and the Oxus, although no such well was known to Vámbéry. Of the position of this well he had no idea, but to his joy, the Kirghiz, on being questioned, said that there was water at Alty Kuduk, or the "Six Wells," twenty miles off, and that Kaufmann had left some troops there.

To this point the party set off at once, MacGahan rightly reckoning on the probability of finding a different kind of commander from Weimarn there. On the way he had to quell a mutiny among his disaffected followers, who presumed upon the bribe of three hundred roubles (£30) he had given them the day before to induce them to slip from the camp with him, and displayed an insolent demeanour. The journey was not accomplished without severe hardships from heat and thirst, but in the end Alty Kuduk was reached, and the exhausted riders received a hearty welcome from the astounded officers posted there. All the food and liquor the hospitable Russians had was placed at MacGahan's disposal, and after a nap the new-comer and his entertainers had a merry time of it. The advent of a stranger from Europe was a godsend to the officers, who were terribly low-spirited at being left behind in the desolate desert, and seemed to have only one pastime—that of "singing, to a most doleful air, a song they had adapted from the German, commencing 'In dem, Alty Kuduk, da ist mein vaterland,' into which they had introduced an astonishing number of variations."

The next day, towards noon, MacGahan was in the saddle again, on the road to the Oxus. The officers tried to dissuade him from the enterprise, assuring him that he could not escape the Turcomans hovering round the army; but although he was not without apprehensions, and Mustruf knew very little more of the way than himself, he felt that there was as much danger from Weimarn's Cossacks behind as from the Khivan horsemen in front. As a matter of fact, only a few hours after his departure from Alty Kuduk, an officer arrived with twenty-five Cossacks and an order to arrest, disarm, and take him back to Tashkent. These were not Weimarn's Cossacks, but a detachment from Perovsky, who had been chasing him for six hundred miles across the desert. Hearing of his departure from Perovsky, an overzealous official at Tashkent had suspended Colonel Rodionoff and ordered an immediate pursuit.

Unconscious that these men were so close behind him, MacGahan rode out of Alty Kuduk on the 27th of May, hoping to reach the river, and consequently Kaufmann's army, the same day. The exact distance to the river was unknown, but he thought it could not be more than fifty, or less than thirty miles. As Kaufmann had only taken two of his six boats, he felt pretty sure he could not yet have crossed, and that he would find him camped on the banks. The thing was to join his force without being captured and cruelly tortured by the Turcomans.

The river was not reached until long after dark. Stealthily drink was given to the horses, and then the party silently withdrew to the dunes to camp and wait for daylight. No fire could be lit for fear of attracting the enemy.

The next morning MacGahan cautiously ascended some hills, 500 feet high, whence the horizon could be scanned twenty miles up and down the river. The dead ashes of many camp fires and the tracks of cannon could be seen, but no army. Riding on, the party suddenly encountered five men on horseback, who, however, instead of attacking them, dashed into the river—there 1,200 yards wide—swam across, and rode off in the direction of Khiva. A little later another band was seen in the valley, twenty strong. This time it was MacGahan who took to flight, luckily without being followed.

At eleven at night, having ridden forty-five miles, the correspondent ordered his exhausted followers to camp and wait again for daylight. All knew that they were in the very thick of danger, that they were in the midst of the enemy, and that having been twice seen from the other side, there might be bodies of horsemen in pursuit of them. The night was an anxious one for MacGahan. All his men would persist in sleeping, and he had to watch alone, "with the murmur of the river for company."

In the morning they were in the saddle by daybreak, and pushed on. A mile beyond they came upon a still smouldering fire—they had halted the night before just in time to keep from falling into a Khivan camp! Riding on a few miles, they were suddenly electrified by a series of reports, at short but regular intervals, which came rolling up the valley of the Oxus, awakening the long silent echoes, like distant thunder. It was the roar of cannon! apparently five miles distant.

His followers, terribly frightened, wanted to hug the river, but MacGahan decided to ride straight ahead to the guns. Ascending the first slope, they cautiously peered over. Nothing could be seen—another hill, a mile beyond, cutting off the view. They crossed the summit, and were riding down to the valley, when five horsemen suddenly came dashing over the hill before them, and seeing the party, wheeled off to the river. The moment was now intensely exciting. Who was on the other side of the hill? What was taking place there?

The sand was so deep, and the horses so

exhausted, that they could not force them out of a walk. While mounting to the summit of the hill the cannonade suddenly ceased. Peering over the top, they saw, two miles in front of them, a number of horsemen, a hundred or so in all, scattered along a line right across their path. While they were deliberating what should be done, two of the horsemen detached themselves from the line and came riding towards them. This was now the most exciting moment of the journey. Believing them to be Turcomans, the correspondent and his companions hid behind the hill—flight was impossible with their tired horses—and prepared for a desperate conflict. The only hope MacGahan had was that he might kill the two Turcomans, catch one of their horses, and dash through the line to the Russians.

Moving cautiously forward, the two horsemen approached to within twenty-five yards of the party, and MacGahan was about to fire, when Mustruf sprang up, gave a shout, and threw up his cap, wild with joy. He had recognised one of the two as a Kirghiz of his acquaintance, and in a few seconds there was a hearty and joyful shake-hands all round.

The Kirghiz were acting as scouts to the Russians, who were only three miles further on, bombarding a fort across the river. Proceeding ahead, MacGahan reached before long a height whence the battle was visible. The Russians were disposed at the foot, half a mile along it cannonading the Khivans on the opposite bank of the river. While he stood watching them a shell exploded among the Khivan cavalry and produced a panic. In a few minutes the Khivans were in full retreat, and the battle of Sheik-Arik—the only severe fight of the campaign—was won.

MacGahan had thus the good luck to descend the hill to the Russians at the moment they were flushed with delight at their victory. In a few minutes he was in the midst of a wondering throng of them, receiving their hearty congratulations at the success of his thirty days' ride across the desert. General Golovatchoff shook hands warmly with him, and invited him to breakfast.

"I suppose," said MacGahan, "I looked as though I needed it, and something more. Hollow-eyed, hollow-cheeked, dirty, dust-covered, unkempt, and ragged—my rifle, which I had carried for a month, slung over my shoulder in a *bandoulière*, had worn my coat into holes—I presented a sorry spectacle among the Russians, who were all spruce in their white coats and caps and gold and silver buttons, as clean and starchy as though they were on parade in Isaac's Square, St. Petersburg. They gave me such a lively account of the dangers I had escaped, that I really began to be frightened. I experienced something of the feeling of the man who, having killed, as he supposed, a fine large wolf, was aghast on being told that he had slain the largest and most magnificent lioness that had ever been seen in the country."

After some tea he called on Kaufmann, who gave him a hearty welcome, and telling him to sit down, said he was a *molodyetz*, or brave fellow. For a day or two he had to live on horseflesh, the army having run out of its supplies, "but," says he, "from the time the Russians had anything to offer me, I never passed a tent where they were eating or drinking that I was not invited to join. From the Grand Duke Nicholas down to the smallest officer in the detachment, they were all the same. I was invited on all hands, twenty times a day, to eat or take tea. Indeed, until I reached Khiva, I made no arrangements for having my servants prepare meals for me, but simply lived on the community at large. And now, as I write, I cannot think of the hospitality which I received without a throb of grateful remembrance. I take this occasion to thank them; to thank not only those with whom I became intimate, but the many whose names I did not even know, but whose kindness and generosity I have experienced, and whose friendly faces I shall not easily forget."

MacGahan's subsequent adventures were interesting, although no more fighting took place until the commencement of the Turcoman campaign. Arriving at Khiva in advance of the Tashkent troops, the united Orenburg and Kinderley columns attacked the city, and after a severe struggle gained a lodgment close outside the walls. This was on the 9th of June. Finding resistance hopeless, the Khan sent a letter to Kaufmann proffering his submission, but the people, and above all the Turcomans, continued firing throughout the night, and the next morning Colonel Skobeleff and Count

Schouvaloff, heading a thousand men, carried one of the gates by assault, after which, clearing the streets, they advanced as far as the Khan's palace. There they learned that Kaufmann, with the Tashkent troops, was making a peaceful and triumphal entry on the opposite side of the city, by the Hazar Asp gate, and immediately returned again.

MacGahan gives a graphic description of the joyful meeting of the Russian conquerors in the midst of Khiva. But more striking still is his account of his adventures the night following the capture of the city, when he lost his way in the Khan's palace, and after blundering into the powder magazine, where the powder was lying loosely about the floor, stumbled upon the harem, the ladies of which entertained him in a most charming manner.

His stay in Khiva lasted five weeks. The Russian troops then commenced the disgraceful campaign against the Turcomans, which is known as the "Yomood massacre." This received political prominence in 1876, when Schuyler published some shocking details he had obtained from an eye-witness, and provoked a rejoinder from Mr. Gladstone which was really an extenuation of Kaufmann's conduct. Into this matter it is unnecessary to go far. Even MacGahan, who was obviously desirous of putting in the best light the actions of those who had treated him so well, cannot help censuring Kaufmann, while his prudently written narrative of the ten days' ravaging with sword and fire of the Yomood settlements, reveals a mode of warfare, to put the matter mildly, repugnant to all feelings of humanity.

The strongest confirmation of the accuracy of Schuyler's statements was afforded in 1879, when Lomakin, who had commanded the Kinderley column in the Khivan expedition, perpetrated the frightful massacre of women and children at Dengeel Tepé.

The Turcoman campaign over, nothing more remained for the Russians to do but sign a treaty of peace with the Khan, and return to their depôts again. On the first of September MacGahan set out with a party of officers for Kazala, and crossing the Sea of Aral in one of the vessels of the Aral fleet, reached in ten days the point where Verestchagin had attempted to detain him in the spring. There he found Mr. Ker, the unlucky correspondent of the *Daily Telegraph*, who had been to Samarcand, and was now on his way home. In a little more than a fortnight MacGahan was again at St. Petersburg.

MacGahan's thirty days' ride across the desert in pursuit of Kaufmann's army is a journalistic achievement which has never been surpassed. Only two exploits approach it in any way—Mr. Archibald Forbes's ride from Ulundi to the African coast, and Mr. O'Donovan's ride to Merv. Both were only of two or three days' duration, and I take it that Forbes's was the more hazardous feat of the two. Archibald Forbes had to ride for a considerable distance alone through a forest swarming with Zulus, with a certainty of death if captured; while Mr. O'Donovan could reckon on the probability that the desire of the Tekkés for English assistance would preserve him from being murdered. But the circumstance that MacGahan underwent greater dangers, and was longer in the desert, in no wise detracts from the merits of his successors. Had Forbes or O'Donovan been placed in the position of Mr. MacGahan, there is little doubt they would have both behaved in the same plucky manner the American correspondent did.

The success of MacGahan rendered the failure of Robert Ker all the more bitter, but there was a peculiar circumstance that enhanced the chagrin of the employers of the latter. Robert Ker sent home some letters padded with extracts from old contributions, and the exposure of this fact by jealous rivals of the *Daily Telegraph* led to an angry controversy, the upshot of which was the journal of Peterborough Court threw over its correspondent and refused to publish any more letters from him. The charge of employing an imaginative pen in Fleet Street to write correspondence ostensibly from Khiva was one that no respectable newspaper could tolerate with equanimity, and the full breast the *Daily Telegraph* made of its relations with Ker completely exonerated the editor and placed the blame in the proper quarter. Ker, shortly after MacGahan's departure from Kazala, proceeded to Samarcand, and on his return home, wrote a work entitled "On the Road to Khiva," in which he made an apology for his misdeeds.

This we cannot but regard as a very lame one, although we hold that it was not his fault that he did not penetrate to Khiva. The mistake he made in going first to the Caspian instead of direct to Orenburg was one anybody might have committed. Khiva lay in a desert 930 miles from Orenburg, 600 from Tashkent, and 500 from Krasnovodsk. The Caspian road was thus the shortest of the three. Had he proceeded at first to Orenburg, he might have spoilt MacGahan's chances, just as the latter by his evasion subsequently spoilt Ker's. Once the Russian officials were put on the alert by the escape of MacGahan from Fort Perovsky, it became almost a matter of impossibility for the trick to be repeated.

Schuyler, who was left behind by MacGahan at Perovsky, went on to Bokhara, and returned home *viâ* Kuldja and Siberia. In Kuldja he met Mr. Ashton Dilke, who had also been on a journey to Samarcand. Dilke, however, travelled more as a tourist than as a pioneer, and as he never enlightened the world with his experiences in Turkestan, his journey was of no very great consequence to the public. MacGahan, Schuyler, and Ker each of them published books of travel on their return home. Of Ker's book little need be said. It consisted of a series of desultory sketches, written in a sentimental and high-flown strain, which any one versed in the literature of Central Asia might have penned in Fleet Street quite as easily as "On the Road to Khiva." But the other two were of a very different character. MacGahan's "Campaigning on the Oxus" is a book of adventure which, from its graphic writing, its charming tone, its never-flagging interest, and its transparent truthfulness, must ever hold its own among works of travel. Schuyler's "Turkestan" was less sensational and less popular. He had comparatively few adventures, but he saw more of Central Asia. And knowing the Russian language and its geographical literature well, and having carefully studied Central Asia in passing through it, he produced a clear and elaborate account of the Russian conquest of Turkestan and its actual condition under Kaufmann's rule, which at once took its place as the standard work on the subject. Some of his views provoked controversy at the time, but there is not an opinion in the book which has not since been supported in a greater or lesser degree by facts, which have been published by the Russians themselves, in regard to their rule in Central Asia.

After his return to Europe MacGahan took part in the Carlist war, in which he narrowly escaped being hanged as a spy, and later on proceeded with a yachting party to Iceland. When he came back to England the *Daily News* secured him as its commissioner to investigate the Bulgarian atrocities. This investigation he carried out in company with Schuyler, who in the interval had been appointed American consul-general in Turkey. The astonishment and horror his accounts occasioned have not yet been forgotten, and undoubtedly had a potent effect in bringing about the Russo-Turkish war. After sharing all the dangers of that conflict and reaching Constantinople with the conquerors, he succumbed to an attack of fever in June, 1878, while nursing a fellow-countryman.

Pages of eulogy might be written on the virtues of one of the most plucky newspaper scouts of modern times. He had in him many of those characteristics which so largely endeared Skobeleff to Russia. He was the Skobeleff of the English-speaking press. Between the two a close and unaffected friendship existed. "When MacGahan died," said a friend of both to the writer the day after Skobeleff's death, "it was impossible to comfort Skobeleff. He wept like a child."

To be wept over by a hero falls to the lot of few men in this world.

CHAPTER V.

CAPTAIN NAPIER'S SECRET MISSION.

English and Russian secret agents in Central Asia—Why should England indulge in cant?—Daood Khan's secret survey of Merv—A black man needs no commendation—Russophobe charges against Russia—Captain Napier's secret journey along the Perso-Turcoman frontier—His confidential report—How it came to be offered to the writer—A Russian staff officer on the value of secret surveys—England ought to have no secret reports—Official statement as to the objects of Napier's journey—His itinerary—Cannot blue-books be made more lively?—Jottings of a native spy—A Persian tailor and a farmer on the position of Russia and England in the East—Results of Napier's survey—England might have had Merv if her statesmen had been wiser—Merv geographically a part of Afghanistan—Napier's opinion of the evils that will result from a Russian occupation of the oasis.

"Of public affairs you have information from the newspapers wherever you go, for the English keep no secret."—DR. JOHNSON to SAMUEL WELCH, 1778 (*Boswell's "Life of Johnson"*).

IN dealing with the rivalry of England and Russia in the East, no charge is more frequently brought against the latter power than the allegation that she everywhere maintains secret agents, and that these enable her to mature her plans for fresh conquests and fresh annexations with an amount of elaborate skill lacking on our part. Russia is the astute power, the power full of guile, the power that works in the dark. England, on the other hand, is too honest to court the gloom and conceal the transactions of her officials. What she does, she does before the whole world, and if she is beaten by Russia in diplomacy, she at any rate can claim that she is always fair, open, just, and honest.

When the history of the Central Asian question comes to be written, which can be only properly and impartially done by some one knowing Russia as well as England, it will be found that after all Russian diplomacy has not been so black as we have been accustomed to believe it, and that further the equivocations and unscrupulosities of Russian statesmen have too often had their counterpart in this country. To go no deeper into the matter on this occasion, we may point out that all along we have employed agents and emissaries quite as extensively in the East as Russia has done, and if the results of their exertions have not been so apparent as in the case of Russia, the cause is to be found in the incapacity of the English Government to utilize their labours in a proper manner. When Grodekoff rides to Herat, or Petrusevitch appears at Sarakhs, or Lessar shows himself at Merv, there is an outcry in the English press about the pioneering operations of Russia, and out comes the stereotyped charge that she astutely employs emissaries and agents all over the East. In nine cases out of ten even the most innocent private Russian traveller is made out to be a Government agent, on grounds often no more substantial than that on which a very clever Russian, knowing England well, sought to demonstrate to us at the Tsar's coronation that O'Donovan was an emissary of our own Government. He proved the matter to his satisfaction this way. O'Donovan was the correspondent of the *Daily News;* the *Daily News* was the organ of the Gladstone Government; *therefore* O'Donovan had relations with the Government, and was under its direction while at Merv. To tell the truth, Russians are so little given to travel, that it is very rarely that innocent private explorers of their race are to be found in the East. If the case is different with ourselves, we should remember that Russians cannot understand a Burnaby riding off to Khiva, or a Valentine Baker to the Perso-Afghan frontier, "for the mere fun of the thing."

Most of our explorers all over the world have been travellers on their own account, and the pioneers in Central Asia have been no exception to the general rule. But there have been secret English agents in that region as well as in other parts of the earth. Major Napier comes under this category, so does Captain Butler, and an excellent representative might be found in Daood Khan, the spy who went to Merv for us in 1870, if we only knew more about him.

Many English politicians make a point of charging Russia on every possible occasion with employing secret agents, overlooking that we have often been as bad as Russia in this respect, if it really is reprehensible to employ secret agents, which we doubt. The Indian Government has always made extensive use of native explorers. One came back a few months ago to India who had been for three years wandering in Thibet, undergoing hardships and privations as a slave, and yet, in spite of physical misery, bringing back an amount of valuable information which should put him in the front rank as a pioneer. But he is only a native, and a black man needs no commendation. A decade ago another native of India went to Merv; he was the first English subject in recent times to penetrate to that mysterious oasis, but his achievement was never heard of until Sir Henry Rawlinson casually revealed it in a discussion following upon a lecture at the Royal Geographical Society.* It seems to us that if we had been as well aware of the

* "Some ten years ago a traveller was sent by the Government of India to those countries of Central Asia. His report had been printed, but never published. His name was Daood Khan. First he went from Sarakhs to Merv, and so on to Tchardjui. Then he came back to Sarakhs, made a circle in Khorassan, and returned by Kelat to Kara Chacha, from whence he crossed the Tejend, and, stopping one day in the desert, on the second day he reached Shahedli, and from there went on to Tash-Robat and Merv. He only spent one day in the desert, and that verified the information which Colonel Stewart had received from the people of the country." —Sir Henry Rawlinson (Proceedings of the Royal Geographical Society, September, 1881)

movements of these and other English emissaries in Central Asia as certain statesmen, a spirit of common fairness would have kept us from continually nagging at Russia for doing what they knew perfectly well our authorities were doing at the same time in the region between Russia and India. Nothing is so exasperating to Russians as the lofty assumption of snow-white morality—they angrily call it cant—which certain English writers and statesmen adopt in these matters. The feeling is a very natural one.

But while asking that more fairness should be displayed towards Russia in this matter, we cannot help drawing attention to one vital difference between her mode of using emissaries and our own. For each power to send its own spies to such uncontrolled points as Merv recently was, no right-minded man will deny to be fair play. But the case is different in regard to Afghanistan, Bokhara, and Khiva. The latter two khanates are under Russia's suzerainty, and since that suzerainty was imposed England has never—so far as I am aware—despatched thither any agents whatever. We have never attempted in any way to undermine Russia's influence in those conquered states. On the other hand, Russia has never been loyal in respecting our suzerainty over Afghanistan, and has repeatedly despatched to Herat and Cabul her secret agents. For such ungenerous and unscrupulous conduct there is no excuse.*

I had nearly completed preparing these sketches for the press, when a reader of the abridged ones appearing in the *Newcastle Weekly Chronicle* asked if I would not give Captain Napier a place among the pioneers. This I had done incidentally, although, for lack of fuller materials, I had been unable to prepare a complete sketch. Napier's report, like Daood Khan's, had been printed, but never published. It was, in short, a secret report, only twenty-five copies had been struck off, and the label "strictly con fidential" had prevented any official writer making use of its contents. To my surprise and pleasure, the inquirer wrote to say that if I cared to go fully into Napier's survey, he

* Captain Venkhovsky's secret mission to Cabul in 1882, discovered by the writer during a chance stay at Kertch, is an instance in point.

would be happy to lend me one of the twenty-five copies.

An eminent Russian staff officer, who had been engaged in several secret surveys, once started in the presence of the writer and several Russian officials the discussion whether any real gain is derived from keeping Government reports secret. "We spend a lot of money," he said, "in obtaining reports of the military defences of Germany, and Germany does the same with us. The reports of both countries are printed, and are supposed to be known only to the officials of the departments concerned, but Germany somehow gets copies of our reports, and we equally somehow get copies of hers. Hence what is the good of secrecy? If our reports were published, the knowledge of the military condition of Germany would not be confined exclusively to a few officers, probably too lazy or too stupid to make use of it, but would be thrown open to the entire army. The army would invade Germany not ignorant of its defences, but thoroughly instructed as to their character. Unrecognised Von Moltkes might at their leisure improvise plans, and in general good would be derived from the reports of the secret surveys, instead of their lying, like mine are, in the dusty pigeon-holes of the General Staff Office, until the information in them rots and becomes useless."

Much might be argued for and against the publication of purely military reports dealing with the armaments of great powers, but where a report embraces mainly geographical matter, as in the case of Napier's, it seems to us absurd to hoard it up. At any rate, this opinion should stand good with England. In Russia, where the policy of the country rests with a few officials, the restriction of secret reports to the perusal of those officials does the State no harm. But the case is totally different with England, where the policy of the hour depends not upon a few officials, but upon the entire public. The better that public is instructed the sounder its policy is likely to be; hence reports such as Napier's ought always to be issued in the ordinary course of state papers.

The matter may be argued on other grounds. General Sir Charles MacGregor proceeds to Khorassan at his own cost, and travelling over most of the ground covered by Napier, obtains information of an identical character, which he places, with innumerable sketches, at the disposition of Government and the public. The *Daily News* sends a correspondent to Merv, and all the data Mr. O'Donovan is able to get is also freely given to Government and the public. On the other hand, Government despatches Napier to the Persian border, and every scrap of information he acquires is jealously withheld from MacGregor and the *Daily News*, instead of their generosity being reciprocated. As most of the Government reports are printed, and the cost of printing chiefly consists in setting up the type, it would be as easy to print two hundred and fifty copies as twenty-five, and the system prevailing therefore cannot be defended on the score of economy. As for private travellers, it is a well-known fact that works like MacGregor's "Khorassan" bring in no profit to their authors, who indeed have to be satisfied if the publication of them does not involve a loss.

The books published by Baker, MacGregor, O'Donovan, and others covering most of Napier's geographical survey, and the establishment of Russian rule over Akhal and Merv having rendered the political matter obsolete, there can be no harm in dealing with the "Collection of Journals and Reports Received from Captain the Hon. G. C. Napier, Bengal Staff Corps, on Special Duty in Persia in 1874," albeit headed in large type "Strictly confidential." The book is octavo, of 350 pages, and comprises ten reports, diaries, memoranda, and notes. In a preface dated 1st January, 1876, the Political and Secret Department of the India Office gives the following reasons for Captain Napier's survey:—

"On the 7th February, 1874, Mr. Taylour Thomson, Her Majesty's Minister at Teheran, reported that a secret raid had been made by the Persian governor of Khaf on Herat territory, and he proposed that a native agent should be sent from Meshed, in conjunction with an agent of the Persian Government, to ascertain on the spot the true state of the case, with a view to obtain restitution of the plunder if proved to be Afghan property. Upon the suggestion of the Government of India" (Lord Northbrook viceroy, the Beaconsfield Cabinet at home freshly entered into power), "it was eventually decided to employ a European officer instead of a native agent, and Captain the Hon. G. Napier was ordered by that Government to proceed to Teheran and report himself to Her Majesty's Minister at that court for special duty. That duty was primarily to report upon the circumstances of the raid made upon Herat from Khaf, but he was also instructed to embrace the opportunity of his journey to Khaf to obtain all available information on the present condition of the Persian frontier, the feelings between the Persians and Afghans on either side of the border, the condition of the Turcoman tribes, the effect of the late arbitration in regard to the Seistan boundary, and on similar matters of interest."

Captain Napier arrived at Teheran on the 4th of June, 1874, about six months after the return home of MacGahan and Colonel Baker. A month later he set out for Meshed, and travelling along the familiar route traversed by Marsh, Vámbéry, and others, reached Meshed on the 11th of August. Here a month was spent in negotiating with the Persian authorities about the Persian raid, of which nothing satisfactory resulted, and this indirect cause of the journey disposed of, Napier made his way to Kelat-i-Nadiri, on the Perso-Turcoman frontier, following in the footsteps of Valentine Baker. From Kelat he slowly made his way to the south-west along the border, visiting in detail every place of importance, until he attained the Caspian at Astrabad. Teheran was reached again on the 21st of December. Here he stayed till March, writing excellent reports, and then proceeded to Calcutta.

The value of Napier's survey consisted less in the amount of new ground he covered, which, in effect, was trifling, than the admirable manner he investigated the country hastily passed over by his predecessors, and the skill with which he drew from Turcomans exhaustive accounts of Akhal and Merv. Both those districts are now so well known that a Murray's guide could be easily compiled for the traveller. By the light of this information one can judge how skilfully Napier achieved his mission. Most of his information had to be drawn from Turcomans unaccustomed to accuracy, or Persians fond of Oriental embellishments; by close cross-examination he sifted the truth from their talk, and evolved an account of the three oases of Akhal, Atak, and Merv, which was surprisingly realistic.

What adventures he had, what his personal experiences were, we have no record in his "Persian Journals." Except to the expert, the book is a dry mass of facts, and the statesmen who used it must have found it weary reading. After all, the usual narrative personal form of travel-writing adopted by private explorers is the most natural, and the best calculated to instruct. Statesmen, however heroic, are but human beings like the rest of us, and find the perusal of drily written blue-books as repulsive as the general public. Perhaps this may account for the small effect produced by reports such as Napier's. Lord Palmerston changed the style of handwriting throughout the public service. It is now the clearest and the best in the world. Why cannot some one in turn insist on officials making their reports more attractive?

Here and there the diaries of native spies are inserted. That of Kazi Syad Ahmed, of Astrabad, is the best, in spite of the bad grammar of the translation, and contains a number of curious entries, of which the following are specimens:—

"Astrabad, Nov. 13th, 1874. I went out for a stroll this evening in company with Mahomed Hossain, merchant, and Ismail, tailor, and when we got to the top of Qila Kandan, which affords a good view of the country around, the tailor exclaimed, 'What a pity it is that Persia has no master! Otherwise thousands of tomans would have accrued from the produce of the forest to the Government treasury.' He then stated that he one day heard one of the Russian consul's servants say that in a few years all this country would be taken by the Russians, who would realize lakhs of tomans from this forest. I then asked, 'Do you expect that Russia will take Astrabad in a few years?' He replied, 'We know it for certain that Russia would take Astrabad and all Persia to-morrow if it were not for the British Minister's flag which is planted in Teheran.' I then said, 'Is this true?' He rejoined, 'Certainly so,' and stated that Russia and England were two rival powers, and had their Ministers in Teheran. The Russian Minister peeped out through his window every morning to see if the English flag was still on high, and finding it so, he is disappointed, but no sooner will he see the British flag hauled down, than he will telegraph to Russia to march troops into Persia, and make it a Russian province like Turkestan. This simple fancy of the tailor amused me very much and made me laugh."

A few days later he met a farmer at a village near Astrabad. "I asked him what the revenue of his village was. He replied as much as the governor could exact. I said how could that be? He rejoined that Persia had no master; irregularity and disorder reigned everywhere. Had Persia had a master, the plain of the Turcomans would not have been made over to Russia, which is so fertile that one maund of seed gives an out-turn of a hundred maunds. He then said that the Turcomans were lucky that they became Russian subjects. They would no longer be subject to arbitrary exactions, and experience the tyranny of Persian rulers. I then remarked, 'How is it that you, being a Mussulman, prefer an infidel government to your own?' He answered, 'Russians are much better than these Mussulmans' (alluding to his governors), and then said, 'Go and see the Turcomans of Tchikishlar, how well off they are; they are getting richer every day.' He said that a single Russian could travel among the Turcomans without any risk, but the Persian governor of Astrabad could not go a few miles without a thousand men."

Captain Napier's survey was attended with one very important political circumstance. Both the Tekké chiefs of Akhal and the Tekké chiefs of Merv made repeated overtures to him to be taken under the protection of England through the medium of Afghanistan. So far as Akhal and the Atak were concerned, this was hardly feasible; but geographically Merv is an integral portion of Afghanistan, and England missed a grand opportunity when Lord Northbrook in India and the Beaconsfield Government at home failed to respond to the wishes of the Mervis.

Already, six months earlier, Colonel Baker had discovered the Tekké Turcomans discussing the chances of an English protectorate. Napier found them ripe for the measure, and warmly seconded Baker's recommendation to the Government.

"The strategical value of the position of Merv," wrote Napier, "requires no demonstration, and its political importance becomes as evident when the question is viewed from the spot. The Murghab river, rising in the mountains of Afghanistan, flows north into the desert of Khiva, and reaching not more than half-way across, it buries its water in the sandy waste. Along its banks live a succession of nomadic tribes, commencing with the Eimaks of Herat, and followed by the Sarik and Salor Turcomans, forming an unbroken chain, connecting the oasis of Merv with the heart of Afghanistan. East, west, and north of the line fertilized by the river extends a waterless desert, forming a natural boundary between Khorassan, of which Merv and the Murghab may be considered merely a salient angle, and the tracts comprising the Uzbek khanates" (of Russian Turkestan). . . . "Its occupation by an aggressive power will open the way to further extensions of influence on what has always been the weak side of Afghanistan, the side of Herat. . . . As to the reasons underlying the evident desire of the Tekkés for an Afghan alliance, there is a very general impression abroad that an alliance with Afghanistan—the Afghans are their co-religionists—means an alliance with England.

I received abundant proof of their desire for a direct connection with us, and I believe that they might be transformed into a peaceful, honest, and prosperous community, and would prove a service of real strength to the border and to the empire."

Not long afterwards General Sir Charles MacGregor, on equally good grounds, advocated the enclosure of Merv within the political limits of Afghanistan; but his words fell flat on the ears of the authorities, and it is too late now to carry the recommendation into effect. Had Napier's secret reports been issued to the public in 1875, the impression is strong on my mind that public opinion would have sufficiently reciprocated the earnest desire expressed to the English Agent by the Turcomans, for something to have been done to save Merv from Russian seizure. As it was, Napier's survey was practically barren of results. It had no influence on public opinion, it added nothing to the published stores of knowledge, and it would appear to have exercised no important influence upon the statesmen at whose instigation it was undertaken.

These remarks apply with equal force to a second journey Napier undertook along the same frontier in 1876. The gallant officer was not to blame for this, but the system which led to his reports being hoarded in secret until they had lost their value.

CHAPTER VI.

COLONEL C. M. MACGREGOR'S SURVEY OF KHORASSAN.

O. K. and the annexation of Khiva—Progress of events in Central Asia—MacGregor's claim to consideration as an authority on the subject—The absurd order forbidding English officers to travel in Afghanistan compels him to journey six thousand miles instead of one thousand—"Good gracious, this man *is* a liar!"—Ride from the Persian Gulf to Herat—Ill-treatment by the Afghans—Turned away from Herat and censured by the English Government—Horrors of Turcoman man-stealing—What the people of Khorassan think of the Russians—The Government forbids him to explore Merv and the Hindoo Koosh — His bitter disappointment — His journey to Sarakhs, and opinion of its strategical importance—Sarakhs the real key of Herat—MacGregor meets Ayoub Khan at Meshed—Confronts him again at Candahar—Rides along the Perso-Turcoman frontier to the Caspian—The real pillars of the empire.

"Le despotisme fait illégalement de grandes choses, et la liberté ne se donne pas la peine d'en faire légalement de très petites."—BALSAC.

AFTER the return of the Russian army from Khiva in the autumn of 1873, there was a lull for a few months in Central Asia; then Russian restlessness commenced again. Early in 1874 Colonel Ivanoff, who had been made commander of the fort Russia had established at Petro-Alexandrovsk, a short distance from Khiva, to overawe the city, moved about the oasis, carrying fire and sword into the settlements of the luckless Turcomans.* These ravages were resumed the following year, and completely crushed the

* In O. K.'s recent work "Skobeleff and the Panslavist Cause" (Longmans, 1883), page 14, occurs the passage—"Before any troops withdrew from the khanate—for, however strange it may appear to those who constantly accuse us of breaking our word in annexing Khiva, there is not one Russian soldier in Khiva to this hour . . ." This is a quibble, which no genuine lover of historical truth, as O. K. professes to be, would have been guilty of. She implies Russia completely evacuated the khanate after its conquest, in compliance with her promise to England. As a matter of fact, Russia established a garrison of 4,000 troops at Petro-Alexandrovsk, two marches from Khiva, on territory previously controlled by the Khan. Burnaby met some of these troops encamped a short distance from the city. Russia assumed the exclusive control of the river watering Khiva, of the military administration of the whole of the surrounding region, and of the foreign relations of Khiva, besides reducing the Khan to the position of a tribute-paying feudatory. A writer who will audaciously imply after this that Russia totally evacuated the country, in the same manner as for instance England evacuated Abyssinia or Candahar, will quibble about anything, and it is a waste of time to argue with such. At present Russia, by pushing a new frontier from the Caspian to Askabad, and thence *viâ* Merv to Bokhara, is wholly enclosing Khiva within its territories. This settles the controversy.

independence of the Turcomans dwelling between Khiva and Merv. In the meanwhile Colonel Lomakin had returned to the Caspian with the Kinderley column, and had been installed commandant at Krasnovodsk in the place of Markozoff, who was put on the retired list for failing to reach Khiva with the Krasnovodsk column. A few months later the Transcaspian military district was formed, with the administrative seat at Krasnovodsk, and Lomakin began to dream of carving a second Turkestan out of Central Asia. Exploring parties were sent out along the road leading to Merv, pretensions were put forward to the control of the Turcomans dwelling south of the Atrek, on Persian soil, as well as to the north of it, and efforts were made to buy over the allegiance of Sofi Khan and other Akhal chiefs to Russia. These operations did not remain unnoticed in England. Russia's violation of her contract not to annex Khiva had provoked mistrust and alarm respecting her future operations. The belief had become general that she needed close watching. Even such an ardent advocate of "masterly inactivity" as the then Liberal viceroy, Lord Northbrook, could not conceal his uneasiness. Both the home and the Indian Governments had refused to countenance Colonel Baker's survey in any way, but a month or two after his return to England—a week or two later than MacGahan's return from Khiva—they despatched to the Perso-Turcoman frontier Captain Napier. This officer paid a flying visit along the Turcoman frontier from Meshed and Kelat to Astrabad, but his report was a confidential one, and he added little to the knowledge that Baker had acquired in 1873. So little of his information was allowed to transpire that it did nothing to allay the public alarm, and in this manner circumstances provoked in due course the appearance of another pioneer in Central Asia.

This was no other than Colonel C. M. Macgregor, a scion of a family that has given so many illustrious officers to the army of India, and who was well known in 1875 as the compiler of two huge works on Central Asia and Afghanistan respectively, which contained, in an admirably arranged and condensed form, the whole of our stock of knowledge of the region. In preparing these works—which regrettably are confidential ones and inaccessible to the general public*—MacGregor had come to know what gaps existed in the topography of Central Asia, and it was to fill in some of these that he prepared, early in 1875, to set out on a ride from India to Russia. A ride from Rawul Pindee to St. Petersburg would have been unique, and would have surpassed any preceding achievement of the kind; but, unfortunately, MacGregor was thwarted in every possible way, and prevented from realizing it—this not by the Russians, but by the obstructive statesmen and officials of his own country.

In the first place, an order existed against officers entering Afghanistan at all—an order which, by the way, still remains in force. The explanation of this was that the Ameer refused

* The whole system of printing confidential reports in England is a farce. They are always known to foreign powers, from whom the "confidential" system is intended to protect them, and the general public are the real sufferers. This is, however, mitigated in a few instances. It is surprising the number of persons, wholly unconnected with the Government service, who have experienced no difficulty in obtaining access to MacGregor's works on Central Asia. In Russia their contents were known long before the Afghan war, and on the outbreak of that conflict, a certain London daily paper published whole columns of matter from the Afghanistan volume, in the form of telegrams from Berlin, humorously heading the information as being derived from the reports of the Russian General Staff.

to hold himself responsible for the safety of any European traveller, and the English Government, to avoid complications, did its best to prevent officers penetrating into the country. Thanks to this, MacGregor, instead of riding straight from his station on the Indian frontier to Meshed, a distance of a thousand miles, had to pursue a roundabout route by sea, involving a journey of six thousand miles. "I may be asked," he says, "why I did not, like Burnes, risk the danger of the shorter route, and I can only give the answer which would be given by scores of my brother officers, among whom the spirit to dare and the heart to do is as strong as ever it was in the days of old. I would gladly have risked all that Afghan cut-throats could have done to me, but one cannot deliberately disobey orders."

MacGregor proceeded down country to Bombay, and thence, on the 26th of March, 1875, went by sea to Bushire, near the head of the Persian Gulf. Having recently lost his wife, the sixteen days' voyage, with no companions on board, was a miserable one to a desolate man, and he was glad to get on shore again—any land, even the wilderness at Bushire, being more lively to him than the restless interminable sea. MacGregor's 3,000 miles' ride commenced at Bushire, his route running direct to Herat, thence to Meshed, Sarakhs, and along the Perso-Turcoman frontier to the Caspian. At Kaziroon, the first important place on the road, he asked, he says, one Hadji Abul Hussun, a merchant, about the famine. "His account was very frightful. Over 1,000 souls, he said, had died in Kaziroon alone, and no attempt whatever had been made to help the wretched people. When I told him that I had been employed in the Bengal famine, and though only part of the rice sent up for relief passed through my hands, yet I had sent up seventy-five krools of maunds of rice, or, to bring it more home to him, 250,000 mule loads, I could see a smile of disbelief come over his features, and he looked at his son as much as to say, 'Good gracious, this man *is* a liar!' So he capped my story by saying that there were ninety million people in Persia. When I asked where they were, remarking that I had come a hundred miles into the country, and certainly had not seen a thousand people, he replied, without a moment's hesitation, 'Oh, they are moving about. I should think they must be, and moving so fast as to be invisible, only I did not say so."

Between Kaziroon and Shiraz a pass 7,600 feet had to be crossed, and beyond Shiraz the ruins of Persepolis traversed. Up to this point so many travellers have penetrated that the country was tolerably well known, but from Persepolis to Yezd, across the desert, no Englishman had ever journeyed, although Trezl, one of General Gardanne's suite, had been along it. From Yezd he made his way to Herat *viâ* Tubbus, Toon, Birjan, and the country south-east of Khaf and Ghurian, not travelling straight, but zigzagging about, so as to effect a thorough survey of the region. No adventures of any note occurred on the way, and the Colonel, well provided as he was with servants and luggage, accomplished the journey across the desert with a considerable amount of hardship certainly, but not with that suffering which had attended Vámbéry's tramp to Khiva or MacGahan's thirty days' chase of Kaufmann. A good geographer, a first-class topographer, and an excellent sketcher, Colonel MacGregor made a thorough survey of the country lying between the Persian Gulf and Herat, noting everything on the way with the eye of a general, and making a sketch of every place or point that might be of importance to any future commander leading a column in that direction.

When close to the Afghan frontier, he wrote to the governor Shere Ali had recently appointed to control Herat in place of Yakoob Khan, who had been treacherously conveyed to Cabul and imprisoned, informing him of his impending arrival, and having spent a night at Pahre, the first village on Afghan soil, set off the next day in undress uniform with the expectation of entering the Key of India by sundown. On his way he was met by an official from the governor, who treated him very rudely and ordered him to retire at once to Persia. MacGregor consented to return to Pahre, but the next day rode on again to Herat, making a halt at Kargan, about five miles from the city, to await an answer to another letter he had despatched to the governor. From the fort attached to the village he had a fine view of the valley of Herat, "which stretched in every direction but the south, one sea of yellow fields and verdant trees. Without going farther it was easy to see the value of Herat to any power with intentions on India, and to recognise the justice of the dictum which termed it the Gate of India. Just as in the minor undertaking of the capture of a city the wise commander will give his troops a breathe on their gaining the outer defences, so must every general coming from the west rest his men a while in this valley. And no better place could be found for the purpose; abundance of beautiful water, quantities of wheat and barley and rice, endless herds of cattle and sheep, good forage, and a fine climate,—all combine to make the Herat valley the most apt place for a halt before entering the desolate country between Farrah and Candahar."

Before long the official arrived who had treated him so rudely the day before, and repeating his insults, ordered MacGregor to return to Persia again. Having no official status, and not wishing to provoke any complications between England and Afghanistan, MacGregor repressed the strong desire that possessed him to castigate the Afghan for his insolent demeanour, and turned back to Persia, this time taking the high-road to Ghurian and Meshed, traversed in 1872 by Marsh. At Ghurian the local Afghan governor expressed his regret that MacGregor had been so badly treated, and did the best that lay in his power to make amends for it. It was to this point—two days' journey from Herat—that Lessar, the Russian railway engineer, penetrated a few months ago. One more march brought MacGregor to Kusan, the frontier outpost of Herat, and the following day, June 24th, he crossed the border into Persia.

On his return to England MacGregor was censured by the Indian Government for going to Herat, but no one acquainted with the condition of the Central Asian Question at the time can read the account of his proceedings without arriving at a very strong opinion as to whom blame was really due in the matter. The recent Russian advance has rendered his survey of the Herat valley, and of the country lying between it and Sarakhs, of the highest national importance. Events—the impending development of which was sufficiently foreshadowed in 1875—have more than justified his action. It is impossible to read his "Khorassan," without, on the one hand, extolling him for his patriotism, and on the other censuring those in power in India who did their best to thwart him. It is such men as MacGregor who build up and sustain empires. It is such bureaucrats as those who censured him, who, by their folly and heedlessness, humble and ruin them.

The journey from the Perso-Afghan frontier to Meshed was accomplished by MacGregor in a week, the route lying through Shuhr-Now, of which road we possessed scarcely any information. The whole of the distance from the Herat valley to Meshed the traveller saw evidences of the disastrous character of the Turcoman forays. Between Herat and Meshed, a distance of 220 miles, there were only 1,000 Persian sowars, or armed horsemen, to protect the country. Through the thin and scattered line they formed, it was the easiest thing in the world for the Turcomans to pass in bands of from ten to 1,000 strong, and hence the whole country was more or less in a ravaged and ruined condition. "There was not a man," MacGregor says of one district, "who had not suffered some loss, and very few of the elder ones who had not been prisoners. One man a month before had lost his wife, two daughters, and a son, by these dogs of Turcomans, and he was in the depths of despair. He knew he could never ransom them; he had nothing, and the price demanded was 3,000 krans. He said if he could only be sure they would take him to the same place, he would go and get taken himself. They all said that if the Kujjurs (the ruling dynasty in Persia) were not such contemptible characters, they would go and take them and release their people; they would all go and fight the Turcomans. But they could expect nothing from the Shah, and they eagerly asked when the Russians were coming, adding, 'May God send them speedily!' This showed how the fame of the Russians in releasing all the slaves in Khiva has spread, and to what extent they have most deservedly gained prestige by it."

At another place: "About half-way on the road we passed a ruined village called Farzabad, which, four years ago, the Turcomans had surprised when most of the men were out, and had carried off every soul—about a hundred—out of it. This information was told me by a man who had lost his wife, three sons, and a daughter, in this way. Poor devil! I pitied him, and could well appreciate the motive which induced him to say, 'Oh, sahib, I wish to God either you or the Russians would come and free us from these devils.'"

The aggressive policy of Russia in Central Asia has certainly been a blessing to the peaceful folk of that region and countries adjoining. The conquest of the Akhal Tekkés has freed half of Khorassan from the scourge of the man-stealing Turcomans, and when the Merv and Sarik tribes are brought under control, the district through which MacGregor passed on his way from Herat to Meshed will be relieved of a curse that has clung to it for centuries. England herself has done nothing to remove that curse; she has done her best to prevent its removal: the whole credit rests with Russia. Hence, is it a matter of surprise that the people dwelling in the country stretching from Askabad to Herat, *viâ* Sarakhs and Meshed, through which a Russian advance will some day no doubt be made, should have a very high opinion of the active Russians, and a very low opinion of the do-nothing English and Persians?

MacGregor talked with these people about the Russians. "Indeed, it is almost impossible to avoid doing so, for directly they know one is English, they commence their usual string of questions with: "When are the Russians coming to Herat?" etc. It has evidently been very industriously spread about in these parts that though we are the most powerful at sea, they are the more powerful on land, because every one I met said the same thing. It is not very easy to answer these people, for they have been told everything that leads to this belief. When I said, 'No, the Russians are not more powerful than us; the only time we ever fought them we thrashed them, and, *inshilla*, we will do it again,' the answer was, 'Yes, but there were four vilayets' (countries) 'against them then; how will it be when you are alone?' Unpleasant as it may be to acknowledge, there is no doubt the prestige is with Russia; and the general opinion is that they mean to take India, and that they will do it.

"In Khorassan there is another opinion which is as prevalent as belief in the Russians, and that is contempt of the Kujjur. This I have heard expressed over and over again, coupled with epithets the reverse of complimentary. So much is this the case that I do not think the Shah need ever hope for an active support from his Khorassani subjects against Russia. I think they would fight against the Afghans or Turks, because they hate them; but they have no reason to dislike the Russians, while all the stories they hear induce respect for that power. They are not, I think, in the least ill-disposed to the English, but they do not think much of them; we are all very well, they say, but we are not going to win."

Colonel MacGregor had a brush with the Turcomans on the way, which might have been attended with serious results had he displayed less nerve and his assailants more resolution. Meshed was entered on the 1st of July, and after a few days' rest MacGregor began to complete his preparations for attempting afresh the exploration of Afghanistan. One of the tasks he had set before him was to ride along the direct road between Herat and Cabul, which no European had ever traversed. His first plan for achieving this enterprise, by proceeding from India to Cabul and thence to Herat, had been frustrated by the order of the Indian Government forbidding any officer crossing the Indo-Afghan frontier; and his second, for riding the other way, from Herat to Cabul, had been baulked by the churlishness of the governor Shere Ali had put in place of Yakoob Khan. He now hit upon a third scheme—to ride from Meshed to Merv, thence try and find his way *viâ* the Oxus to Kolab, and afterwards return back to Bamian, cross the Koh-i-Baba range, emerge on the Herat-Cabul road a few days' ride from Cabul, and make his way to Herat along the course of the Hari Rud valley. Such a survey would have been a splendid one. We should have learnt from the cleverest reconnoitrer of the day the actual character of the country lying on both sides of the Hindoo Koosh, and the condition of all the roads running through Afghanistan from Russia to India. We shall never have another such opportunity as MacGregor had in 1875, and if ever there be an early conflict between Russia and England in Central Asia, we shall be compelled to fight our rival either ignorant of the characteristics of many of the roads, or else dependent on information obtained by Russian pioneers, who had no unpatriotic bureaucrats to restrain and thwart them.

There is every reason to believe that MacGregor's survey would have been crowned with success, but for the ill-advised action of the Indian Government. MacGregor committed an error of judgment in telegraphing to Mr. Aitchinson, the Foreign Secretary at Simla, the scheme of his intended journey. A few days later, when on the point of quitting Meshed for Merv, a carrier arrived from Teheran with some letters for him. The first that caught his eye was an official one—it was from the British Minister at Teheran, and ran thus: "I have the honour, by the direction of His Excellency the Viceroy of India, to inform you that you are prohibited from travelling in Afghanistan or Turkestan, or going beyond the boundary of Persia."

"The letter," says MacGregor, "dropped from my hand, and for a moment I felt quite sick with the bitter disappointment these words caused me. Picking it up, I again and again read it, still with a faint scintillation of hope that it might not quite exclude me from all further enterprise. But the words were only too clear, 'You are not to enter Turkestan or Afghanistan, or go beyond the boundary of Persia.' It was clear I was debarred from going anywhere of the smallest interest, or offering the least hopes of distinction; and then I remembered Mr. Aitchinson's frigid rejection of my offer for *any information*, and I confessed, with bitterness, that I had been forewarned.

"I had been forewarned, but I had, in the days when the spirit of adventure rose high in me, not heeded the warning. I argued, 'I can understand their not wishing to send me on a formal mission; I can quite understand the frame of mind which would make a man think it is better to save a few rupees *in his time* than spend it on a venture which may only bear fruit *after* he has gone; but surely, when I have not asked for the expenditure of one farthing, or even asked for any protection entailing one iota of responsibility on Government, I shall be let alone, even if it should become known that I proposed to extend my travels.' But the result proved otherwise. Whether that letter was due to the sole unaided intellect of him from whom the order emanated, or whether I owed it to the promptings of any one seized by the curse of jealousy or the more withering canker of overzeal, it proved the extreme to which 'masterly inactivity' could go. Hitherto there had been some charm in the trip. The unknown in geography has always to me the same witchery that the candle has to the moth, or the flash of a woman's eye has to the hardest man. But this was all at an end, and it was with a sickening feeling that I remembered I was hundreds of miles away from civilization, separated from it by miles of dreary wastes and melancholy burnt-up hills; that I had marched all these miles, endured all these hardships, risked my health and my life, and spent my hardly won coin, for nothing. It never occurred to me to disobey the order, and I trust no soldier will think it ought to have occurred to me. It was so curtly distinct that it could admit of but one interpretation. It was perfectly clear that my further journey must cease unless I chose to resign my commission.

"'Please, sir, breckfuss ready,' was my

incomparable boy's practical attempt to break the reverie into which I was plunged, sitting half stunned by the bad news which the courier had brought me. Some letting off steam was absolutely necessary, so I d—d my boy, much to his astonishment, cursed Persia and the Persians, in which he heartily concurred, and—for one must keep within bounds in recording one's thoughts of superior officers—wished those who had ordered me were at the bottom of the sea, with the millstone 'masterly inactivity' round their necks."

Judging from the fate of MacGregor and other English military explorers, no English officer desirous of taking in hand a survey ought to inform the Government beforehand of his intentions, otherwise he is sure to have them frustrated. As for any hopes of Government support, he may make up his mind at the outset that he will receive a chilling refusal, accompanied by the inevitable order forbidding him to carry out the most cherished part of his scheme. The happiest course for a would-be military explorer to pursue is, to hold his tongue until he has accomplished his self-imposed mission, and then to inform the

Government of it. Captain Marsh did this, and rode without hindrance from the Caspian to India. MacGregor adopted the contrary plan, and had his survey blighted.

Prohibited from quitting Persia, MacGregor all the same did not omit to make use of even the limited opportunities left open to him. A Persian relief was about to march to Sarakhs, and the explorer arranged to accompany it thither. With the exception of Burnes, no Englishman had ever been over the whole of the ground, and a whole generation had passed away since Burnes had journeyed through Sarakhs on his way from Merv to Meshed. In 1873, Colonel Valentine Baker had wanted to survey Sarakhs, but had been compelled to give up the idea, owing to a delay in the despatch of the relief he meant to have gone with. MacGregor was luckier, and leaving Meshed July 18th, he reached Sarakhs on the 27th, without encountering any adventures on the road.

Sarakhs is of vast importance to India. It is the next strategical point the Russians must take or turn in their advance from Askabad upon India. It is of really greater value than

Merv, and since the conquest of Akhal has acquired the title of the Key of Herat. Merv is the key of Herat to a force advancing from Turkestan upon Herat, Sarakhs to an army advancing from the Caspian. As an advance from the latter quarter is more probable than from the former, it follows that Sarakhs possesses greater significance than Merv. This significance was recognised by MacGregor in 1875, before even the Russians had established a hold upon the country inland of Krasnovodsk. "I think a glance will show," he wrote, "that in the complications which must arise ere the Russo-Indian question can be deemed settled, its future is likely to be a stirring one. Placed at the junction of roads from Herat and Meshed, by the Hari Rud and Ab-y-Meshed valleys respectively, and at the best entrance to the province of Khorassan from the north, it cannot fail to exercise a very serious influence on the momentous issue of the above question. This must happen, whether it falls into the hands of the friends of England or into those of her foes. Whether Russia uses Sarakhs as a base for offensive measures against Herat, or England for a defensive outpost to defeat any such operations, that position will be heard of again. And if my feeble voice can effect a warning ere it is too late, let it here be raised in these words : *If England does not use Sarakhs for defence, Russia will use it for offence.*"

The day after his arrival at Sarakhs, he induced the authorities to give him a couple of hundred horsemen—the fear of the Tekkés was such that no one dared show his nose outside the fortress without an escort—and with them MacGregor rode out across the Tejend some twelve miles in the direction of Merv. " It was with a very reluctant heart I returned again," observes the explorer. "Beyond lay an endless desert, and deserts have equally a disturbing effect on me with unknown ranges of mountains : I always want to look beyond. And so it was the spirit of adventure said, 'Ride on; true, these people won't go with you, but *qu'importe?* go on by yourself. It would be fun to ride quietly by yourself into the Tekké den'; but then rang out those words which were still rankling in my breast, 'You are not to enter Afghanistan or Turkestan.' So I had to come back."

MacGregor wanted to have gone from Sarakhs to Kelat-i-Nadiri, the jutting point of the Khorassan highlands, sixty miles west of Sarakhs, to which Baker had penetrated in 1873, and from one of the castles of which he had been able to see Sarakhs, thanks to the amazing clearness of the atmosphere and the flatness of the Atak oasis intervening. He could not persuade the relieved guard, however, to proceed thither on its way back to Meshed, and had to return with it to that city; thence making his way again to the border to Kelat by another road, less exposed to Turcoman raids than the Sarakhs one. While waiting at Meshed for the necessary permission to proceed to Kelat, he one day came across Ayoob Khan, whose salute he duly returned. Ayoob, whose brother Yakoob, of Herat, had been treacherously imprisoned by Shere Ali, and who himself was an exile, seemed half inclined to call on MacGregor to stop, but seeing that he did not encourage the idea—for fear of causing more complications with the Indian bureaucrats—he desisted. The next time the two met was at Candahar, Ayoob then commanding the Afghan army that had beaten Burrows at Maiwand, and MacGregor one of the three brigades that avenged that disgraceful disaster.

Leaving Meshed on the 7th of August, MacGregor reached Kelat in five days, and after making plans of the strongholds and defiles of the khanate, turned off in a westerly direction in the footsteps of Colonel Baker, not spending his time in sport, however, but utilizing every opportunity for mapping and sketching the country. Kelat, Deregez, Kuchan, Budjnurd—the chain of khanates lying adjacent to the new Russian province of Akhal—were each dealt with in such a thorough-going manner that it is a question whether there is any other part of Central Asia so well surveyed as this particular section, unless, indeed, it be the ground which MacGregor had previously passed over, or which he subsequently traversed in making his way to Shahrood and Astrabad. From Astrabad he visited the island of Ashurada, proceeded thence by sea and road to Teheran, and so journeyed on to Tiflis *viâ* Tabreez. From the capital of the Caucasus he pushed through the Dariel defile to Vladikavkaz, the terminal point of the

Russian railway system. Thence he made his way to Rostoff and Kharkoff, and afterwards through south-west Russia to Vienna and London—splendid finishing touches to his enterprise—having during his eight months' exploration accomplished one of the most important surveys, judging it by its results, that any English or Russian officer has effected in the region lying between Russia and India.

After his return to England, MacGregor published his "Journey through Khorassan," and shortly afterwards was despatched by Lord Salisbury on a fresh survey. A most interesting account of this journey has just been published by Messrs. W. H. Allen and Co., under the title of "Wanderings in Balochistan." Almost directly after his return to India from this expedition, he was sent to the frontier to take part in the Afghan war, and earned laurels as chief of Roberts's staff and brigadier-general of one of the three columns that crumpled up Ayoob Khan at Candahar. At the close of the war he was made major-general, a K.C.B., and Quartermaster-General of India, in which post he has a useful career before him, and from which many believe he will ultimately force his way to the highest military position in the East.

It is a satisfaction to know that, however much English statesmen may blunder, we have got in India men like General Sir Charles MacGregor to resist any eruption from the North that may some day take place, under the auspices of the Tchernayeffs and the Kaufmanns of Russia. If it be true that such men are the real supporters of our power in India, then the nation cannot be too proud of them.

CHAPTER VII.

CAPTAIN BURNABY'S RIDE TO KHIVA.

Russian operations in Turkestan from the time of MacGahan's return to Burnaby's departure from London—The aim of the English officer—His advantages over other explorers—The railway to Orenburg—Burnaby's journey to the Sea of Aral—The ride thence to Khiva—The exploit not so difficult as commonly imagined—The dangers at Khiva overstated—The Khan of Khiva of Vámbéry's time, of MacGahan's time, and of Burnaby's time—The interview between the Khan and General Kaufmann—A tiger with pared claws—Burnaby unjust to the Russians—His interview with the Khan of Khiva—The Khan at the Tsar's coronation—Burnaby stops too long at Khiva, and is arrested by the Russians—His experiences at Fort Petro-Alexandrovsk—His journey home—Review of his "Ride to Khiva"—Value of his exploit—England and her Burnabys.

"Next the more temperate Turkmans of the South,
The Tekkes and lances of Salore,
And those from Atrek and Caspian sands,
Light men, and on light steeds, who only drink
The acrid milk of camels, and their wells."

MATTHEW ARNOLD

COLONEL C. M. MACGREGOR, foiled by his own Government in penetrating to Merv, arrived home from his eight months' ride on the 15th of November, 1875. Fifteen days later another pioneer set out for the same strategical point, hoping to reach it, not from the southern side of Central Asia, as MacGregor had striven to do, but from the northern, or Russian side. This was no other than Captain Fred Burnaby, of the Horse Guards Blue, who, thanks to the enterprise of his publishers and the advertising skill of the proprietors of a certain pill, has acquired a wider renown as a dashing explorer than any other traveller of modern times.

The previous pioneer in the direction traversed by Burnaby had been MacGahan, who returned home from Khiva in the autumn of 1873. The close of that year and the greater part of 1874 passed over without any striking events in Turkestan. The Russians, having been almost incessantly engaged fighting since 1860, needed a little breathing time to consolidate their conquests, and for eighteen months after the fall of Khiva did little beyond improve communications, organize garrisons, fix the relations between themselves and the natives, and prepare for further movements in the direction of India.

On two sides of Turkestan—east and west—the Russian Government sought to extend its dominions: on the east against Kashgar, where Yakoob Beg had carved an independent Mussulman state out of China and had entered into close relations with India, and on the west against the Turcomans dwelling within the triangle formed by Krasnovodsk, Khiva, and Merv. In 1873, 1874, and 1875 Colonel Ivanoff, MacGahan's good friend, led successive ravaging parties against the Turcomans of the oasis of Khiva, while Lomakin conducted expeditions up the Atrek and across the left flank of the oasis of Akhal to the sandy wastes of the Ust Kum. A notion prevailed in those days that it would be an easy matter to divert the Oxus into the Caspian, and thus open up a grand waterway from the Baltic and Volga to the riverine towns of Afghanistan and Bokhara. Hence these expeditions had for their object the subjugation of all the nomads of the country lying between the lower Oxus and the Caspian, so as to facilitate the accomplishment of this undertaking.

But while Russia was crushing the Turcomans on the west of Central Asia, and making preparations on the east for a war against Yakoob Beg of Kashgar, in order, according to Schuyler, that Kaufmann might buy the goodwill and court influence of Skobeleff by giving him an opportunity to win a few laurels, a storm suddenly burst upon Turkestan with a force that threatened for the moment to sweep away the power of the invaders. The people of Khokand, the bravest of the Turkestanis, without any warning, rose up against their pro-Russian ruler, the tyrant Khudoyar Khan, established a government of their own, and put masses of troops so rapidly in motion that a panic seized upon the authorities at Tashkent, and many feared a repetition of the Indian mutiny. However, Russia had in Kaufmann, Skobeleff, and Abramoff three officers who were equal to any emergency ; forces were concentrated, the revolted territory invaded, the crushing battle of Makram fought, and the enemy driven back from stronghold to stronghold, until at last the Khokandese leader sued for peace, which was granted at the price of the cession of the Namangan district, and £410,000 in cash. This conclusion of the struggle did not please the people of Khokand, and before the ink of the treaty was dry, outbreaks and outrages commenced again, and the Russians had to undertake an enterprise which has always been regarded as one of the most harassing and inglorious operations of war—pacify a brave and independent race, dwelling in a highland country, offering every facility for a prolonged and stubborn defence. The incapacity of the commander—General Trotzky—to whom the task was confided, only aggravated the situation, and things were in this condition, that Russia was preparing for a winter campaign against the Khokandese, to be followed by operations in the spring against Kashgar and Akhal, thereby pushing on at three points towards India, when Captain Burnaby set out from London on the 30th of November, 1875, to see what the Russians were doing in Central Asia.

The task Captain Burnaby imposed upon himself to achieve, to ride through Khiva to Merv, was a difficult and dangerous one, but he had many advantages which previous pioneers had gone short of. December was the coldest season of the year for travelling across the Central Asian steppes, but he had for his guidance the experiences of Major Abbott, who had ridden from Herat to Merv and Khiva during the winter of 1839, to say nothing of his own personal acquaintance with winter life in Russia. If the snow and the frost were trying, they were hardly more so than the blazing heat of summer, which MacGahan experienced; and the snow, at any rate, secured him against the possibility of death from thirst. His route from Kazala to Khiva lay through Kirghiz camps, and from Khiva to Merv through Turcoman ones; but MacGahan had shown that he had nothing to fear from the former, while our relations with the Merv Tekkés were so friendly that, barring the possibility of an armed rencontre without a preliminary parley to explain matters, he had little to fear from the latter. Besides, he had Mr. MacGahan himself, who had been over the whole ground subsequently traversed, to coach him for the ride; he had Mr. Schuyler again to assist him when he got to St. Petersburg; and finally, on his arrival at Khiva, he could count on a Russian garrison being within hail in the event of the Khan attempting to ill-treat him. Add to these advantages a knowledge of Russ and Arabic,

A SNOW-STORM IN THE DESERT.

[*To face page* 182

a magnificent physique transcending that of most men, and plenty of money to secure himself as much as possible against the discomforts of the journey, and it will be seen that Burnaby was very much less handicapped than many of his predecessors. We are not saying this in a carping or disparaging spirit, but it is hardly possible to treat of the exploits of a number of men in one and the same arena without instituting comparisons between them. Burnaby, in setting out for Khiva in 1875, did not have before him that black prospect of danger and death which MacGahan had had in starting on his thirty days' ride from Perovsky in 1873, or Vámbéry, in trudging from Teheran in rags to the torture dens of Central Asia ten years earlier.

Captain Burnaby set out from Charing Cross the last day of November, 1875, with eighty-five pounds of luggage. The journey to St. Petersburg and thence to Orenburg was accomplished without any difficulty, and the delays that occurred at the latter place were nothing more than most travellers experience in a strange land in equipping themselves for a distant expedition. In 1875, the railway from the Volga to Orenburg was not yet finished, and thus from Samara to that point Burnaby had to travel by the post road.* Since then the locomotive has penetrated to the Ural border of Russia, and one can travel from London to Orenburg under circumstances of greater comfort and ease, so far as the Russian and German sections are concerned, than one can from London to Newcastle. But the moment Orenburg is reached, all comfort is at an end. Beyond, to the eastern limits of Turkestan, extend the undulating plains, known as steppes, more or less grassy, in the direction of Siberia, but assuming a desert character in the neighbourhood of the Aral Sea, the Syr Daria and Oxus rivers, and west of them to the Caspian. The winter season being at its height, these steppes were covered with snow, and were far better adapted for travelling than in summer time, when the creaking and jolting of the *kibitka* or *tarantas* make one sigh for the smooth gliding of the sledge. There was no regular road. The post

* The writer may mention that he spent the autumn of 1875 at Orenburg and in the Ural region abutting upon the Kirghiz steppes, returning to England shortly before Burnaby's departure.

stations were little better than cowsheds, and, barring the halt at Orsk, the journey from Orenburg to Kazala, 664 miles, was but little more than a twelve days' continuous race across the snow, broken by breakdowns, snowstorms, quarrels with the post-masters, and other similar accompaniments of travel in Asiatic Russia —hardships and inconveniences that thousands of Russians, officers and officials, their wives and their families, recruits and time-expired soldiers, have experienced year after year since Yermak first conquered Siberia three centuries ago, and which these mute inglorious Burnabys will have to undergo without recognition or reward for a generation or so to come, until the iron horse replaces the steppe galloway, the metal road the camel track, and the inhabitants of far-distant towns of Siberia and Central Asia participate in the blessings of railway-travelling.

"You will get on very well as far as Kazala," had said MacGahan to Burnaby, "and then you will have to pull yourself together and make your rush; it is to be done, although the odds are rather against you." But, on reaching Kazala, Burnaby was very civilly treated, the new commandant, Colonel Goloff, not only offering him every assistance, but placing at his disposal a Cossack escort. The pioneer thanked him for the proffered escort, but refused it, seeing in it a dodge to convey him straight to Petro-Alexandrovsk, a Russian fort sixty miles from Khiva, where good precautions would be taken to prevent him entering the Khan's capital. It is a question, however, whether there was so much guile in Goloff as Burnaby imagined. The fact that he let him depart from Kazala without placing any restraining watch at all over his movements, showed that he had none of that desire to hamper him which had possessed Verestchagin when MacGahan and Ker had stopped at the place. No one could have expected him to have ruined his own career by openly doing his utmost to bring an English officer—possibly a secret agent—face to face with the Khan of Khiva. Short of this he did his best for Burnaby, who might perhaps have more gratefully acknowledged it; and it was largely owing to his help that the pioneer was able to leave Kazala, on his ride to Khiva, on the 13th of January, 1876.

The cold was intense, but Burnaby, his servant Nazar, and the guide were warmly clad, had excellent horses, and, unlike MacGahan, were provided with three camels, conveying a warm *kibitka*, or Central Asian tent, and plenty of food and clothing. Thanks to these things, the 370 miles' journey to Khiva was done in thirteen days, with comparatively little discomfort, considering the season of the year, and with not a tenth of the hardships MacGahan had undergone. Of danger there was none whatever. MacGahan had proved the Kirghiz nomads to be both harmless and hospitable, while the terrible ravages Colonel Ivanoff had been perpetrating year after year among the Khivan Turcomans had completely crushed every bit of spirit out of the latter. The steppes stretching to Khiva were as safe as the steppes of South Russia, and were traversed by Burnaby with as little incident and adventure as one would experience in the latter region. The weather, extremely cold when they started, grew warmer afterwards, and save on one or two occasions, the party were able to pass the night in the cosy tents of the nomads or the comfortable one of their own.

"It would never do to enter Khiva alone and unprotected," Colonel Goloff had said to Burnaby at Kazala. "Why, the Khan would very likely order the executioner to gouge out your eyes, or would keep you in a hole in the ground for five or six days before he admitted you to an audience. The Khivans are very dangerous people." These words have been taken *au sérieux* by many, but they were evidently only jokingly uttered by the Colonel, and were no doubt really accepted as such by Burnaby. Khiva, as a matter of fact, was just as safe as Kazala. The Russians had not only overrun the Khivan oasis and crushed all the disorderly elements in it, but 3,000 or 4,000 of them were posted within sixty miles of the Khan's capital, under the command of an officer who was known to be as fearless and as swift in hitting as any in Central Asia.

The people of Khiva had never been as fanatically disposed towards Europeans as the Bokharans had been; the Russian prisoners and slaves had been treated well by them; after the fall of Khiva the people and the Russian soldiery had mingled on excellent terms; and the Khan, both during that period and subsequently, had seen so much of the Russians that it was altogether inconceivable to any one knowing these things—and Burnaby knew them—that he should act towards the traveller as he would certainly have acted towards Vámbéry, twelve years earlier, had he penetrated his disguise. Vámbéry went to Central Asia as a scientific spy; his danger was increased by the very disguise he wore, for the people of every country resent their religion being trifled with, and had it been found out anywhere in the East that his dervish rags were the rags of an impostor, the enraged Mussulmans would have torn him to pieces. If he had been seized and imprisoned at Khiva, hopeless captivity or a cruel death, without possibility of rescue, would have been his lot; whereas, in the case of Burnaby, the Cossacks would have been in Khiva a few hours after anything happening to him. On the whole, therefore, the ride to Khiva was a comparatively safe exploit, and cannot by any means, either as regards adventures, hardships, or results, be compared with the rides of MacGahan and MacGregor, or of Mr. O'Donovan into Merv. Had there been danger at Khiva, Burnaby would have undoubtedly faced it, but it was an injustice to other explorers to talk of his ride as being the foremost of its kind, as was done by many newspapers on his return home.

The Khan that Burnaby visited was the ruler Vámbéry had had to confront and bless in his dervish rags twelve years earlier. Vámbéry called him a tyrant, and candidly confesses what a fright he was in during and after the interview. One can easily realize his sensations, taking into consideration the fearful risk he ran. The Khan had only to utter the words "Alib barin" ("Away with him")—words daily pronounced by him against offenders for the most trifling crimes—and the dervish would have been remorselessly dragged away by the executioners to be slaughtered. During his interview with the Khan, Vámbéry could have hardly failed to compare himself to a mouse in the presence of a cat.

The case was altogether different when the Khan was seen the second time by European eyes. Said Mahommed was then the mouse, and General Kaufmann the cat. Escaping from the city on seeing further defence useless, the Khan decided a few days after the capture of Khiva to return and give himself up. This was ten years almost to a day from the time Vámbéry had inwardly trembled before the despot. MacGahan was the eye-witness of the scene.

"The Khan rode humbly into his own garden, where Kaufmann was seated on a raised platform of brick under the elms. When he reached the end of a short avenue of young poplars, leading up to General Kaufmann's tent, he dismounted from his richly caparisoned horse, and came forward on foot, taking off his tall sheepskin cap, and bowing low as he approached. He ascended the little platform, where he had probably often received the respectful homage of his own subjects, and knelt down before Kaufmann, who was seated on a camp-stool. He then retired a little further on the platform, which was covered probably with one of his own carpets, and remained kneeling. It should be observed that the Khivans do not sit cross-legged like the Turks, but in a kind of half-kneeling posture, like that of the Kirghiz, and it is in this posture that they eat, talk, and confer. In kneeling, therefore, the Khan did not adopt a posture of humility, but simply one of respect.

"A man about thirty, with a not unpleasant expression of countenance, when not clouded by fear, as at present; large fine eyes, slightly oblique, aquiline nose, a very thin black beard and moustache, and a heavy sensual mouth. Physically, he is decidedly powerful, fully six feet three high, broad-shouldered in proportion, and weighs, I should say, between two hundred and fifty and three hundred pounds. He was dressed in a long khalat, or tunic, of bright blue silk, and the tall sheepskin cap of the Khivans. Humbly he sat before Kaufmann, scarcely daring to look him in the face. Finding himself at last at the feet of the Governor of Turkestan—the famous Yarim Padishah (Half-King)—his feelings must not have been of the most reassuring character. The two men formed a curious contrast. Kaufmann was not more than half as large as the Khan, and a smile, in which there was apparent a great deal of satisfaction, played over his features as he beheld Russia's historic enemy at his feet. I thought there never was a more striking example of the superiority of mind over brute force, of modern over ancient modes of warfare, than was presented in the two men. In the days of chivalry, this Khan, with his grand form and stalwart arms, might have been almost a demi-god ; he could have put to flight a regiment single-handed, he would probably have been a very Cœur de Lion, and now, the meanest soldier in Kaufmann's army was more than a match for him.

"'Well, Khan,' said Kaufmann, smilingly 'you see I have come to see you at last, as I wrote you I would, three years ago.'

KHAN. "'Yes ; Allah has willed it.'

KAUFMANN. "'No, Khan, there you are mistaken. Allah had very little to do with it. You have brought it upon yourself. If you had listened to my counsel three years ago, and acceded to my just demands, you would never have seen me here. In other words, if you had done as I advised you, Allah would not have willed it.'

KHAN. "'The pleasure of seeing the Yarim Padishah is so great, that I could wish nothing changed.'

KAUFMANN (with a laugh). "'The pleasure, I assure you, Khan, is mutual ; but now let us proceed to business. What are you going to do? what do you wish to do?'

KHAN. "'That I leave to you to decide in your great wisdom. If I could wish for anything, it would be to become a subject of the Great White Tsar.'

KAUFMANN. "'Very well, you shall not be his subject, but his friend, if you will. It only depends upon yourself. The Great White Tsar does not wish to deprive you of your throne. He only wishes to prove to you that he is too great a Tsar to be trifled with, which I hope he has shown to your satisfaction. The Great White Tsar is too great a Tsar to take revenge. Having shown you his might, he is ready to forgive you, and let you retain your throne under conditions which you and I, Khan, will discuss another day.'*

KHAN. "'I know I have done very wrong in not granting the just demands of the Russians, but I was ignorant and ill-advised. I will know better in the future. I thank the Great White Tsar and the illustrious Yarim Padishah for their great kindness and forbearance to me, and will always be their friend.'

* This magnanimous tone did not altogether coincide with the onerous conditions of peace afterwards imposed on the Khan.

KAUFMANN. "'You may return now, Khan, to your capital. Re-establish your government, administer justice, and preserve order. Tell your people to resume their occupations and their work, and they will not be molested. Tell them that the Russians are neither brigands nor robbers, but honest men; that they have not come to carry off their wealth, nor violate their women.'

"After mutual questions about each other's health, and wishes for each other's prosperity, expressed in the most flattering language, the Khan retired, and returning to the city resumed his ordinary occupations. The first visit was followed by several others, at one of which the Khan assisted at the review of the Russian troops. It was amusing and interesting to watch the curious and astonished expression with which he looked at the filing past of the Russian troops. Their solid, regular tramp, and the short, queer shout which they uttered without turning their heads, when addressed by Kaufmann, gave them to his eyes a something very mysterious and diabolical. He reminded me of a half-frightened, half-curious child, watching some strange thrilling Christmas pantomime.

These, then, he must have thought, are the men who are conquering Central Asia ; before a handful of whom, whole Mussulman hosts went down at Samarcand like grass before the scythe; these the devils, twelve hundred of whom took Tashkent, a town of a hundred thousand inhabitants, by storm, with a loss of half their number ; before whose unholy breath the religion of Islam is disappearing from the earth."

After the Khan's claws had been pared by the Russians, he was no longer the terrible sovereign he had been in Vámbéry's time. There was as much difference in the Said Mahommed of the two epochs as existed between Cetewayo in the height of his despotic power and the respectable portly old gentleman who subsequently visited England to ask to be restored to his country. There was a certain amount of risk incurred by Europeans in visiting Cetewayo when he was engaged in hostilities with England ; but there was absolutely none after he became a humbled vassal, conscious of his inability to withstand our arms. Still more so was this the case with the Khan of Khiva, for the Russians had not only deprived him of his army, but had posted in the Khanate a force capable of occupying his city with the greatest ease forty-eight hours after the perpetration of any outrage. Anybody who knows intimately Russian officers in general, and the commandant of Fort Petro-Alexandrovsk in particular, will agree with us that Ivanoff would have hurried to rescue Burnaby with as much speed and eagerness as if he had been a fellow countryman in distress.

But there was absolutely no fear of the Khan misbehaving himself, and if Burnaby gained at the time extra *éclat* by setting forth in vivid colours a danger which never existed, there is no reason why he should not be deprived of it in measuring his achievements with those of other men. He had with him MacGahan's book, and in "Campaigning on the Oxus" the Khan was shown to have developed excellent traits of character after his conquest by the Russians. He had further talked before starting with MacGahan and Schuyler—the latter well posted up in the latest events at Khiva—and they could hardly have failed to tell him that there existed no longer in Khiva any fanatic spirit against Europeans, and that the reports in the Russian newspapers represented the Khan as ruling the Khanate in an exemplary manner, and treating all visitors with consideration and respect. Hence there could be no possibility of a repetition of the cat-and-mouse scene immortalized by Vámbéry; and, to be plain, Burnaby's entry into Khiva was of itself not a whit more remarkable than the visit of an English tourist to the capital of any Indian feudatory prince.

While magnifying the danger he ran in penetrating to Khiva, *before* reaching the city, the traveller subsequently ascribes the groundlessness of his fears to the calumnies of the Russians. In describing the gallows at Khiva he says: "I must here remark that many of the cruelties stated to have been perpetrated by the present Khan previous to the capture of the city did not take place; indeed, they only existed in the fertile Muscovite imagination, which was eager to find an excuse for the appropriation of a neighbour's property." How far this was correct, the reader can judge for himself by referring to Vámbéry's account of the gouging out of the eyes of the Tchaudor Turcomans, which Vámbéry, the Russian-hater, as he has been called, himself saw perpetrated. No Russian account of the Khan's administration was worse than that depicted by Vámbéry, and hence Burnaby must be adjudged to have calumniated the Russians when he imputed to them the dissemination of wilful mis-statements of the Khan's mode of rule.

On nearing Khiva Burnaby despatched a note to the Khan announcing his approach, and the morning after his arrival an escort of honour was sent to the house he had put up at to conduct him to Said Mahommed's presence. The Khan was in a *kibitka*, in the courtyard, reclining against some pillows and seated on a handsome Persian rug, warming his feet by a circular hearth filled with burning charcoal. He raised his hand to his forehead as the traveller stood before him, a salute which the latter returned by touching his cap. He then made a sign for Burnaby to sit down by his side.

Burnaby describes the Khan as "taller than the average of his subjects, being quite five feet ten in height, and strongly built." He thus makes him five inches shorter than MacGahan calculated him. The writer saw the Khan in 1883 at the Tsar's coronation, and he was certainly over six feet high, towering above most of the Russians at the balls and ceremonies,* although there were splendid specimens of the latter gathered at the imperial festivities. "His face," says Burnaby, "is of a broad massive type; he has a low square

* The Khan, with the other representatives of Asia, lodged in an hotel almost opposite the one at which I put up at Moscow. I was continually seeing him, although I had no opportunity of speaking to him, and so far as I could ascertain, he had nothing to complain of respecting his treatment. The only occasion that he seemed to me to have his vassal condition made manifest, was on the day of the Tsar's entry into Moscow. He then rode with the Asiatic deputation in front of the procession, mingled with 140 other Asiatic subjects of the Emperor. His size and weight were unpleasantly brought home to me one night at the conclusion of a court ball. The grand staircase of the Kremlin Palace was crowded with departing guests, when Said Mahommed appeared at the top with the Bokhariot prince and his suite. Waiting in vain a few minutes for a passage to be cleared for him, he decided to carve one for himself, and plunged down the staircase, like a burly Yorkshireman from the gallery of a London theatre. It is needless to say that the ladies and their cavaliers discreetly avoided arresting his course as far as they could help, but here and there pressure compelled them to bar his advance, and it was in executing a flank movement round one of these obstructions that he came in contact with my person, and left painful impressions of his weight.

forehead, large dark eyes, a short, straight nose" (or rather an aquiline), "with a coal-black beard and moustache. An enormous mouth, with irregular but white teeth, and a chin somewhat concealed by his beard, and not at all in character with the otherwise determined character of his face, must complete the picture. He did not look more than eight-and-twenty" (his real age was thirty-five), "and had a pleasant genial smile, and a merry twinkle in his eye, very unusual amongst Orientals; in fact, a Spanish expression would describe him better than any English one I can think of. He is *muy senpatico.* I must say that I was greatly surprised, after all that has been written in Russian newspapers about the cruelties and other iniquities perpetrated by this Khivan potentate, to find the original such a cheery sort of fellow." This was very bad of the Russian newspapers, but it should not be forgotten that when we English caught Cetewayo and tamed him, we discovered that, after all, he was not such a bad fellow as he had been previously painted by the English press, omitting to remember, as Burnaby did with Said Mahommed, that there was all the difference in the world between Cetewayo the ignorant despot and Cetewayo enlightened by his conquerors.

Burnaby's interview with the Khan is so well known that it need not be repeated here. The Khan expressed himself dissatisfied with the Russians, which feeling one can readily understand, for they had stripped him of most of his glory and reduced him to the condition of a governor of a town. Recently he has grown more reconciled to his conquerors, with whom he has become better acquainted since he journeyed to Russia to attend the coronation of the Tsar. If he returned home from Moscow and St. Petersburg thoroughly impressed with the might and magnificence of the Emperor, which he is said to have done, he must certainly have carried back with him a lively recollection of the kindness and consideration shown him, and the care taken on all occasions to prevent him realizing that he was a conquered prince.

Burnaby stopped some days at Khiva. Had he contented himself with a mere halt, and pushed on at once to Merv, he might have gained the renown which he had set out to seek and which in after years fell to Mr. O'Donovan,

THE KHAN OF KHIVA, AS HE APPEARED AT THE CORONATION OF ALEXANDER III.

[To face page 202.

of being the first European to penetrate to the "Queen of the World" in modern times. But instead of going ahead he decided to turn off towards Bokhara, where there was comparatively little fresh to be seen, and infinitely greater chances of being interfered with and turned back by the Russians. This resolve sealed the fate of his enterprise. While he was preparing to go to Bokhara, two Russians appeared at Khiva with a summons to repair to Fort Petro-Alexandrovsk, and the will of the commandant being law in Khiva, Burnaby had no other alternative but to obey it.

Six hours' ride the next morning brought him to Anca, a market town forty miles from Khiva, and a short journey the following day to the Russian fort. There Burnaby found that a telegram had arrived for him from the Duke of Cambridge, ordering his immediate return home. The document had been waiting for him several days at the fort, and in the event of his having gone first to Petro-Alexandrovsk he would have never seen Khiva.

"A little later, an officer brought a message from Colonel Ivanoff, to say that he had returned from shooting and was waiting to see me.

He is a tall man, considerably over six feet in height, but very thin, and of a German type, his whiskers having a decided Teutonic appearance. I was received by him at first a little stiffly, but his demeanour soon changed, and he began to laugh about my journey.

"'Too bad,' he said, 'letting you get so far, and not allowing you to carry on your undertaking.'

"'It was lucky,' I remarked, 'that I did not come here first.'

"'Yes,' said Ivanoff; 'when I received the despatch, and found that you did not arrive, I sent back a special Tartar courier to Kazala, to say that you had probably gone on to Bokhara, and had thus given us the slip; but we should have caught you there,' he continued.

"'It is the fortune of war,' I said. 'Anyhow, I have seen Khiva.'"

Burnaby says Ivanoff here winced a little, but within the wince there may have lurked a facial shrug of satisfaction. Burnaby had set out to visit Merv, and Ivanoff had caught him before he got there. As for Khiva, it had been for some time out of the running, and a survey of it was only of limited value.

Whether Russia was justified in preventing Burnaby reaching Merv, and whether the Beaconsfield Government were right in yielding to the diplomatic pressure exercised by Russia to bring about his recall, are points over which much argument might be expended. One feature of the affair, however, stands out clear. Numerous Russian pioneers were overrunning Central Asia at the time, and the English Government seem to have at once responded to the Russian demand, without endeavouring to obtain reciprocal treatment at the hands of their rival.

Bound to obey the command of the Duke of Cambridge, Burnaby had to prepare at once to return home, and that, according to Colonel Ivanoff's decision, by the shortest way, which was almost identical with the route he had previously traversed. Escorted by Cossacks, he safely accomplished the desert journey, three hundred and seventy-one miles, in a little over nine days, and with his arrival at the postal track at Kazala, his adventures, properly speaking, came to an end.

From one point of view his recall was advantageous. He reached home in the very nick of time to give his adventures to a public greedy for anything fresh about Russia. Far less exciting and graphic than MacGahan's "Campaigning on the Oxus," or Vámbéry's "Travels," Burnaby's "Ride to Khiva" secured, thanks to this circumstance and the enterprise of his publishers, an immensely wider circulation than either of those works. As a record of travel, or as regards the new and original matter contained in it, his work will not stand comparison with either MacGregor's "Khorassan," or O'Donovan's "Merv Oasis." But neither of the latter books has been popular, or has had adequate justice done it: the one because it was not light reading, and ushered into the world with a flourish of trumpets, and the other because it failed to appear until public interest in the exploit achieved had nearly died away.

It is impossible, we think, for any thoughtful person to weigh the achievements of the various Central Asian pioneers without arriving at the conclusion that Burnaby has been, in comparison with other explorers, very considerably over-praised for his ride. The exploit on which his reputation mainly rests admits of three divisions:

the journey from England to Kazala, the seven hundred miles' ride across the desert to Khiva and back, and the visit to Khiva itself. The first part was no great achievement, as the road to Kazala is yearly traversed by hundreds of Russians, and every winter Russian ladies—the wives of officers—may be seen doing what Burnaby did in his sledge. Of his entry into Khiva enough has been said to show that there was nothing dangerous about the enterprise. In this manner the pith of Burnaby's exploit is confined to the three hundred and odd miles' ride across the snow-clad desert from Kazala to Khiva, and the ride with the Cossacks back again. In performing this, Burnaby simply did what Central Asian merchants constantly do throughout the winter, and what, as a matter of fact, is done almost every week by Cossacks or their officers. From a Russian point of view, therefore, there was nothing remarkable about Burnaby's ride to Khiva. Scores of Russian officers might be enumerated who have performed rides in Central Asia more unique in every respect than his.

Even if we compare the exploit with the achievements of English officers, it will not be a difficult matter to find plenty of instances surpassing it. To go no further than the limited arena selected for this book, his seven hundred miles' level ride through hospitable camps of tamed Kirghiz will not bear comparison with Marsh's 1,400 miles' ride through Persia and Afghanistan to India, flanked by Turcoman robbers and wild tribes most of the way, and attended at intervals with rough mountain travelling. Nor can it be placed alongside MacGregor's 3,000 miles' ride through the most unsettled parts of the Perso-Afghan region. Yet such is the capriciousness of fame, that while every schoolboy knows Burnaby by his ride to Khiva, not one Englishman in a hundred thousand is aware of Marsh and MacGregor's exploits.

In our opinion, the true merit of Burnaby's achievement consists in this—that an officer of wealth and rank could be found to leave his home at the gayest season of the year, and spend his holidays in performing a distant and arduous journey, amidst the severest climatic conditions, to reconnoitre the military position of a rival country, at his own cost and risk, for the sake of a State which, judging by its treatment of previous explorers, would accord him no reward or thanks for his trouble. It is this self-sacrifice, enterprise, courage, and patriotism which has given the name of Burnaby a special and splendid significance in our language. To the majority of Englishmen Burnaby's name is not so much associated with exploration of strange countries, as typical of a class of officer ready at a moment's notice to secretly ride off and reconnoitre the position of England's enemy, no matter in what part of the world that enemy may be. MacGregor and Marsh, Baker and Stewart, were all of them Burnabys, and if any one has been transcended by the others in his exploits, the fact will be seen on examination to be largely due to circumstances over which the pioneer himself had no control. When MacGregor returned from Herat in 1875, we knew all we wanted to know for the moment about the southern side of Central Asia, and Burnaby would have wasted his energies in proceeding thither on another 3,000 miles' ride. But clouds had gathered over the northern side of the region. Burnaby took it to be his mission to dispel these mists, and without hesitation set off straight for

Khiva. In like manner when, after his return home, a public desire was manifested for a knowledge of the actual state of things on the Armenian frontier, where war was brewing between Turkey and Russia, Burnaby patriotically responded to the appeal, and rode through Asia Minor to Kars.

Such officers are invariably snubbed and disdainfully treated by the Government of the day, whether it be Conservative or Liberal, and they are scarcely ever rewarded for their trouble; but, in spite of the foolishness of their rulers, Englishmen possess a spirit of patriotism which nothing can quench, and whenever the outposts of the Empire are menaced, a Burnaby is sure to be found in the thickest of the danger calmly stalking the enemy.

CHAPTER VIII.

GENERAL PETRUSEVITCH AND THE TURCOMANS

Events in Central Asia after Burnaby's return home from Khiva—Butler appears on the scene disguised as a Chinaman—Napier's operations—Career of General Petrusevitch—The question of the diversion of the Oxus into the Caspian Sea—Its importance for Russia—The Oxus of the past and the Oxus of the future—General Glukhovsky's explorations—What may come of the restoration of the ancient waterways and irrigation canals in Central Asia—Petrusevitch's survey of the Perso-Turcoman border—Political preponderance in Afghanistan the coveted prize of the Caucasus school of administrators—Policy of Stolietoff, Markozoff, Lomakin, and Petrusevitch in the Transcaspian region—Skobeleff on the disadvantages of border conflicts—Anecdote of General Lazareff—Anecdotes of Petrusevitch while at Krasnovodsk—The siege of Geok Tepé—Death of Petrusevitch—Romantic circumstances connected with his end.

" In the field of proud honour, our swords in our hands
Our king and our country to save,
While victory shines on life's last ebbing sands,
O ! who would not die with the brave ? "

ROBERT BURNS.

BURNABY's return home coincided with the close of the Russian operations in Khokand, and the annexation of the territory (March 2nd, 1876), under its ancient name of Ferghana, with Colonel Skobeleff as its governor. This ended the Russian encroachments in the Pamir direction, and Kaufmann began to prepare for the long meditated seizure of Kashgar, while Lomakin, controller of the Transcaspian territory, sought once more to bring the Akhal Tekkés under the sway of the White Tsar. Of Kashgar we possessed abundance of information through the journeys thither of numerous pioneers, and the Embassy headed by Sir Douglas Forsyth; and, in excess, the Russians were so dilatory in making an attack on Yakoob Beg that there was little to tempt an adventurous officer to proceed to such a distant region. But the case was different with the Perso-Turcoman frontier, where the mysterious oasis of Merv still continued to act as a magnet. After the return home of MacGregor in 1875, and while Burnaby was making his way to Khiva, Captain Napier continued to move about the border in his capacity of Government agent, and early in 1876 Captain Butler appeared on the scene also, disguised as a Chinaman. Napier's operations were secret, and attracted no notice in England, while it was not until 1878 that a few scanty newspaper paragraphs drew attention to Butler's journey. That journey we shall deal with anon, in describing his better known secret mission of 1878. For the moment we give precedence to Petrusevitch, who explored the Perso-Turcoman frontier on behalf of Russia in 1876 and again in 1878.

Nikoli Grigorivitch Petrusevitch commenced his career as an artillery officer the year after Alexander II. ascended the throne (1857), and having served a few years in the army of the Caucasus, was appointed in succession to various administrative posts, in which he manifested remarkable qualities for controlling and civilizing the hill tribes. After the fall of Khiva his geographical attainments led the Government to despatch him beyond the Caspian to explore the old bed of the Oxus. For years previously it had been a moot question with *savants* whether the Oxus had ever run into the Caspian or not; and if so, whether the waterway could not be re-established between Central Asia and the Caspian, which was believed to have existed in the time of the ancients. The question was a very fascinating one, especially for Russians. The river Volga is the main artery of Russian life—the Tiber of the Russian empire; it is joined to the Baltic by a magnificent series of canals, permitting the passage of barges of 2,000 tons and steamers 200 or 300 feet long, and after a course of 2,150 miles through the heart of Russia, empties itself into the Caspian Sea. Hundreds of huge barges yearly make their way up the Volga to the Neva, and on the other hand steamers and barges from the Neva proceed down the Volga to its mouth, whence the goods are transferred to ships and conveyed to various parts of the Caspian. English people are accustomed to look upon the Caspian as a remote appendage of Russia, with but little or no life in it ; but Russian commerce is rapidly developing along its shores and a great marine springing up on its waters.

In ancient times Indian wares used to be conveyed through Cabul to the Oxus, down which they floated to its mouth, which mouth either opened into the Caspian Sea, or was situated close alongside it. Recent Russian explorers are of opinion that the Oxus ran about half way across the Aral-Caspian desert, and that the waters of the Caspian Sea extended up the Krasnovodsk Gulf a considerable distance inland, almost touching it. In those days Central Asia was covered with magnificent cities. Forests and gardens existed in the place of barren deserts, and a vast trade was transacted between India and Europe by means of the Oxus waterway. If, by any means, that waterway could be re-established, and vessels could convey Indian wares by water direct from Bokhara or Afghanistan to the banks of the Neva, Russia's power would be immensely increased in Central Asia, and she would doubtless derive a large profit from her conquests.

These considerations led the Russian Government in 1874 to despatch Petrusevitch from Krasnovodsk to examine the old course of the Oxus from that direction, while General Glukhovsky pursued a similar series of investigations from the side of Khiva. The operations were attended with no remarkable adventures, and bore no satisfactory results, for much of the desert could not be surveyed on account of the hostility of the Akhal and Merv Tekkés. It will not be until Merv is pacified and the entire region examined by engineers that Russia will take upon herself the task of attempting to establish a waterway between the Oxus and the Caspian. But already the surveys of Petrusevitch and a number of less known explorers and topographers, the levelling operations of Glukhovsky, extending over a period of seven years, and the recent investigations by Lessar of the region between Sarakhs and Merv, and Merv and Khiva, have shown that a deal of the water of the Oxus that wastes itself in the Aral can be diverted half way across the desert without spoiling Khiva, that probably a branch can be established across the desert higher up from Tchardjui towards Merv, that the surplus waters of the Murghab or Merv river can be twisted towards the Tejend, and those of the Tejend again towards Askabad; so that if a real navigable waterway cannot be successfully established, the existing desert between the Oxus and the Caspian can be irrigated into cultivation in such a manner, that a more or less cultivated expanse will some day be formed between the Caspian and Khiva and the Caspian and Oxus, *viâ* Merv. When these improvements are effected, which, according to Lessar, can be done at a relatively small outlay, the face of that part of Central Asia will be entirely changed. The clayey plains now marked "deserts" will be turned into grassy steppes like those of South Russia, and the herds of cattle and horses that are now disappearing from South Russia, owing to the encroachments of agriculture, will appear again on the fertilised plains of Turkmenia.*

Petrusevitch's exploration of the Transcaspian deserts provoked a strong desire in his heart to effect this transformation, but there seemed little hope of it ever falling to his lot to achieve it. He was but a mere geographer, and although the survey he conducted in 1876, and again in 1878, along the Perso-Turcoman frontier, in the footsteps of Baker and MacGregor, added slightly to his fame as an explorer, still it did not open out to him any influential administrative career. For the sake of his topographical knowledge he was retained at Tiflis as counsellor to the Caucasian Government, and to a certain class of mind this would

* An important effect is likely to be exercised on the climate of Central Asia by the reforesting of Turkestan, commenced under the auspices of General Tchernayeff. In the spring of 1883 upwards of 100,000 trees were planted in Southern Turkestan.

have been an adequate recompense for the work he had achieved; but Petrusevitch was ambitious. He wished to act as well as to advise. In common with MacGregor and Baker, Butler and Napier, his travels along the Perso-Turcoman border had impressed him with the idea that it was in Russia's power to carve a great province out of Turkmenia.* He saw as clearly as our gifted explorers the golden opportunities that lay within Russia's grasp. Once the whole of the Turcomans were brought under Russian control, it would not be difficult for the Governor administrating their territory to secure political preponderance in Persia and Afghanistan.

Suddenly things shaped themselves in his favour. For years previously affairs had been mismanaged in the Transcaspian region. The first administrator, Colonel Stolietoff, he who had been the first to land and establish Krasnovodsk in 1869, had failed to give satis-

* The distinction between Turkestan and Turkmenia should be clearly borne in mind by the reader. The former appellation is applied by Russia to her province in Central Asia, ruled from Tashkent and including Khiva and Bokhara; and the latter to the Turcoman region, with Merv, east of the Caspian, controlled by the government of the Caucasus.

faction to the Government, and had been superseded in the second year of his administration by Colonel Markozoff. The two years' career of this officer was still more unfortunate. His harsh and domineering manner inflamed against Russia all the Turcomans who were not within the immediate reach of the Cossack, and although he conducted several reconnaissances that were successful so far as topographical results were concerned, still he left behind him, wherever he went, ill-will; which cost Russia a whole series of campaigns against the Akhal Tekké tribe. In 1873, the column he led from the Atrek to co-operate in the general advance upon Khiva collapsed from heat and want of water when half way across the desert traversed by Vámbéry, and he reached Krasnovodsk with only a skeleton of his original force. For failing in this enterprise he was placed upon the retired list of the Russian army, and a successor appointed in the person of Colonel Lomakin, who had successfully led the Kinderley column to Khiva.

The new administrator introduced quite a different policy. "The Turcomans say that where Markozoff threatened and used force," reported Napier in 1874,* "Lomakin calls round him the chief men of the tribe, and opening their hearts by a liberal display of hospitality, together with more valued proofs of his good will and earnests of his generous intentions for the future, explains to them his wishes and exhorts them as allies and friends of Russia to aid him. With a good military reputation and a sufficient force maintained at Krasnovodsk, the method adopted by the latter is no doubt best calculated to ensure the good will of the Yomood tribe for the present, and its future subjection."

But Lomakin's "good military reputation" did not proceed from qualities of his own, but from the borrowed lustre of such men as Skobeleff, Grodekoff, and other brilliant officers who had served as his subordinates in the march upon Khiva, and who had mainly contributed to the success of the column. When Lomakin came to act against the warlike Tekkés with no clever assistants to guide his operations or retrieve his errors, his incapacity became exposed at once. The more he fought the worse he fought. On the other hand, every

* Napier's Journals, page 31.

campaign left the Tekkés more enlightened, and better able to cope with European foes.

Speaking on this point, Skobeleff said to the writer a few months before his death: "It is a mistake to engage in frequent wars against border tribes, for they become accustomed to your mode of fighting, and each time grow more difficult to crush. A general who conducts European troops for the first time against savages can subjugate them with the greatest ease, with a minimum of loss and a maximum of effect. But if in reprisals for border raids he keeps advancing and retiring, each successive expedition becomes more difficult, until at last the pacification of the country, which, if a thorough policy had been pursued at the outset, would have been a mere military promenade, is impossible without a long and arduous war."

The policy Skobeleff deprecated was precisely the one pursued east of the Caspian by Lomakin. How far he himself was responsible for it cannot be defined. Fully occupied with the completion of the conquest of Turkestan, the Imperial Government was probably disinclined to take in hand the sweeping subjugation of Turkmenia. Besides, every movement the Cossacks made beyond the Caspian was loudly denounced by the English press, and statesmen of both parties recommended that an advance upon Merv should be regarded as a *casus belli.* These two considerations were probably responsible for the circumstance that Russia, instead of conquering Akhal after the Khivan campaign, sought to bring the Tekkés of that oasis and the adjacent Turcoman tribes under her control by diplomatic means, aided by a yearly display of force. Unfortunately for her, this policy produced the opposite effect to that intended. Observing that the Russians always retired after their yearly reconnoitring of the Turcoman region, the Tekkés lost their respect for them, while Sofi Khan of Kizil Arvat, Tekme Sardar of Beurma, and other leaders who accepted from time to time Lomakin's offers of hospitality, learned the principles of European warfare in the Russian camp. Thanks to the knowledge the Tekkés acquired by their yearly conflicts with the Russians and the visits of their leaders to their camps and forts, they grew so expert, that from being only able to fight on horseback in 1873, they were sufficiently advanced in warfare by 1879 to successfully resist the invaders from behind earthworks, and to establish a powerful fortress the following year, which took Skobeleff nine months in preparations and three weeks in continuous siege operations to subdue.

From the close of the Khivan campaign to 1877, Lomakin reconnoitred yearly the Akhal region, with more or less unsatisfactory results. In 1878, a larger expedition than any previous one was beaten at Khoja Kalé, and compelled to retreat, under very disastrous and humiliating circumstances, to Tchikishlar. The following year, Russia concentrated at the mouth of the river Atrek an army of 25,000 troops, to retrieve the defeat, and placed the force under General Lazareff, who had distinguished himself in the capture of Kars.* But Lazareff dying shortly after the departure of the expedi-

* A Russian officer attached to the expedition, whom I met at Skobeleff's funeral, narrated to me the following anecdote to show the difference between Lazareff and Petrusevitch. When on the point of setting out to assume the command, Lazareff asked Petrusevitch to draw up for him a proclamation in the Turcoman language, counselling the enemy to submit. After some days Petrusevitch brought the general a dozen sheets of foolscap covered with writing, and handed it to him. "What's that?" demanded Lazareff. "The Proclamation," replied

tion from the coast, Lomakin, as the senior officer of the force, resumed control of the operations, and hurrying on to Dengeel Tepé, or Geok Tepé, was so shockingly thrashed by the Tekkés that the Government had no alternative but to withdraw him completely from the Transcaspian region. General Tergoukasoff was thereupon sent to take over the command of the remnants of the Atrek army, until the Government had decided when and in what form to conduct another expedition, and Petrusevitch was ordered to Krasnovodsk to replace Lomakin in the civil administration of the country.

At Krasnovodsk, Petrusevitch earned golden opinions by his admirable conduct.* He had none of the usual characteristics of the Russian frontier official—he did not drink, or smoke, or play cards, or intrigue with women; his honesty was beyond question, and the natives found in

Petrusevitch, beginning to read from it in Russ a series of arguments why it would be better for them to surrender. "Stop!" exclaimed Lazareff. "I don't want to send them a book. Put that in the archives, and just write half-a-dozen lines, telling them that we mean to have their country, and that if they don't submit at once we'll smash 'em"!

* During my recent journey to the Caucasus I heard nothing but good of Petrusevitch.

him a warm and zealous protector. A Russian gentleman, who visited him at the great stone house Lomakin had constructed as the official residence at Krasnovodsk, thus describes what he saw there :—

"On reaching the Governor's house, the orderly told us to pass through the drawing-room to the cabinet beyond. Before we had even reached the half-opened door of this a pleasant voice called out to us to enter. As we did so an officer in green uniform rose from a table loaded with books and papers, and advanced to meet us. It was General Petrusevitch—a man a little above the medium height, with a rosy face, a long, light-coloured beard, a broad, handsome forehead, and a pair of bright intelligent grey eyes. From the two book-cases, crammed with books, and the piles of books scattered about everywhere, it was easy to see that the General was a person of literary tastes.

"After transacting business, we had a talk, and I willingly accepted Petrusevitch's invitation to dine with him. The company consisted chiefly of military men. General attention was excited during the dinner by the remarks of an engineer, who had just returned from surveying the course of the projected railway across the steppe to Kizil Arvat. He laid great stress on the fact that, although this was the first time he had ever undertaken long marches in a waterless country, he had nevertheless always been able to keep four or five miles ahead of his escort without feeling any inconvenience from it, and hence considered that most of the talk he had previously heard of the difficulties of desert marching was pure moonshine. Petrusevitch, who was listening attentively with bended head, here suddenly interrupted the boaster with the inquiry :—

"'And what, my dear sir, let me ask, did you carry on the road ?'

"'Carry ? Nothing,' replied the engineer.

"'Nothing ! And a soldier, you know, has to carry a rifle, cartridges, water, provisions for several days, his great coat, etc. You are now returning to St. Petersburg. May I beg of you to eliminate from your conversation all such boasting as this, since there are quite enough persons there already who consider the precautions superfluous we are taking to secure the comfort of the troops during their impending march under a burning sun?'

"Receiving intelligence that a large distilling apparatus, established by the Caucasus and Mercury Company to supply Krasnovodsk with water, had become, after a stoppage of two months, a complete failure, in consequence of which the railway works had had to be suspended, Petrusevitch put his hand to his head and exclaimed: 'The devil only knows what's to be done. It is only the press that could help us in this—the newspapers would at least serve to expose the culprits.' At this moment the Policemaster of Krasnovodsk entered, and announced that the man who had stolen the five-rouble note (10*s.*) had been caught. 'There you are,' exclaimed Petrusevitch ironically, 'we can always catch a man who steals a five-rouble note; but only let us try and find out who is to blame for erecting worthless boilers to the distilling apparatus, and we are sure to fail. Everybody has an excuse for himself, and does not hesitate to lay the blame upon the Almighty.'"

Three months after this Skobeleff arrived at Krasnovodsk, and preparations were at once made for the campaign. Petrusevitch took a prominent part in the task of organizing the expedition, and when the final advance took place he proceeded to the front as one of Skobeleff's immediate assistants. His aid was invaluable in the reconnaisances that preceded the investment of Geok Tepé, and he greatly distinguished himself at the capture of the outlying fort of Yangi Kala. Two days after the occupation of this point, Skobeleff decided he would not make a direct attack on the fortress, but approach the walls by a regular siege. To divert the attention of the Tekkés from the laying of the first parallel on the night of the 3rd of January, Petrusevitch was ordered to attack with a force an outlying position some distance to the right of the Russian camp. This was tenaciously held by the Tekkés, and the general, in riding into an enclosure to animate the Cossacks, was struck by a bullet and fell dead from his horse.

The death of the explorer was all the more untimely and melancholy from the circumstance that only a few days previous he had had the happiness of finding that he had secured the affections of an amiable lady, who had joined

DEATH OF GENERAL PETRUSEVITCH.

[*To face page* 228.

the force as a hospital nurse with a number of others, headed by the Countess Miliutin, the daughter of the Minister of War. Skobeleff was bitterly vexed when he heard of his death. He had such a warm regard for Petrusevitch that he could not control his emotion before the troops. By his orders, all the officers and men who had fallen in the fight were carried to a point outside the camp to be buried, and after a funeral service had been performed over them, the whole of the cannon belonging to the army fired a simultaneous volley into the fortress, whence, says a Russian writer, "cries and groans directly afterwards issued, showing that our iron tears had not been shed in vain."

At the close of the siege the body of the general was sent to the Caucasus, to be buried in a little village belonging to one of the hill-tribes in Daghestan he had ruled with such success in the earlier part of his career. Krasnovodsk, from which he had meant to superintend the works for irrigating and rendering fit for colonization the country lying between the Caspian and the Atrek, has been abandoned by his successor. The Governor of Transcaspia rules to-day at Askabad, 350 miles further east of Krasnovodsk, and 350 miles nearer India. Nothing for the moment is being done to carry out Petrusevitch's colonization project in the country between the Caspian and Atrek, but the notion of twisting and diverting the rivers in the steppe to render them subservient to Russian interests has passed from Petrusevitch to General Komaroff, who is busy striving to shape the Tejend in such a manner as to create a waterway from Askabad to Merv on the one hand and to Herat on the other.

CHAPTER IX.

CAPTAIN BUTLER, THE SECRET ENGLISH AGENT.

The remarkable siege of Geok Tepé—Excitement occasioned in England and Russia by the fighting—Captain Butler claims that he fortified the place—Never near it—The public and explorers—Butler's journey along the Perso-Turcoman border in 1876—Sent again in 1878 to lead the Turcomans against the Russians—Butler a wrong agent for a mission of this kind—O'Donovan upon his pretensions—Some of his alleged adventures in Persia—The English Government placed in an awkward position by his disclosures of his mission—Their effect on the policy of Russia in the Akhal Tekké region—The Government throw him over—Fate of Butler—Another of O. K.'s misstatements—Effect of the journeys of Butler, Baker, Napier, and MacGregor on the Turcomans of Akhal and Merv—The trouble they caused Russia and the barrier they opposed to her operations—What English officers may do to strengthen and defend the Empire.

"Before mine eyes thou hast set, and in mine ear
Vented much policy, and projects deep
Of enemies, of aids, battles, and leagues."

MILTON.

In the opening month of 1881, a remarkable conflict took place on the confines of Transcaspian Persia, which provoked considerable interest and sensation in Europe. A tribe, which all travellers had concurred in describing as unfit to fight behind walls, although excellent warriors on horseback, suddenly improvised a Plevna, and, notwithstanding that they had no artillery and only short-range muskets, while the enemy—commanded by Russia's best general—possessed seventy cannon, and were armed with breechloaders, maintained for three weeks such a desperate defence, that for a time it seemed as though the invaders would at length be driven back, baffled and beaten, to the Caspian. During this exciting crisis, a letter appeared in the *Globe* newspaper, in which the writer affirmed that—" In truth I can claim with pride that for two and a half years at least, by constructing the fortifications of Geok Tepé, I have helped a brave and heroic people to retain their liberty ; and my constant prayer is that my friends (the Turcomans) will act as heroically at the two spots further east I have chalked out for them as they are acting within the beleaguered earthwork of Geok Tepé." The writer of this letter was Captain Francis Butler ; the place he said he fortified he never cast eyes on or was near in his life; and the two points—as strongly fortified as Geok Tepé—he said the Russians would find further east have never yet been found by their generals or explorers.

There are two tendencies in people with regard to their views of travel. One is to exaggerate the dangers and difficulties of a journey in foreign parts; the other to speak disparagingly of the accuracy and achievements of explorers. Thus, Burnaby's ride to Khiva has often been spoken of as a unique achievement, instead of regarding it as an exploit transcended by hundreds of others, and possessing in all its essential features nothing out of the common of every-day travel in Asiatic Russia. On the other hand, it has almost invariably been the fate of travellers who have penetrated to unknown or little known places to have discredit cast upon their statements. We laugh at the King of Siam who lost his patience when the European spoke, among other marvels, of rivers being frozen over in winter in the Far West; but the same spirit of incredulity prevails in more enlightened communities; and thus Livingstone had to fight on his return from Africa with easy-chair geographers, who believed they knew more about the regions discovered than he did; Vámbéry had to endure seeing in print that he had never been in disguise to Khiva; and more recently hints have been uttered that Mr. O'Donovan's adventures at Merv had their origin in his Irish imagination. In such cases as these the happiest course a traveller can pursue is to hold his tongue and leave it to time to confirm his statements. Explorers in the footsteps of Livingstone have long ago proved the accuracy of his writings; the Russians invading the Khanates visited by Vámbéry in 1863 have found that he really was there, and that the state of things at the time was as he described it; and Alikhanoff and other pioneers have penetrated to Merv without discovering anything to impugn the accuracy of Mr. O'Donovan's assertions. But there are travellers and travellers—travellers who describe truthfully what has occurred to them, and travellers who indulge so largely in embellishments that, owing to the difficulty of separating the truth from the false admixture, the public are obliged to reject their statements altogether. To the latter category would appear to belong Captain Butler, one of the most unfortunate travellers in recent times.

Captain F. W. H. Butler, of the 9th Foot, spent his leave in the spring of 1876 on the Perso-Turcoman frontier, travelling in the disguise of a Chinaman. This he adopted owing to his ignorance of Persian, and the knowledge of Chinese he had picked up while commanding the coolie corps during the Taeping rebellion. On his return to India, he placed at the disposition of the Government notes he had taken (which, owing to the travels of Baker and MacGregor over the same ground, could have had geographically but little that was new in them), and this led Lord Lytton, in 1877, to despatch him again to the Perso-Turcoman border. According to Lord Lytton, he was simply sent to ascertain the state of things at Merv; according to Butler and his friends, he was ordered thither to lead the Turcomans against the Russians in the event of a conflict between England and Russia in the East. One thing is very certain: the mission was of a very delicate character, and required great discretion on the part of the accredited agent to prevent his Government being compromised by it. Whether the Viceroy was right or wrong in dispatching Butler to Merv is a question that may be argued by itself. Had the English Government supported Baker in 1873, had the Indian Government permitted MacGregor to have gone ahead in 1875, had the home authorities, finally, left Burnaby alone in Khiva in 1876—there would have been no need of dispatching a secret agent to survey Merv in 1877. But statesmen ought not to be discouraged in their attempts to retrieve their blunders. We think that Lytton was quite justified in sending an explorer to Merv in 1877, and had he chosen a traveller of discretion like MacGregor, a survey might have been secured without in any way wounding the susceptibilities of Russia. Captain Butler, however, was the worst person adapted for a mission of this kind, and compromised England in a manner that gave Russia a ready retort to our constant charges of frontier intrigue against her in the East.

What route the captain took along the

border, and what actually occurred to him, are points on which nothing reliable has transpired. Butler himself has never written anything, and we believe that the military authorities at home threatened him with the loss of his pension if he published any account of his proceedings. The official report he furnished the Government was found to contain so much unreliable matter that it could not be trusted at all, and of the many accounts that appeared in 1879 in the Indian and English papers of his operations, some of them clearly inspired by the captain, the palpably false was so mixed up with the real that they were of little value to the investigator. In one of these it was said he had been within forty miles of Merv, whereas it is known that he never penetrated beyond the border; and as for the statement that he fortified Geok Tepé, Skobeleff and other Russian officers not only laughed at the notion—although it would have been a good point for Russia if she could have proved that Butler had built the defences—but even Mr. O'Donovan felt bound to deny its accuracy. Butler, he says, in his "Merv Oasis," tried to go to Akhal, but failed. "He never got nearer the Tekkés than Deregez. That he did his best to go forward I am aware. In the attempt, I am told, he wounded one of the cavalry who tried to prevent him. Akhal Tekkés or Merv Tekkés he never saw on their own ground. The letter to which I allude says that, according to the captain's own statement, he denies having *armed* the Tekkés; he only imparted to them a slight knowledge of drill and field fortification. Unless the captain be possessed of some mesmeric power of instruction, some 'mystic might which breathes through sundering distance,' I am at a loss to know how he imparted even the small modicum of knowledge which he admits to have imparted, to people within reach of whom he never came nearer than a hundred miles."

It seems tolerably certain that Butler gave a very exaggerated account of what he did on the Perso-Turcoman frontier, and allowed extraordinary stories to go forth of his adventures. Boulger, in his "England and Russia in Central Asia," gives one of them. "Making the Persian frontier form his base, Butler explored the passes of the Kuren Dagh, accompanied by a young Englishman, Mr.

Henry Hammond. Of the difficulties and dangers encountered by this gallant officer we know little, but the following incident will show that they deserve the epithet of hair-breadth. Early on the day following his arrival at a village beyond Kuchan, the Persians ordered a body of sixty soldiers into the fort, where they deprived Captain Butler and his companion of their arms and luggage; while on the morning following this, the governor of the place, with some forty men, took them to a spot in the glen, and, after separating them, ordered Captain Butler to dismount, as he was about to be shot. With this request he refused to comply, adding that, if he were to be shot, he would give the signal to fire by taking off his hat. The governor thereupon cocked and presented his gun, but he put it down in astonishment when the captain took off his hat, and in admiration of his courage asked him to be their chief. The governor was subsequently flogged and dismissed from his post."

In spite of such problematical adventures and doubtful geographical discoveries, Butler attracted no notice as an explorer until his quarrel with the Indian Government. It had been intended by Lord Lytton that his mission should be a secret one, but the Russian Government got wind of it,* and made representations which caused our authorities to order Butler home. On his arrival in India he made a claim for money in excess of the sum supplied him by Lord Lytton for the journey, which the Indian Government refused to allow him. Consider-

* Writing to the Marquis of Salisbury, under date July 3rd, 1878, our Ambassador at St. Petersburg, Lord Augustus Loftus, said:—" M. de Giers, the head of the Russian Foreign Office, admitted that he had sent M. Bakouline, the Russian Consul at Astrabad" (who had treated Colonel Baker so hospitably in 1873), "to watch the movements of Captains Butler and Napier, who were reported to be inciting the Turcoman tribes to hostilities against Russia. I (Lord A. Loftus) stated to M. Giers that Captain Butler was a mere traveller on his own account" (the Ambassador was apparently unaware Butler was the paid agent of the Viceroy; whether the home authorities were equally ignorant is doubtful), "and no agent of Her Majesty's Government, and that urgent orders had been sent to him by the Commander-in-Chief in India to return to his military duties. M. de Giers, who appeared to be well informed both in regard to Captain Butler and Captain Napier, stated that he was aware that Butler had been recalled, but that, nevertheless, he had refused to obey the orders he had received" (which seems to have been correct), "and was persisting in his intention to visit the Akhal tribes. He referred even to the letters which Captain Butler had addressed to certain Turcoman chiefs, of which His Excellency had evidently received copies."

ing that Butler, in excess of failure, had furnished reports on which no reliance could be placed, the decision has a certain amount of justification. But Butler did not subscribe to this view; he allowed statements to go forth that he had been a secret emissary sent by Lytton to lead the Turcomans against Russia; that he had been thrown over because the Viceroy had not the moral courage to support him in the face of Russian remonstrances; and that the only reward he had received for his geographical discoveries, his hardships, and his narrow escapes from death, was that he had been sent back to his regiment in disgrace, with several hundred pounds of expenses disallowed him.

The press in England and India took the matter up, and unluckily the controversy started at a moment when the Liberals were doing their utmost to discredit the acts of the Beaconsfield Government in India. The case of Captain Butler thus served as an admirable weapon in the hands of those who vehemently oppose all action against Russia in Asia. This did not tend to improve the feeling which had grown up between the Indian Government and Butler. But the worst was to come, and this treatment, too, from the very opponents of Viceroy Lytton, Butler had been helping so much by his disclosures.

We have seen that his divulging of his secret relations with Lytton had embarrassed the Conservatives while in office. Having offended one party he proceeded to offend the other, by writing to the *Globe*—at a moment when the Liberals, now in power, were endeavouring to eliminate all friction between England and Russia, and when Russia was watching with breathless suspense the deadly conflict at Geok Tepé—that it was he who had been instrumental in causing so much trouble to Skobeleff by fortifying that place, and further that the invaders would find two more strongholds, planned by him, to the east of it. This disclosure seriously embarrassed the Foreign Office authorities, for however much the new Government might disapprove of the acts of the old one, it could not shake off England's responsibility for what Butler said he had done in the Akhal oasis. England stood convicted, on the showing of Butler, that an officer on active service had gone to Akhal when the Akhal Tekkés were at war with Russia, and had assisted the enemy by building a powerful fortress. Further, his letter made it appear that England's diplomatists had repeatedly passed off on Russia an officer as a private and harmless traveller, who, by his help to the Tekkés, had caused Russia one great disaster at Geok Tepé, and the greatest siege known in modern times in Central Asia.

Russia attached so much importance to Butler's letter that it was telegraphed *in extenso* to Skobeleff, and occasioned reconnoitring expeditions being sent out in the direction of Merv in search of the other two Geok Tepés the officer had spoken of as existing east of the beleaguered fortress. According to General Soboleff * it even brought about the occupation of Askabad, and although some doubt may be expressed on this point—for the conquest of Akhal would have been incomplete without the seizure of that place—it is very probable that Russian statesmen availed themselves of the circumstance to justify Skobeleff's operations beyond Geok Tepé, which provoked so much excite-

* Interview with General Soboleff, head of the Asiatic Department of the General Staff—"The Russian Advance towards India."

ment at the time. At any rate, Butler's letter was a splendid one for Russian diplomats to make capital out of, and the probability that the opportunity was seized upon is sustained by the rapid punishment that overtook the writer of it. A few days after the letter appeared in the *Globe*, Butler was placed on the retired list, and he was not even allowed to take the title of major, to which he was almost, if not entirely, entitled. When Mr. Labouchere brought his grievances before the House, the Marquis of Hartington defended the course the authorities had taken, and still further damaged the reputation of the officer by stating that "official information received from other sources by the Government of India had thrown considerable doubt on the accuracy of Captain Butler's report of his proceedings on the Perso-Turcoman frontier, which report further contained no information of value." This may be said to have closed Captain Butler's career, and since then nothing has been heard of him and his grievances.

The English public is always ready to sympathise with an individual ill-treated by the State, and had Butler swerved less from the path of accuracy his grievances would have stood a chance of being listened to. But, as the case stands, it is difficult to accord him very much sympathy. The English public likes to think that an English officer is incapable of deceit, and that his word can be taken in any matter without suspicion of diplomatic reservations. Butler stands convicted of having asserted he fortified a point which he was never nearer to than 100 miles, and which, as a matter of fact, he had no hand, direct or indirect, in defending. If a man, in giving evidence, is proved to have been guilty of untruth in a matter susceptible of testing, it is commonly the case to disregard what he says on other points where tests cannot be applied. But, in excess of the principal misstatement about Geok Tepé, Butler made other assertions in his report which could be tested and have their falsity exposed by officers like MacGregor, who had been over the same ground, or by the native agents our Teheran legation maintained in Khorassan. It is rare, when a man comes back from his travels, that the public have to tell him, "We cannot believe what you say;" and the fate of Captain Butler should serve to deter other pioneers from attempting to secure notoriety by other means than that of hard, honest, genuine exploration.*

Before completely parting with Butler, it will not be out of place to point out the very important effect his presence alone had on the Perso-Turcoman frontier, apart from any of his actions. It is not too much to say that if Baker and MacGregor, Napier and Butler, had never put in an appearance on the north-east Persian border, Russia would have been spared

* In O. K.'s recent book, "Skobeleff and the Slavonic Cause," Madame Olga de Novikoff says (page 325):—"The Atrek frontier was the line along which your Central Asians and ours elected to fight out their battle. *An English officer, Lieutenant Butler, fortified Geok Tepé.*" Considering that the talented authoress had read "The Russian Advance towards India," having at least taken extracts from it from beginning to end, it show show unreliable she constantly is with regard to the accuracy of her facts, that she should have boldly asserted, for sake of argument, what she must have known to be untrue. In the "Russian Advance" Butler's claim is gone into at length, and not only is it proved by English evidence that he had nothing to do with the fortification of Geok Tepé, but General Skobeleff, the chief of his staff, General Grodekoff, and the clever engineer officer who went over the whole of Butler's ground on the frontier, Captain Masloff, in their conversations pooh-pooh and ridicule the notion as the claim of a braggadocio. Yet knowing all this, O. K. writes in her glib, confident way, "Butler fortified Geok Tepé"!

a whole series of Turcoman campaigns. The visits of these officers cost Russia millions of money, and hundreds of lives. This is a historical fact which has never been properly examined, even by the Russians themselves, and it is worth looking into for a few moments, if for no other reason than showing what immense harm our Burnabys can do a rival power.

From the close of the Khivan campaign in 1873, when Russia first began to prepare to conquer the Tekké Turcomans of Akhal and Merv, up to the time Skobeleff laid siege to Geok Tepé, not a year passed without some English officer or other moving along the Turcoman border from Sarakhs to the Caspian. All these officers, without exception, were strongly opposed to Russia's advance eastward, and although they never helped the Turcomans with money or weapons, or, with the possible exception of Butler, actually promised them English aid, still they encouraged them to resist the Russians, and by continually asking them if they would not like to accept an English protectorate, etc., raised expectations of assistance from India. Up to the very day of the investment of Geok Tepé, the Tekkés believed officers would arrive from Candahar to lead them against the enemy; and when the stronghold was captured, a splendid white charger, richly caparisoned, was found in a stable, which the defenders had kept all along for the expected English commander.*

Had Colonel Baker and his successors not visited the Persian border, the Turcomans, left to themselves to arrange matters with the Russians, would have no doubt submitted within a year or two of the fall of Khiva. The opposition existing in England to their annexation, and the efforts of our legation at Teheran to protect them, would have been unknown to the Tekkés, and without this stimulus they must have been soon discouraged in their unequal struggle for independence. But the incessant visits of warlike English officers altogether changed the condition of things. They made no secret that both England and England's legation at Teheran were striving to save them from the Russians. Anybody who

* Skobeleff gave this to the Emperor shortly before his death.

has read the books of these pioneers, and knows anything personally of the writers, can easily imagine them saying, in their brave soldierly style—"Don't you give in to the Russians. England is doing all she can to prevent them taking your country, and if you can only hold out long enough, there's a chance that she'll step in and help you lick them."

Such language as this, held out year after year, could not but have the effect of buoying up the Turcomans, and causing them to fight with greater vigour. Putting ourselves in Russia's place, it is easy to understand why she felt all along aggrieved at the presence of these officers on the Turcoman border, and why she was always complaining of them. It is no exaggeration to say that the journeys of Baker, MacGregor, Napier, and Butler did more to arrest the Russian advance than all the solemn deliberations of successive English cabinets, the sackfuls of diplomatic correspondence, the miles of parliamentary speeches and questions, and the myriads of newspaper articles published on the Central Asian Question between 1873 and 1881.

Their efforts were in vain. Abandoned by

England, the Turcomans had no other course but to surrender. But the check the presence of the four English officers occasioned to Russia's growth was something—something of which they may well be proud. If they failed to save Akhal and Merv, they at least caused a dissipation of Russian energy, which otherwise might have been expended in bringing our rival closer still to India. This is a great fact, and it may be made a greater one, if borne well in mind by other English officers desirous of serving their country outside the narrow channel of military routine.. Wherever our Empire is threatened, wherever our interests are imperilled—in Africa or in Asia, in Madagascar or Tonquin, on the Gambier or the Niger, bordering Afghanistan or the confines of Corea, thither ought English officers swiftly to make their way, to ascertain the secret operations of rivals, to expose their malevolent designs, to restore by their presence faint-hearted nations, and by their letters and their books keep England alive to her obligations to her Empire. Most officers have money. Most of them have leisure. All long for distinction. With an Empire widening every day, in every part of the earth, and daily inviting more and more the attacks of jealous rivals, it ought not to be difficult at any time for an officer to find something to do to add to its lustre and ennoble his name.

Yes, our Burnabys, our Bakers, our MacGregors, our Gordons—these are the real pillars of the Empire. These are the men who confer provinces upon England, who risk their lives to guard them. When the world is a little older, and the working-man's vote is worth more than the statesman's opinion, then the splendid achievements of such men will be more generously appreciated, and the warm English feeling expended to-day on torpid, stupid, unpatriotic party politicians will be directed towards heroes, whose steady undaunted patriotism, in face of public indifference and bureaucratic disdain, conveys a moral as grand as their careers.

CHAPTER X.

PASHINO, THE SECRET RUSSIAN AGENT.

The Russians before Constantinople—Conference in their camp to discuss the utility of striking a blow at England through India—Dispatch of Russian officers from the army to Central Asia—Pashino sent to India to find his way to Cabul—Career of Pashino—Interpreter to the Ameer Abdurrahman Khan—Pashino's journey round the world—An incident at the Tsar's coronation—Private Russian travellers in India—Their fewness—Pashino's views of the administration of India—Nonsense written on India by Englishmen—Evil results in India and Russia—Pashino, stopped on the Afghan border, returns to Constantinople—By his conduct spoils his subsequent career—Becomes a pauper and a cripple—Rewards given by Russia to her explorers.

"*Constable.* If the English had any apprehension, they would run away.

Rambures. That island of England breeds very valiant creatures; their mastiffs are of unmatchable courage.

Orleans. Foolish curs! that run winking into the mouth of a Russian bear, and have their heads crushed like rotten apples."

SHAKESPEARE, *Henry V.*

EARLY in 1878, the Russians drove back the Turks helter-skelter to the southernmost points of the Balkan Peninsula, and settled down in the outskirts of Constantinople. Resistance from the Turks they had no longer to fear, and they would have undoubtedly occupied and annexed Tsargrad but for their knowledge that such an act would provoke England to war. Hence they checked their advance when in sight of the coveted city, and entered into diplomatic negotiations with the Sultan and his supporters. For a time it seemed as though no *modus vivendi* would be arrived at, and it was during this period that a conference was held in the Russian camp to discuss the utility of striking a blow at English power in India. The result of the conference was that Colonel Stolietoff was sent *viâ* Tashkent to Cabul, to set the Afghans in motion against India; Colonel Grodekoff was despatched to help Kaufmann, and subsequently pushed on to Herat; and Gospodin Pashino was supplied with funds to proceed to India, thence to make his way *viâ* Peshawur to Cabul, and join Stolietoff there.

Pashino was one of those restless mortals who can never settle to anything long, and who, in spite of great gifts and the incessant smiles of fortune, always misuse their opportunities. Originally a student at the St. Petersburg University, he was sent to the Tartar University of Kazan on taking his degree in 1856, and spent several years in philological investigations. In 1861 his knowledge of Oriental languages led the Russian Government to secure his services, and send him to Teheran as junior secretary to the Russian Embassy, where he may probably have rubbed against the ragged dervish Vámbéry in his walks about the streets, and perhaps wondered at the European features of the *hadji*. In 1866, the newly-conquered territory of Turkestan having been formed into a province distinct from Orenburg, with a Governor-General of its own, Pashino was removed from Teheran to Tashkent to serve as agent of the Minister for Foreign Affairs. Shortly after his arrival, the present Ameer of Afghanistan, Abdurrahman Khan, fled to Samarcand, and Pashino was appointed as interpreter to him. "At that time," he says, "I was the only person in Turkestan who understood the language of Abdurrahman Khan. Consequently everything he wished to say had to pass through me, and there was no one with whom he could be on more familiar terms than myself."

Had Pashino possessed the qualifications of a diplomatist, he would have undoubtedly, owing to his knowledge of Oriental languages, risen to the high and confidential position on Kaufmann's political staff which was subsequently occupied by Herr Weinberg. But he was rash, headstrong, egotistical, and loquacious, and these defects rendered him ill-adapted for the intrigues which Kaufmann was always conducting in Central Asia. Shortly before the expedition against Khiva in 1873, he returned to Russia, and proceeded thence to India. Who supplied the funds for the journey, and what the object of it was, are points on which no information is forthcoming; but the following year, when he undertook a second journey thither, his expenses were specially defrayed by the Tsarevitch, now Alexander III. This time Pashino returned home through Persia.

Shortly after his arrival at St. Petersburg, one of the Khludoffs, the richest of the Moscow cotton-spinners, decided to send his son on a journey round the world, and engaged Pashino to accompany him.* A third time, in the course of his travels, he paid a visit to India, and also made his way to the Burmese Court, where the King spoke in very contemptuous terms of the English to the Russian visitors. When he returned home, the Turkish war was at its height, but he did not long

* On the day of the Tsar's coronation I was stopping for a while in one of the stands near the Uspenski Cathedral in order to watch the Emperor proceed thence to the palace, when a very shabby and dissipated young man made his way to the reserved seats immediately behind me, close to where Mr. George Augustus Sala, in court costume (his cocked hat and dirk causing the spectators to take him for a British admiral), was busy penning the wonderful account that was to appear the next morning in the *Daily Telegraph*. "I cannot understand," observed the correspondent of another paper to me, "how, with all their precautions, the authorities should have allowed such a dissipated-looking person to come to this stand. He looks just the very sort of man to make an attempt on the Emperor's life." I rejoined with some equally uncomplimentary remarks, shortly after which the person referred to got up, and calmly observed, in a casual sort of way, in English, "You're making plenty of notes to-day." It was not the first time a similar *contretemps* had occurred to me in Russia, and therefore, without being abashed at his having understood our conversation, I ignored what we had said and fell to interrogating him. It then came out that he was a son of one of the cotton-spinning Khludoffs—his father had four mills—and was cousin to the young man who had been escorted round the world by Pashino. The latter he knew well, and he gave me some interesting particulars about him.

remain inactive. At the instigation of Skobeleff, his services were secured, and, with an audacity altogether Russian, he was instructed to proceed through India to the court of a prince, who was afterwards to be instigated by Stolietoff to make a descent upon the English dominions.

Luckily, we had at the time officials at Peshawur who were not afraid to act upon their own responsibility. Pashino was stopped by these, and refused permission to proceed through the Khyber to Cabul. In vain he made an outcry about stopping "a private traveller," the Peshawur authorities were inflexible, and their action was upheld by the Government at Simla.

"Look at Pashino," said a leading official of the Russian Foreign Office to me in 1882, on my expressing regret that the Russian Government would not sanction my proceeding to Askabad. "Look how Pashino was treated. Although a private traveller, engaged in scientific pursuits, he was stopped at the post of Peshawur and refused permission to cross the border into Afghanistan. If your Government objects to private Russian travellers in India, can you wonder at our Government objecting to private English travellers in Central Asia?"

I pointed out that England did not object to Russians visiting India, but that she considered they ought to keep out of Afghanistan—hence his argument was a fallacious one, since he mixed up the zone between Russia and India with India itself. Russians could go to any part of India, but English travellers were not allowed to move freely about Turkestan. The movements of the travellers of both nations in the unabsorbed region of Central Asia were quite a different matter.

But the real point at issue, whether Pashino was a harmless private traveller or not, was settled a few days later by a letter from that person himself to one of the St. Petersburg papers, in which, after paying a tribute to the memory of General Skobeleff, he mentioned that it was due to the action of the deceased general that he had been furnished with funds, and sent from the Russian camp to India to make his way to Cabul.

It is a curious circumstance that, although Russians take a great interest in India, few of them have visited it. Probably not more than half-a-dozen have penetrated to it during the last quarter of a century, and, so far as I am aware, no Russian book of travels has been written on the country during that period. Pashino contributed many articles to the newspapers on his return home from his various journeys, but these were not of a very solid or durable character. Russians, however, naturally attach more weight to the opinions of one of their own countrymen who has visited India than to the views of any number of English writers. Pashino holds that we cruelly oppress and exploit the people of India. The administration, he says, is composed of the needy scions of the English nobility and their retainers, who are purposely sent to India to enrich themselves at the expense of the natives. Were any European succour forthcoming, the people would rise *en masse* against the English and sweep them into the sea. As for the English army, the soldiers and officers acquire such effeminate ways after being a few years in the East, that a hardy enemy advancing from the North would experience little difficulty in defeating them. Altogether, according to him, our rule in India is neither respectable nor strong, and when Russia and India touch one another it will not long prevail against the forces operating against it from within and without.

These opinions are not very dissimilar from those expressed after the Khivan campaign by Captain Terentyeff in his notorious work, "Russia and England in the Struggle for Markets in Central Asia," and still more recently by General Annenkoff in his "Roads to India," General Soboleff in the Russian General Staff history of the Afghan war, and, finally, by Skobeleff himself in his "Project for the Invasion of India." To us these errors are palpable, but they are not so to the Russians. After all, they are not very much worse than the misconceptions and errors prevailing in the majority of books of tourist travel written by English people on Russia. Nor are they, indeed, worse than a deal of nonsense on India that is often published by Englishmen. In the *Nineteenth Century* for July 1883 is an article, coming under this category, entitled "The Spoliation of India." A full translation of this subsequently appeared in the *Novoe Vremya*, and must have confirmed many Russians in their belief that we heartlessly exploit our Eastern dependency. English writers in discussing Indian affairs should remember two things—that their words may provoke disaffection in India, and in Russia stimulate a desire to promote the emancipation of the country. The impression is quite strong enough already in Russia that the natives would eagerly greet a deliverer, without Englishmen going needlessly and unpatriotically out of their way to render it stronger.

When Pashino returned to Constantinople, the Russians were evacuating the extremity of the Balkan Peninsula, and he proceeded on board one of the transports to Odessa. In the meanwhile, Stolietoff had induced Shere Ali to fight England by the promise of aid from Russia, and after a short struggle the unhappy Ameer had fled from Cabul to Mazar-i-Sherif, accompanied by the Russian embassy. Stolietoff was summoned home, and placed upon the retired list in disgrace for having involved Russia in such difficulties in Cabul. Shortly afterwards occurred the murder of Major Cavagnari at Cabul, and Pashino was summoned from Odessa to Livadia to personally give to the late Emperor an account of Afghan affairs.

After a while he was sent to Tiflis, and here a fresh career, accompanied by rapid advancement, might have fallen to his lot, but for the defects of his character. No traveller has been more befriended than Pashino has been; yet, in spite of his knowledge of Oriental languages and Eastern countries, the Russian Government, which is ready to make use of any instrument, could do nothing with him. Deprived of the support of the Tiflis authorities, he made his way to St. Petersburg, and tried to earn a few roubles by writing *feuilleton* articles for the newspapers. Before long he quarrelled with this support, and, throwing it up, was reduced to the condition of the direst necessity. A few months ago, in crossing a street, he was knocked down and run over by a carriage, and is now a cripple in the paupers' ward of one of the St. Petersburg hospitals.

Such is the melancholy termination of the career of a man who, had he made better use of his opportunities, might have risen to a high and lucrative position in the Russian service. The Russian Government is always ready to secure to itself any individual possessing knowledge likely to forward its interests. A man who displays talent in any particular line can always count in Russia on being rewarded in due course by an appointment under State. We manage these things differently in England. The occasion is extremely rare that the Government incorporates within itself the talents of outsiders. It does not even encourage its own servants to distinguish themselves. The case of Colonel Stewart is the only one we can call to mind of an English explorer in Central Asia being rewarded on his return home by a special appointment. The rest have got no thanks, and have considered themselves lucky if they have escaped the snubbing inflicted on Colonel MacGregor. On the other hand, there is not a single Russian explorer who has not been rewarded in some shape or form by the State. Among them few have had better avenues to advancement opened out to them than Pashino, and if his career has ended in sickness and poverty, the blame is more on his side than on that of the Russian Government.

CHAPTER XI.

GRODEKOFF'S RIDE TO HERAT.

Grodekoff and the English fleet at Ismid—Central Asia the best place for settling the Eastern Question—Russia's plan for attacking us in India in 1878—Grodekoff and the expedition to Khiva—Narrowly escapes death by thirst—Grodekoff small in body but strong in spirit—A school chum of Skobeleff's—Preparations at Tashkent for the march to India—Burnaby's ride and Grodekoff's compared—Incapable of supporting a disguise—Ride from Samarcand to the Oxus—Quarrels with the Afghans—Brave demeanour of Grodekoff—His perilous position at Mazar-i-Sherif—The Afghan conquest of the Uzbeks—The Russian uniform at Cabul—Grodekoff's ride to Herat—Reception there—Importance of his survey—His reward—Shares with Skobeleff the last Turcoman campaign—A visit to Grodekoff the morning after Skobeleff's death

---

"Chiefs of the Uzbek race
Waving their heron crests with martial grace;
Turcomans, countless as their flocks led forth
From the aromatic pastures of the north;
Wild warriors of the turquoise hills—and those
Who dwell beyond the everlasting snows
Of Hindoo Koosh in stormy freedom bred,
Their fort the rock, their camp the torrent's bed."

"*Lalla Rookh.*"

EARLY in 1878 a slightly-built officer of quiet demeanour might have been seen one morning quietly reconnoitring the English fleet at its anchorage at Ismid. The Russians and the English at that time stood face to face before Constantinople—the one menacing it with their army and the other protecting it with their fleet. The reconnoitrer was a pioneer of the army, and as he surveyed the iron-clads lying at anchor he probably thought then, as many had done before him, that since the army could not attack the fleet and the fleet could not assail the army, why not fight out the struggle for the mastery of rival interests on some ground accessible to both nations? In other words, why not seek to settle the Eastern Question on the plains and hills intervening between Russia and India?

If anyone had been desirous of demonstrating how closely the destinies of Turkey and Central Asia are connected with each other, they could have scarcely chosen a better subject to hang their arguments upon than the gazer at the ironclads. The slightly-built officer of quiet demeanour had hastened fresh from the conquests of Central Asia to participate with his friend Skobeleff in the crusade against Constantinople; and the Turks now being defeated and crushed, he was about to proceed back to Central Asia to take part in Kaufmann's march to Cabul and India. The aim and scope of that expedition had been settled at a conference in the Russian camp directly after the arrival of the army before Constantinople. Stolietoff was to make his way to Cabul and enlist the sympathies of Shere Ali against us. Kaufmann was to follow in due course with three columns, and the Russians and Afghans combined were to make a descent upon India; the natives of which, it was expected, would rise on their approach and welcome them as deliverers. To retain and rule India was a matter that did not enter the Russian plans. All that Russia wanted was to see us ejected from India. India lost to us, she believed we should at once descend to the condition of another Portugal or Holland. She would then be left without her bitterest and strongest rival to pursue her policy of territorial extension in Europe.

To co-operate in the expedition against India, the slightly-built officer of quiet demeanour was despatched to Tashkent. As has since transpired in some reminiscences published by Captain Masloff, Skobeleff strongly believed at the time in the utility of an expedition from Turkestan to India, and the officer being his closest and dearest friend, naturally knew more about his views and plans than any other person. Grodekoff had not only been a chum of Skobeleff's at school, but had served with him throughout most of his career. They had been subalterns together in the Caucasus: they had marched together to Khiva in 1873—Grodekoff as chief of the staff of the Mangishlak or Kinderley column (Lomakin's), and Skobeleff as commander of the cavalry.* Two years later, Skobeleff had

* Grodekoff narrowly escaped death from thirst in this campaign. MacGahan says of the march of Lomakin's column:—"The 9th and 10th of May were days of terrible suffering. It seemed almost as if the whole column were about to die of thirst. The well of Kol-Kinir, at which it arrived on the evening of the ninth, was so deep that water could only be obtained very slowly, and thus but a small portion of the detachment could be supplied. It was now evening, and the troops had had no water since mid-day; nor was any to be obtained until they reached Alpai-Mass, a distance of thirty-five miles. On the evening of the 9th and the morning of the 10th, both the soldiers and the beasts had to remain without water. Under these circumstances the march to Alpai-Mass began. By midday of the 10th, when the heat was most violent, the horses began to sink, their riders hung on to them helplessly, and even the officers of the

waged the Kokandese war, with Grodekoff as his principal assistant, and when the Turkish conflict had broken out they had journeyed together to Europe to co-operate in it. To look at Grodekoff, one would have regarded him as the last person in the world to be the hero of so many arduous achievements. Our Burnaby is of gigantic proportions; MacGregor has a powerful, massive physique; MacGahan was

---

staff were losing hope; for Alpai-Mass was still about fifteen miles distant—that was, a march of four hours. Lomakin ordered a halt, and everybody, even the officers with their horses, sank down helplessly into the burning sand. Not a drop of water was left in the column; round about, as far as eye could reach, there was nothing but white sand. Lieutenant Stumm, in describing the scene to me, said that at this moment his senses were beginning to reel and the fever to mount to his brain. While all were still in this miserable condition, two wild forms were suddenly seen on a sand-hill far away in the distance. Colonel Lomakin had found a dried-up channel, and sent forward two Kirghiz, who discovered a small well—the Kuruk—at the distance of about a mile to the north. Just as the men, with the staff, had refreshed themselves, news came that the portion of the troops which had been left behind under Grodekoff, three miles and a half from Ilte-Idshe, were unable to proceed any farther, and were now lying exhausted on the sand. At once every animal which could be ridden was sent back, with every and any sort of vessel that would hold water; and it was only after the troops had been thus relieved that they were able to resume their march, after a narrow escape from death."—*Campaigning on the Oxus*, page 210.

noted for his endurance and strength ; and it is a question whether any of the pioneers we have spoken of were less endowed with physical qualities than Grodekoff. But Skobeleff, as is well known, would allow no one to belong to his "set" who was not remarkable for dauntless courage, and the eagerness with which he availed himself on all possible occasions of Grodekoff's services is a proof, if any were needed, that within the frail form of that slightly-built officer of quiet demeanour there lurked a spirit that could be relied upon to confront danger with unswerving and unquenchable heroism.

On his arrival at Tashkent from Constantinople, Grodekoff found the inhabitants in a great state of excitement at the impending march of the troops to India. In his interesting account of the journey of the Russian Mission to Cabul, Doctor Yavorsky, who accompanied it as physician, and subsequently attended Shere Ali in his last illness, tells us that the army was wild with excitement at the idea of attacking the English in their Eastern Empire. The officers seemed to entertain no doubt that, in company with the Afghans, and aided by a timely mutiny, they would be able to eject us permanently from India. Whether Grodekoff shared this view or not, he does not say; but all the same he marched with the army to the Bokharan frontier, to a town called Djam, where the enterprise came to an end with the receipt of the news of the conclusion of the Treaty of Berlin.

Greatly to their chagrin the troops in consequence were ordered to march back to their quarters again, and the English, in the words of Doctor Yavorsky, "were allowed to continue their oppression of the natives of India a little while longer." Grodekoff's appointment also lapsing, it became necessary for him to return to St. Petersburg to the General Staff, and by that weary road *viâ* Kazala and Orenburg, traversed already half-a-dozen times by himself, and which, owing to official corruption and carelessness, had become one of the worst in the Russian dominions; which is saying a good deal. One can easily imagine him, therefore, casting about how to attain Russia by some other route. Nearly all the roads radiating from Turkestan in the direction of Russia had been more or less surveyed by topographical officers, and nothing was to be gained by adopting any of them in preference to the Orenburg-Kazala track. But there was a new way to Russia which promised honour and promotion to him who should be the first to traverse it. That road lay through Herat.

We have seen how contemptuously General Sir Charles MacGregor was treated by the Indian authorities, when he sought in 1875 to ride to Russia from the Indian border *viâ* Herat. Colonel Grodekoff, in making a similar request to *his* Government, was not only thanked for proffering it, but was offered funds for his journey. This offer, for various reasons, he declined, but he accepted twenty silver articles for presentation to the Afghan authorities on the way. The moment was a very opportune one for the journey. The Russian Embassy was at Cabul; Shere Ali and the people were hostile to the English and favourable to the Russians; and both still had sufficient faith in Stolietoff's rash promises of Russian assistance to sustain the belief that they would comport themselves towards explorers from Turkestan with civility and attention. All the same, the Afghans are naturally so churlish and suspicious that they treated Grodekoff at times as a prisoner, and the well-known character for blood-thirsty fanaticism they acquired during the Afghan war displayed itself repeatedly in plots to murder him because he was an infidel. Owing to these circumstances, his ride was an exceptionally dangerous one—infinitely more dangerous than Burnaby's ride to Khiva or Marsh's ride through Herat to India, although less so than MacGahan's chase of Kaufmann's army. Burnaby's ride did not begin till he got to Kazala, on the Sea of Aral, and it was of only 370 miles' distance through pacified and orderly country. On the other hand, Grodekoff's ride from Samarcand to Astrabad was over 1,200 miles long, of which 400 lay through a turbulent and little-known country, ruled by the most fanatic of the Afghans, and raided upon by the Turcomans of the Murghab and Merv, who, if they had caught the traveller, would have revenged upon him the harshness Kaufmann had displayed towards solitary marauders of their clans caught in the outskirts of Khiva.

Colonel Grodekoff set out from Samarcand

on the 9th of October, 1878, accompanied by an interpreter, a native servant, and a groom; the four rode on horses, and led with them three others, two bearing their luggage in packs, and the third acting as a reserve. The Colonel did not imitate many European travellers, and carry with him an arsenal of weapons. All the party had to protect them was one cavalry Berdan with 100 cartridges, and a Smith and Vesson revolver with a dozen charges—in all 112 cartridges, to carry them across 1,200 miles of country, flanked half the way by nomad tribes.

No disguise was adopted by the traveller. "I travelled in my uniform, concealing neither my nationality nor my rank. I neither sought to hide the march route I intended to make on my way to the Caspian. I believe that in the circumstances in which I at the time found myself placed, this was the best means of travelling in Asia. Any masquerade that I might have adopted would have only impeded my movements, on account of my unsatisfactory knowledge of Oriental languages, and my ignorance of the ceremonial observances which Mussulmans make use of at almost every step."

The ride through Bokhara to the Oxus was unattended with any adventure, and on the 18th of October he crossed over into Afghanistan. His first *rencontre* with the Afghans was not a wholly satisfactory one. "On touching the shore I was met," he says, "by the Eeshagasi, or Chamberlain, Shah Sevar Khan, with the officers of the cavalry escort that had arrived the evening before. This personage invited me to enter one of the tents, of which, as I have said, there were two. I approached the nearest, in front of which was posted a guard; but had hardly got to the door of it when one of the men flashed his sword over my head. Not understanding what he meant by this, I demanded an explanation of the Eeshagasi, who replied that admittance into that tent was prohibited because it contained prisoners. I thereupon angrily asked him why he had not warned me of this in time. As an apology, the Eeshagasi struck the sentry, but I interposed with the remark that the man was not to blame for doing his duty, but only the Eeshagasi himself, who ought to have shown me the road."

Although, as we have said, Grodekoff was of

puny physique compared with the ordinary run of travellers, yet his pluck would not allow him to stand any nonsense from the Afghans. The Eeshagasi wanted him to halt a couple of days on the river bank, instead of going on to the administrative town of Mazar-i-Sherif, 70 miles distant, from whence the Afghans had come, and tried to argue Grodekoff into acquiescence.

But Grodekoff was immovable. "I put it to him that if I remained a night in such a marshy spot I should be sure to catch ague or fever; and that I had a long journey before me which I could not accomplish if I fell sick on the road. The Eeshagasi then promised to remain only until the evening, saying that by that time would certainly arrive from the Governor-General an answer to the message he had sent him. But I knew it could not possibly arrive by then, and gave this plainly to the Eeshagasi to understand. Seeing my obstinacy, the Chamberlain fell into despair. He would only keep me waiting a few hours, he said. He would give orders to kill a sheep and prepare dinner for me. In reply, I refused to have any dinner except at the next station. Then raising my voice, I exclaimed, 'Is there to be an end of this or not? I am tired of all this nonsense. Immediately—this very moment—either I go on to Mazar-i-Sherif, or else I cross over again to Bokhara. But remember, mind, you shall answer to the Ameer for not letting me go on to the town.'"

The Eeshagasi, thereupon, gave way, and they started. "While we were making one of the halts on the road for the men to drink, I continued advancing alone. After a few seconds the Afghans commenced shouting to me to stop. Pretending not to hear them, I continued leisurely riding on. Presently three soldiers dashed up to me. I replied to them that it was not my place to conform myself to their wishes, but their place to conform themselves to mine. Did they not know who I was? The soldiers fell back, and I resumed my solitary ride. When the men had finished drinking, they had a race to catch up with me. I then took the Eeshagasi severely to task. Did he think I meant to run away? How did he come to take that thought into his head? Had I not entered his country of my own free will? Where should I escape to, and how could I get away? The Eeshagasi excused himself. The thought had never entered his head that I should escape. He had only been concerned about my safety. 'What nonsense you talk,' I replied. 'Put an end to this farce. You can see round you for miles. There is not a single man in view. How could there be any danger? Accept it as a rule from this moment, that I am not compelled to conform myself to you, but you to me."

At Seeyageerd they halted for the night, Grodekoff being lodged in a house alongside the Eeshagasi's. Two sentries were placed in front of his quarters, with orders not to let him go out of their sight, and to follow him wherever he went. The danger the explorer ran from these men was shown when he went outside into the courtyard after dusk to have a chat with the officers. "If I had my way," said one of the sentries as he passed, "I would cut that Infidel (Kafir) to pieces." These words were uttered in the hearing of two Afghan officers, but they took no notice of them.

Chatting a short time with the officers, Grodekoff returned to his lodgings to have supper, and afterwards safeguarded himself for the night by barricading the door with boxes, locking it securely with the key, and placing his revolver close at hand in readiness for any emergency.

The night passed over quietly. The next morning Mustapha the interpreter told him that, while cleaning his boots the night before, he had overheard the soldiers discuss whether they should not murder him. Said one, "Let us go and kill the Kafir. What matters what happens afterwards—you know what awaits us in future life if we kill an Infidel." Said another, "Yes, but you see the Russians will exact revenge. They will seize the whole of the country; then that will be bad for all." To this the first retorted, "Can't we say that he never crossed the river?" "No," replied the second Afghan; "because the Bokharans will say they delivered him whole into our hands. Besides, he is not a little man. He is a colonel, and the Russians know where he is and all about him. Let us give over thinking about taking his life."

When Grodekoff went into the courtyard to perform his toilette the Afghans gathered round as spectators. In course of time he proceeded to clean his teeth, upon which one of them, more inquisitive than the rest, demanded of Mustapha, "What's that brush made of?"

"Pig's bristles," replied Mustapha.

The Afghans fell back in horror, and commenced spitting violently, to express their disgust at using the hair of such an unclean animal for cleansing the mouth. Fearing their fanaticism would provoke the Mussulmans to some outrage, Grodekoff hastily beat a retreat, inwardly resolving for the future to perform his toilette in private.

When they arrived at Mazar-i-Sherif Grodekoff was escorted through the town more like a prisoner than a guest, in spite of his sarcastic protests. Fifteen years earlier Arminius Vámbéry had entered the same town disguised as a dervish. In the interval the Afghans had conquered the country down to one side of the Oxus, and the Russians down to the other. Mazar-i-Sherif, close to the historic ruins of Balkh, had been chosen as the administrative centre of the new Afghan province by Shere Ali, who little imagined that he would eventually end his career there, a fugitive from his own capital.

The people of the country were Uzbegs, described by Vámbéry as the "best race in Central Asia." When the cry was raised by the Liberals in 1879 that we were stealing away the independence of the Afghans, it was conveniently overlooked that a large portion of Afghanistan was made up of recently conquered states, whose inhabitants were bitterly opposed to their Cabul masters. Vámbéry found this feeling prevailing at Herat. Grodekoff found it existing throughout the whole of Afghan Turkestan.

"These people are crushed and degraded in every possible form by their conquerors," he says. "The Afghans treat them as inferior beings. It is quite a common thing for the Afghans to resort to their whips, or to the butt-end of their rifles, in their dealings with the subjugated people. I often saw Afghan soldiers, wandering without employment from village to village, fall upon the unfortunate defenceless Uzbegs, and without any obvious pretext whatever, thrash them most unmercifully. And how they used to bully them, when they made the inhabitants bring food and fodder for themselves and the escort! Having been impressed by the might of Russia in conquering Khiva and Bokhara, the Uzbegs living on the left bank of the Oxus imagined that the advance of the Russians upon Samarcand would not terminate there; and to this day believe that sooner or later we shall cross the river and impose our administration upon Afghan Turkestan." If they did this, they would possess themselves of all the outposts of India north of the Hindoo Koosh. "Hearing from a thousand lips, from the Russian Mussulmans resorting to the shrine of Ali at Mazar-i-Sherif, of the blessings of Russian order and Russian right, and of our humane relations with the conquered natives of Russian Turkestan, the Uzbegs do not manifest any fear towards us, but desire our presence. This I saw clearly enough in the warm reception accorded me by the Uzbegs wherever I went; not to speak of what I heard from the lips of those who artfully managed to pass through the Afghan guard and approach my side. Said they to me, 'Are the Russians coming soon? Would to God that the time could be hastened for our deliverance from these Afghans! Tell us—is it not true that the Russians are coming now to Afghanistan? Is it not true that troops are following behind you?'"

The Governor-General, or Lueenaib, of Afghan Turkestan, was Khosh Deel Khan, a handsome, well-built, well-dressed young man of thirty, who had married a sister of the Ameer Shere Ali. He received Grodekoft courteously the day after his arrival, but told him firmly in indirect terms that he would have to regard himself as under restraint until instructions arrived from the Ameer. He would not let him go forward, he would not let him go back, and it was only after some very hot language between the two, that Grodekoft resigned himself for the moment to the situation.

The next day the Lueenaib sent to ask it Grodekoff would lend him his uniform, the shape of which pleased him so much that he wished to have one made like it. The uniform was given and the following day returned with thanks. "When the English entered Cabul,' says Grodekoff, "they found among other things a Russian uniform, which occasioned immense sensation and alarm throughout India and England. It is quite as likely as not that this uniform was no other than the one the Governor-General had had made for himself."

The ten days' imprisonment to which Grodekoff was subjected at Mazar-i-Sherif was not borne tamely by the Russian officer. The Afghans refused to take a letter from him to General Kaufmann, they tried to decoy his interpreter Mustapha into the Ameer's service, and every night increased the guard placed over him to confine his movements. Grodekoff, on his part, gave full vent to his anger, denounced the Afghans as "a lying, treacherous lot," and declaring he would find his way to the court of the Ameer to expose the Lueenaib's conduct, drove out of his presence the secretary of the Governor-General. Things looked so bad at last that the traveller held a council with his men, and decided if an answer did not come from Cabul in a fortnight to fight through the cordon at night and try to escape to Bokhara.

The arrival of a message from Shere Ali, ordering him to be treated with distinction and assisted in every way in accomplishing his mission, changed the state of affairs in a moment. Henceforward he experienced no more trouble at the hands of the Afghans, and was conducted to the limits of the country at the Ameer's expense by officers specially appointed to wait on him, accompanied by an escort of honour, which on the Turcoman border assumed the proportions of a powerful cavalry force.

On the 29th of October Grodekoff set out with forty troopers on his way to Herat. The journey occupied eighteen days, and was unmarked with striking incidents or adventures of any kind. At the town of Saripool the people gave the Russian an ovation, and well he deserved it, for everywhere along the road he did his utmost to protect them from the violence of the Afghans. Instead of winking at the malpractices of the officers escorting him, he rated them soundly for their misconduct. The city of Maimene, which in Arminius Vámbéry's time had been a flourishing capital of an independent Uzbeg state, with 25,000 inhabitants, he found to be in ruins, the Afghans having left only a tenth of the people alive. From Maimene to Herat the country was more or less ravaged by the Turcomans, to protect Grodekoff from whom 300 Afghan cavalry soldiers were assigned. This section of the ride was the most important of all to English statesmen, as Grodekoff ascertained for them the condition of a country unvisited for fifteen years by a European, and which ere long must become the subject of frontier arrangements between England and Russia. He himself does not advance the view, but his facts point clearly to a definite opinion, that from Merv to Herat the turbulence of the tribes is calculated to provoke a Russian movement upon the Key of India.

It is a cardinal point of Russia's Asiatic policy not to allow wild tribes to disturb her frontier. If they refuse to behave themselves, she crushes them and annexes their country. This brings her in contact with fresh tribes, and of course the process has to be repeated, and cannot but be repeated until her border reaches that of some powerful state. Grodekoft s ride showed that turbulent tribes exist all the way from the Russian Turkestan and Transcaspian borders to Herat, and that unless we assume the responsibility of controlling them their conduct must lead in due course to the advance of the avenging Cossack to the principal bulwark of India.

At Herat Grodekoff received a warm reception, reminding one of the cordial welcome accorded to Captain Marsh in 1872 by Yakoob Khan. The Governor-General was Sardar Mahomed Omer Khan, who had succeeded Yakoob Khan on the treacherous seizure of the latter by his father Shere Ali, and who had so rudely turned back Colonel MacGregor in 1875. Handsome apartments were given the traveller, and fifteen servants appointed to wait upon him.

This large number took away the breath of Grodekoff, who is a man of extremely simple habits, and is content with a single partitioned room when at home. "I was quite staggered when they were ushered in a body into my presence. Among them, for instance, was one who only assisted me in washing my hands, another who only swept the room, a third who only looked after the lights and nothing else; and so on. This division of labour was striking. The fifteen could not understand at all how Mustapha could prepare tea, clean my boots, light the candles, etc., with no one to assist him. In Herat a man is of no value. He is not protected against the Turcomans; he is dragged from home as a conscript, and perhaps spends the whole of his life in handing round tea or preparing the *Kaliana*, or water pipe, for his superiors. To protect the doors of the Armoury, the Afghans place four men, where one would be sufficient.

"At the entrance to my lodgings was posted a sentry. An hour after the departure of the Sardar, Djan Mahomet came to enquire whether it was necessary to keep the man on guard. I might keep him there or I might send him away, just as I liked. There was no danger to be feared from any one. I said, 'Of course, send him away.' In this manner, for the first time since the 19th of October, that is to say, from the moment I first set foot on Afghan soil, I felt myself a free man, and no longer a prisoner."

Grodekoff's brief description of Herat is worth repeating. "It is a very large city, and does not cede in size to Tashkent. It contains 50,000 people. Among the cities of Central Asia and Khorassan, Herat, by its buildings, occupies a place next to Meshed. The city is surrounded by walls twelve yards high, with a shallow ditch outside. There are no outer defences of any kind; nothing that would call to mind the fortifications of a European city. In its present condition Herat is not in a position to defend itself against a European army; since at a mile to the north it is commanded by heights, from which it could be bombarded by artillery. It is reckoned to possess immense strategical importance."

During his three days' stay at Herat every facility was accorded to him to examine the city, and he was able to make a thorough survey of its fortifications. The importance of this lay in the fact that for five years no European had been inside Herat, and as since Grodekoff's visit five more years have elapsed without any other traveller entering the Key of India, his work is the latest one on the subject. Russians have been often unjustly reproached with keeping the fruits of their surveys to themselves. In proceeding from the Oxus to Herat, Grodekoff traversed districts never explored before, and which, being of importance for England to know, Russia had every temptation to remain silent about. Yet, within a short time of Grodekoff's arrival home, the Russian Government published a beautiful map of his march route for the insignificant sum of fifteen copecks, or 4½*d.*

From Herat to the Caspian Grodekoff proceeded along a road previously traversed by Vámbéry, Marsh, Baker, and MacGregor, and without further adventure completed his two months ride at Astrabad early in December. On his arrival at St. Petersburg he was greeted not with the official snubs and scoldings accorded to MacGregor and Burnaby, but with an audience of the Emperor, an order of Knighthood, and an appointment in the General Staff Office.

The following year he penned some slight hasty sketches of his "Ride to Herat," which the writer issued in an English form. The work was warmly greeted, and was classed by some reviewers with Burnaby's "Ride to Khiva." But this was hardly fair to Burnaby. Comparing one ride with the other, we think few will question that Grodekoff's was considerably more dangerous and important than Burnaby's. But when we compare the accounts of the two rides it is impossible not to admit that Burnaby's vigorous and graphic account of his experiences throws Grodekoff's narrative altogether into the shade.

Early in 1880 Skobeleff was appointed to

revenge Lomakin's defeat at Geok Tepé, and Grodekoff—now major-general—accompanied him as chief of his staff. At the close of the war he received a decoration corresponding to a K.C.B. in this country, and settled down at St. Petersburg to write an elaborate history of the conflict.

* * * * *

I saw him a number of times during this period, and he always evinced the utmost readiness to give me information about the siege. One visit I paid him has melancholy associations that can never fade from my memory.

It was a joyous July morning in 1882, and I arrived at his lodgings in full flow of spirits after a pleasant walk down the Nevski. His man met me at the door with a blank face and the enquiry—Had I not heard the news? What news? That Skobeleff was dead. That he had died at Moscow early that morning.

Thinking he had been misled by a passing rumour I said, "Nonsense; he's alive and well at Minsk. I am going to see him on my way home from Moscow. He's not at Moscow at all."

But the news was too true. The man had himself carried the fatal telegram—the first received at St. Petersburg—to Grodekoff, and knew by heart every word of the message Abadzaeff, Skobeleff's orderly, had sent him, acquainting him with the news, and asking for instructions. He had seen Grodekoff rise from his history with exclamations of amazement, sorrow, and despair, and hasten with the intelligence to the Government.

Proceeding to the General Staff Office I found the news had been confirmed, and on my way home called again at Grodekoff's lodgings to leave a message of condolence. In the interval, however, he had returned, and hearing my voice came into the corridor to greet me. The corridor was dark, and did its best to conceal with a kindly gloom the pallid face and tears of the Russian Burnaby.

"Do not go for a moment," said Grodekoff; "in my room is Captain Masloff, whom I think you know. Enter for a moment. It is, alas! a chamber of sorrow and dead hopes."

I entered the room. Several officers were assembled in it, all bearing visible traces of grief on their faces. Most of them were heroes of Skobeleff's last campaign—the greatest of his exploits, in the opinion of those who knew him best—and the carpet they stood on—a splendid Turcoman carpet—was a bit of the spoil of Geok Tepé. In this room Skobeleff had spent his last days before leaving St. Petersburg for the interior. In the easy chair by the window, overlooking the Bolshaya Morskaya, he had sat for hours reading the manuscript of the history of the siege of Geok Tepé Grodekoff was writing for the Government. It was a great history of a great achievement. Although only half written, large piles of manuscript covered the chairs and the tables in the room; maps and plans of priceless value were scattered on a table near the door—maps of every inch of the conquered Turcoman territory and the adjoining Persian region, plans of the new Russian fortresses in the Transcaspian territory, with every detail of armament filled in. More information lay on that little table than the skilfulest and most energetic military spy could have carried away from the Transcaspian region, after a prolonged survey of it. When I saw these treasures scattered about, I felt thankful I had refused the invitation of Grodekoff's servant to wait in the room till his master returned home.

In our conversations Grodekoff had never manifested any disinclination to withhold information or to show me maps and plans. Like Skobeleff, Grodekoff has such a frank and confiding nature, that I do not think any suspicions would have had much chance of taking root in his breast. All the same, it was a satisfaction to me to know that I had not unconsciously put myself in a position to provoke them.

After a few words of condolence I came away. Subsequently I saw Grodekoff a number of times during the funeral at Moscow and the burial at Spasskoe Selo. I doubt whether anybody felt the loss of Skobeleff so much as he did.

Skobeleff's death blighted the career of many promising officers, and it seemed at the time as though Grodekoff would suffer with the rest; but a short while ago, Tchernayeff accomplished a great work in conjunction with Senator Giers in expelling from Turkestan the corrupt and effete administrators who had made the misrule of the region a byword in Russia, and among the new officials selected to take part in the purer *régime* was the Russian Burnaby. As military governor of the Syr Daria district, where he has already distinguished himself by his administrative ability, he does not exercise a direct control over the political and military forces that are impelling Russia towards India; but he may rise to higher posts in due course, and perhaps attain the coveted dignity of Governor-General of Turkestan. If he does, it is a satisfaction to know he will be among those—and they are not so very few in Russia as is sometimes imagined—who deprecate any interference with our interests in India, and earnestly desire the two rival empires to become friends.

If there were more Grodekoffs in Russia and more Grodekoffs in England, the Central Asian question would rapidly become extinct.

CHAPTER XII.

O'DONOVAN'S DASH TO MERV.

The Afghan war—The Russian conflict beyond the Caspian—Life of Mr. O'Donovan described by Mr. Joseph Cowen, M.P.—His Fenian experiences—Proceeds to Central Asia—Watches Lazareff's campaign in 1879—Is expelled the Russian camp—Wanders about the border—Skobeleff refuses to let him join his expedition—Proceeds to Deregez to join the Akhal Tekkés at Geok Tepé—Misses the siege—Decides to ride off to Merv—The Oasis described—The real character of Mr. O'Donovan's great enterprise—His services to the English Government—The very man the country needed on the spot—The ride to the river Tejend—Bivouacking in the desert—Experiences during a storm the night before reaching Merv—Excitement provoked by his arrival—Suggestions to murder him—His sufferings from the curiosity of the people—Examined by a council of the chiefs—His five months' residence at Merv—A decorated prisoner—Finally escapes the Oasis—Fate of Merv—Mr. O'Donovan's influence upon the solution of the Merv Question—His exploit compared with the achievements of other pioneers—The "Merv Oasis."

"There is a strange fascination attached to this Central Asian exploration. Merv, which is now an accumulation of dirty Tartar huts, was the original seat of the old Iran civilisation. It was the cradle of the imaginative creations wrought out in the historical romances of Persia. Now, probably, it is the darkest spot in the civilisation of the old world. I think it was Volney who predicted that a time would come when some traveller like himself would sit down on the banks of the Seine, the Thames, or the Zuyder Zee, amid silent ruins, and weep for a people inurned, whose greatness had been changed into an empty name. Macaulay, Shelley, Keats, Horace Walpole, and others rendered a similar idea in much the same language. Mr. O'Donovan, in his wild and venturesome ride through the weird deserts of Turkestan, came across the ruins of old temples and the remains of decayed fortresses and viaducts of ancient cities, and has realized the dream that the French philosopher outlined for this country a century ago."

MR. JOSEPH COWEN, M.P.

COLONEL GRODEKOFF, on his way home from his ride to Herat, reached the Afghan frontier on the 21st of November, 1878, the day that the English by their assault and capture of Ali Musjid practically began the Afghan war. Long before he had reached the Caspian the victory of Peiwar Kotal had brought the campaign to a decisive termination; and had our statesmen known their own minds as to the policy they meant to pursue, and given *carte blanche* to our generals to carry it out, there would have been an end to bloodshed on the Afghan border even before Grodekoff arrived at St. Petersburg. But fate had determined that there should be an epoch of muddle and massacre, ending in disgust and tarnished prestige, on the English side of Central Asia; and an epoch of muddle and massacre, ending in a grand military and political triumph, on the Russian side of Central Asia. The latter was beginning to open when Grodekoff traversed the Caspian the first month of 1879. A few weeks later officers and officials might have been seen hurrying from the Caucasus to the river Atrek, to prepare for the great expedition that was to retrieve the defeat Lomakin had experienced the previous September at the hands of the Tekkés. In their wake followed an Irishman, whose wanderings had arisen from his Fenian proclivities, and who was fated to show England that men of his stamp may render greater services to the Empire than the vote-mongering Members of Parliament that had passed the coercive laws and kept at bay reforms, causing the Fenian movement and the traveller's exile.

The early career of Mr. O'Donovan has been aptly described by Mr. Joseph Cowen, M.P.,* and may be appropriately repeated. "The romantic life of Mr. O'Donovan is one

* The London letter of the *Newcastle Daily Chronicle*, July 19th, 1881.

among the many illustrations that are constantly occurring to demonstrate either the inability or the unwillingness of conventional Englishmen to appreciate the special capacities of the Irish character. Able Irishmen are driven by the common prejudices into seeking distinction in all manner of out-of-the way paths. Mr. O'Donovan, whose letters are still the talk of the town, is the son of the famous Dr. O'Donovan, the Irish scholar and antiquary. He was educated at one of the Queen's colleges in Ireland, and was intended for the medical profession, though I do not know that he ever qualified. His father commended him and his brothers to the care of a countryman who held a high position in the constabulary service. The influence of officialdom seemed to have the opposite effect from what was intended, as the sons all took to the reverse of official pursuits. Mr. O'Donovan became associated with the Fenian movement in its earliest and darkest days. He was an active agitator and organizer, and during the operation of the Coercion Bill passed by Lord Russell's Administration in 1866 he was arrested and detained in Mountjoy prison, for twelve months, I believe.

Through the intercession of the gaoler, who in early life had been a sympathizer with the Young Ireland Party, Mr. O'Donovan was released on condition of his going to America. He went, but returned shortly after, and was imprisoned for ten months in Limerick Gaol for possessing arms in a proclaimed district. Out of prison a second time, he came to England and engaged in reorganizing his fellow-countrymen for political purposes. During that time he visited the North of England, and amongst other places lived for a short period in Newcastle. I believe he was concerned in the very enterprise that led to the arrest and the ultimate sending into penal servitude for fifteen years of his friend Mr. Michael Davitt. The Government strove to arrest him a third time, but he succeeded in escaping, and went to France. During the war between France and Germany he took the side of France, and was a volunteer in the army of the Loire, under General Aurelles de Paladine. He was taken prisoner along with Mr. Finigan, the member for Ennis, at the battle of Orleans. After the war he returned to Paris and acted for a time as the correspondent of English newspapers. He then took an appointment as correspondent for a combination of English and Irish newspapers, and went to Spain to the Carlist war. While there he got into prison again, being suspected by the Carlists of having political as well as journalistic designs. He was released through the intercession of Cardinal Cullen with Don Carlos. His engagement with the English newspapers having terminated, he became correspondent for the *New York Herald.* On the breaking out of the Russo-Turkish war, he became correspondent for first one newspaper and then another. His last engagement was with the *Daily News*, and he represented that paper during the campaign of Mukhtar Pasha in Armenia.

"The letters in which Mr. O'Donovan describes his journey to Merv are vividly and graphically written. The style is humorous, picturesque, and attractive. In a very fascinating way much interesting and valuable information is conveyed. I do not know any special correspondent whose letters have surpassed them in interest and attractiveness—certainly none where the adventures of the correspondent have been more marvellous and the risks and dangers he ran greater.

"Mr. O'Donovan is well known to some of your readers in Newcastle, and he is much esteemed for the geniality of his disposition, his courage, attainments, and ability. He has inherited his father's linguistic accomplishments. He is only about 35 or 36 years of age. Accident has made him a newspaper correspondent. If events had run in another groove he would probably have been a Home-Rule member of the House of Commons and denounced daily as a vulgar, illiterate, ill-tempered irreconcilable by the very newspapers and the very men who are now extolling his ability and admiring his daring. If this had not been his *rôle*, he would have been one of the 'dissolute ruffians' that Mr. Forster and the Liberal Government would have confined in Kilmainham. It is an unhappy thing for the English people that they cannot or that they will not recognise the power of such men as Mr. O'Donovan, and instead of winning them to the service of the State, drive them into rebellious courses."

From the above it will be seen that the

special correspondent of the *Daily News* was already a seasoned traveller when he set out from Trebizond on February 5th, 1879, for Central Asia.

His route across the Caucasus was identical with that pursued by Marsh and Baker, and the journey possessed no features different from the ordinary every-day travel in Russia. At Baku Mr. O'Donovan found General Lazareff and his staff on the point of starting across the Caspian, and received a warm invitation to accompany them. The base of the expedition had already been established at Tchikishlar, at the mouth of the river Atrek, close to the Gomüch Tepé whence Vámbéry started on his tramp across the desert to Khiva in 1863. In the interval the Russians had conquered the pirate Turcomans of the coast, established several small forts up the river Atrek, and settled down in stone buildings at Krasnovodsk. Little difficulty had been experienced in subjugating the littoral tribes, but those of the interior, and particularly the Tekkés, were not to be dissuaded from their slave-catching forays except by a display of force. The Tekkés were divided into two powerful bodies, one located along the Persian frontier in an oasis stretching from Kizil Arvat to a little beyond Askabad, and the other in the oasis of Merv. To get to the former or Akhal oasis, it was necessary to march up the Atrek and Sumbar rivers for 200 miles, traversing country having in the dry season the characteristics of a desert, and then crossing the highlands at the end, to descend to the oasis and advance in an easterly direction another hundred miles through the settlements of the Tekkés to their stronghold at Geok Tepé.

The greatest difficulty of the undertaking consisted in conveying across the desert a sufficient body of troops to carry on successful war in the oasis. Lazareff spent the whole of the spring and summer in endeavouring to accomplish this portion of the task, Mr. O'Donovan all the time remaining at the Russian camp or paying visits to the outposts. At the outset, the Russian commander made the fatal error of landing his troops on the desert coast in advance of his supplies, with the result that as fast as he deposited the latter they were consumed, and he was unable to accumulate a sufficient stock to allow an advance to be made. While striving to overcome this difficulty sickness broke out among the troops, and in the end, at the close of the summer, an advance could only be made with 4,000 troops out of 25,000. On his way to the front to lead the expedition Lazareff fell ill and died, and Lomakin, who succeeded him, only penetrated to Geok Tepé to experience a terrible defeat, and be driven back with the enemy at his heels to the shore of the Caspian. While this brief but disastrous campaign was waging, O'Donovan was lying ill with dysentery at Baku, and he only recovered in time to meet the remnants of the army returning to the camp at Tchikishlar. A few days later, Lomakin's successor, General Tergoukasoff, decided he would have no journalists about him, and expelled the *Daily News* correspondent from the Russian camp.*

* Mr. O'Donovan pays the highest compliment to the trustworthiness of the Russian newspaper correspondents attached to the force, by leaving this campaign undescribed in his "Merv Oasis," although he had been specially sent to describe it. Their story will be found in "The Disastrous Russian Campaign against the Turcomans." I may remark in passing that it would be easy to publish full and graphic accounts of most Russian wars, by ransacking the Russian press and literature. What is often spoken of as "the silence of Russia regarding her operations" is really nothing

Throughout the rest of the winter, Mr. O'Donovan led a miserable life in the villages on the Atrek border and in Astrabad. The only way he could get intelligence of the Russian movements was to go spying about the Atrek, where he was in imminent danger of being murdered by the numerous Turcomans prowling about; and by audaciously dropping in upon the Russians in camp now and again on various pretexts, and getting expelled afresh —although not without having seen with his vigilant eyes what was going on. After months of weary waiting, during which Ter-goukasoff was invalided home, and temporarily replaced by General Mouravieff, Skobeleff arrived to take charge of the expedition, and O'Donovan made a final application to be allowed to accompany the force. The refusal he received the *Daily News* "special" ascribes to Skobeleff's own disinclination to have correspondents attached to his army; but, as a matter of fact, Skobeleff was quite free from

more than English ignorance of Russian journalism and literature. It is unfair for political writers to charge Russia with want of candour and stealthy movements, when the blame really rests with their own ignorance of the Russian language.

any prejudice of this kind against the press. His hands were tied by the Minister of War. We have seen what a warm friend he was of MacGahan, another *Daily News* correspondent; and Forbes—a third—makes no secret of the good treatment he was always receiving at the hands of the gifted Russian general. Mr. O'Donovan was not the only correspondent disappointed. Before leaving St. Petersburg Robeleff had to give an unwilling refusal to several old and intimate friends, whose company he would have enjoyed during the tedious campaign.*

Finding it hopeless to attempt to see the war from the Russian sphere of operations, Mr. O'Donovan set off for the Perso-Turcoman border to watch the conflict from the enemy's side, from the fortress of Geok Tepé.

To accomplish this journey he had to increase his equipment and obtain permission of the Persian authorities, and this involved roundabout travelling *viâ* Teheran and Meshed,

* Apart from these and Mr. O'Donovan, General Skobeleff also refused permission to the writer, who desired to join the expedition to write a historical account of the operations.

by the route Colonel Baker had taken in proceeding to the Turcoman frontier. When he got to Deregez, negotiations had to be opened with the Akhal Tekké chiefs for permission to cross the border to Geok Tepé, and these were still in progress when Skobeleff surrounded the fortress, and prevented Mr. O'Donovan's scheme being realized. Had the *Daily News* "special" been as prompt in riding to Geok Tepé as he subsequently was in riding to Merv, he would have reached the fortress some time in advance of the Russians, but even his bitterest enemy cannot wish that he should have put himself in such peril. Had he pushed on to Geok Tepé, he would have been warmly greeted—Skobeleff found in the fortress a splendid charger with magnificent trappings that was to have been given him—but a claim would have been made on his services equally dangerous for him to have assented to or refused. The Tekkés would have expected him to have taken a leading part in the defence, and had he refused would have no doubt tortured and killed him; treating him perhaps in the manner they subsequently did Bombardier Nikitin, a soldier captured during one of the sorties on the Russian trenches, who, for refusing to show them how to fire the mountain guns they had taken, was skinned alive and left to die by inches. On the other hand, had he assisted the Tekkés, he would have stood a good chance of being killed during the bombardment, or shot by the Russians afterwards.

Mr. O'Donovan thus found himself in a position very similar to that which made Mr. MacGahan resolve on his desperate chase of Kaufmann's army. "I had spent," says Mr. MacGahan, "so much of the *New York Herald's* money that I felt morally obliged to push forward. . . . The position of a correspondent is often a very embarrassing one. He embarks, perhaps, on an enterprise without fully counting the cost, or foreseeing or appreciating half the difficulties to be encountered in its accomplishment, and then feels obliged to put on a brave face and carry it out at whatever risk, when in his inmost self he knows that if he were a free agent he would be among the very last to undertake it. In this way he often gets a reputation for foolhardiness, or pluck, or perseverance, or cheek which he really does not merit." For two years Mr. O'Donovan had been stationed on the Perso-Turcoman frontier by the *Daily News*, for the express purpose of viewing the fighting between the Russians and the Tekkés, and, from causes beyond his control, had seen nothing of the two campaigns waged almost under his very nose in the interval. Had he returned home after the fall of Geok Tepé, he would have been thanked for rendering useful services, but could hardly have been congratulated on achieving brilliant ones. The *Daily News* "special" felt that something was required of him to crown his mission with success. What that something was, it was impossible for him to ignore. England at the moment was possessed with a burning curiosity to know what the mysterious stronghold of Merv was like, and was anxious for some one to be on the spot to inform her what the Russians were doing inimical to her interests there. Had he returned home he would have undoubtedly been asked on all sides—"Why did you not go to Merv?" and I take it to be a very fine instance of devotion to duty, that he should have unhesitatingly decided on doing what he felt was required of him, although the country he was about to render such a signal service to had treated him as a conspirator against, and a traitor to her interests. It is, of course, quite in keeping with England's sense of gratitude that he should have never received any thanks for rendering her this service.

The oasis of Merv lies about 130 or 140 miles across the Turcoman plain from the Persian border. At a distance of a third of the way the plain is traversed by the river Tejend, the fertile oasis along the banks of which constitutes a convenient resting-place on the road to Merv. A man can ride the fifty miles to the Tejend in a night, and the eighty or ninety miles thence to Merv in a day and a night. This is severe exertion for a European, and both O'Donovan and Alikhanoff were knocked up in achieving it; but the Turcomans are constantly performing the feat, and arrive at their journey's end without displaying any symptoms of fatigue.

On the maps the country intervening between Persia and Merv is called a desert, but this is a word, conveniently used by geographers to fill up blanks in their maps, which in most instances requires to be accepted with limitations. It is not a desert, for example, like Sahara, which is a real desert in every sense of the term. Nor is it a desert like the Kizil Kum, the sandy region between the Aral and Khiva traversed by MacGahan, which is a Sahara in summer, but over which at other seasons the traveller may pass, helped by the autumn rains, the winter snows, or the thaws and floods of spring. For some distance from the Syr Daria river traces of irrigation works exist, and Russians entertain hopes of restoring to fertility at least a third of the road across the Kizil Kum to Khiva.

The "desert" lying between Persia and Merv would be better called a "wilderness." It is a clayey plain, interspersed by sandy patches, which is capable, provided water be forthcoming, of taking its place among the most fertile regions of Asia. Two rivers empty their waters into it,—the Tejend and the Murghab; the former coursing through Herat and burying itself a third of the way between Persia and Merv, and the latter giving life to the Merv Oasis. Could the water supply of these rivers be increased and properly distributed by irrigation canals, the whole of the country would become like Merv and Tejend. The sandy patches would be simply blemishes, such as exist at present in those two oases, and in the oasis of Khiva. On the other hand, if the water supply of the Murghab and Tejend were cut off, the oases of Merv and Tejend would become barren like the rest of the wilderness. Russian engineers are of opinion that by improving the irrigation system, and storing the rains, it might be possible to reduce the amount of wilderness to a minimum.

The Merv Oasis has an area of 1,600 square miles, or a little smaller than the island of Trinidad, and sustains a quarter of a million or so of people, belonging to the Tekké Turcoman tribe—cousins of the Tekkés of the oasis of Akhal (their original home), occupied by Skobeleff.

When O'Donovan set out for Merv, the Russians had conquered the whole of the oasis of Akhal, and had occupied points in the adjacent oasis of Atak, also, like Akhal, lying along the northern border of Persia, at the foot of the Khorassan highlands. The belief was general

TURKOMAN CAMP.

To face page 312.

that Skobeleff meant to occupy the whole of the Atak district, and then march across the wilderness to Merv.

Paradoxical as it may seem to many reviewers who considered the disturbed condition of the country one of O'Donovan's chief difficulties, the anarchy prevailing was really a circumstance that helped him in his enterprise most. Skobeleff's terrible victory at Geok Tepé had struck such terror into the hearts of the Turcomans, that it had caused them to suspend all their forays and border outrages, while it had further driven to Merv the leader of the Akhal Tekkés, Mahdum Kuli, the very chief O'Donovan had been negotiating with for permission to go to Geok Tepé. If taken for a Russian, he might hope that the fear the Tekkés entertained of their enemy would exercise a check on their murderous proclivities; while, if accepted as an Englishman, he could almost positively rely upon the desire of the Tekkés for an English advance from Candahar to Merv to cause them to give him a hearty welcome.

But all the same Mr. O'Donovan's enterprise was of no mean order. He had not, like Burnaby, simply to keep himself warm for 370 miles, and then, having comfortably ridden his ride, helped along by the camps of the Kirghiz, those taverns of the desert, refresh himself, tourist fashion, in Khiva. His ride, it is true, was only half as long as Burnaby's, or, if we add the Atak stretch, two-thirds of Burnaby's distance ; and he had no cold to contend with. But he had to escape in the first place from vigilant Cossacks on the one flank, and hostile Persians on the other, their opposition preventing him making any arrangements in advance with the Merv Tekkés, and depriving him of a proper escort. Having got clear away from the Persian border, accompanied by a couple of cut-throat servants and four unreliable Turcomans, he had to slip through the Tejend oasis, where large numbers of fugitives from Geok Tepé were assembled, and then pounce upon the people of Merv in such a fashion as to prevent his being sent back before he had seen something of the mysterious community. It was quite a toss up what reception he would obtain at Merv. There were certain chances in favour of a friendly one, but the enterprise was undoubtedly full of serious risk. Apart from the purely political considerations of the moment, for nearly forty years no European, except the French photographer Blôqueville, captured with the Persian expeditionary force in 1861, had entered Merv; and no European had visited the oasis since it had been occupied by the Tekké tribe. What would these Mussulman robbers say to the uninvited Frenghi? All the imaginary dangers which beset Burnaby's ride to Khiva were real ones in O'Donovan's case.

Before riding away to Merv, the special correspondent of the *Daily News* traversed three parts of the Atak oasis, travelling from Askabad in the direction of Sarakhs. Mehna, his starting-point, is 132 miles from Askabad, and fifty-two from Sarakhs. From Merv it is about one hundred and forty miles distant. Baker, MacGregor, and Napier had descended from the Khorassan border hills to a point here and there of the Akhal and Atak oases, but I believe O'Donovan was the first European to proceed along the whole country from Askabad to a ride short of Sarakhs. Askabad was occupied by the Russians directly after he visited it, and for a long time it seemed as though they would push on towards Mehna. As many doubts prevailed respecting the condition of the Atak oasis, the political relations of the scanty Turco-Persian population scattered in settlements along it, and the real designs of the Russians in the region, the information that O'Donovan sent home before going to Merv was of priceless value to the English Government. For us to have had an officially recognised agent on the border might have been embarrassing to the two Empires. What the Government wanted was simply information respecting what was going on in the region. It did not want to have any official dealings with the Turcomans. O'Donovan supplied the information without involving the English authorities in any way. He was just the very man the country and the Government needed on the spot.

When he started off for Merv he seriously believed that the Russians would not be long before they advanced upon the oasis. We now know, from Skobeleff's statements and the character of his operations,* that the belief was

* Skobeleff simply made preparations to reduce Geok Tepé and occupy the Akhal oasis—nothing more. During the last days of the siege his power for offence had so far diminished, that many of his staff believed he would have to abandon the enterprise.

groundless, but it was a belief that was held by every Turcoman in Merv, and by nearly every Englishman in England. It was this that gave supreme political importance to his enterprise; but it also increased its danger. Had the Russians really advanced, the snare he had escaped in not going to Geok Tepé would have entrapped him at Merv. The Tekkés would have made him help them, under the threat of death if he refused. Compliance with the order involved the risk of death from a Russian bullet during or after the siege.

Courageously facing all these dangers, O'Donovan quitted Mehna late in the evening of February 28th, 1881, and rode all night in the direction of the Tejend oasis. The night was dark at starting, and in course of time dense blackness blotted out the plain, hiding the travellers both from friend and foe. The party consisted of two servants—a Persian and a Kurd—and four Turcomans, the latter as truculent-looking personages as O'Donovan had ever seen in the course of his varied career. No adventure marked the fifty miles' silent passage of the plain, and the bank of the river was reached in the morning, just before dawn.

To ford the Tejend being impossible in the dark, the party had a short nap amidst the tamarisks, and early after daybreak proceeded again on their journey. On the opposite side of the river lay the plain, stretching unbroken for ninety miles to Merv—"Not a sandy plain, but an argillaceous expanse. Wherever the wind gives rest all kinds of grasses and leguminous plants grow luxuriantly in the shifting soil, especially in the neighbourhood of the river or after a series of rainfalls. The sandhills of this so-called desert are but as the dust-heaps of a much-frequented high road in Europe. With an adequate water-supply it would be as productive as any of the heavier soils known in other climes."

After an hour's ride from the river they halted to have breakfast, and while tea was being made the Turcomans amused themselves in chasing some boars. The meal consisted of tea, rough griddled bread, and bits of indurated cheese, hardened to the consistency of horn. Spending half-an-hour over this, they saddled and set off again, the plain now being covered with a forest of tamarisk, "whose gnarled stems were often four inches in diameter, and whose withered remains strewed the plain for many a mile with fuel sufficient for a whole army corps. The accumulated growths of half a century were there mingled with the still living bushes. I noticed in some places small houses built after the fashion of American log huts, and intended as sun shelters for passing caravans. Great heaps of tamarisk stems were piled up as landmarks and as signals to following companions. Whatever the dearth of water in the place might be, there certainly was no lack of the means of producing fire."

Towards midday the heat became very intense; and although the small water-skin which they had filled at the Tejend sufficed for themselves, the horses suffered greatly from thirst. Finding the rainpools along the road dried up, they scattered themselves over the plain, but were unsuccessful in discovering any traces of wells. Regaining the road again, they pushed on, and after two or three miles found a small pool, with a sufficient supply for their horses. This difficulty in obtaining water is a feature of the whole of the Central Asian territory unoccupied by the Russians. The latter, on seizing new districts, sink artesian wells and construct reservoirs along all the main routes, thus removing at a stroke the drawback of ages to safe and rapid travelling in this part of the East. What O'Donovan suffered on the way to Merv, early Russian pioneers suffered in exploring the road to Askabad. Thanks to the Russian military engineer, one need not concern himself any longer about water in travelling to Askabad, and this will be the case in due course with Merv also.

During the afternoon league after league was traversed without any new feature becoming apparent, and as evening wore on the party entered quite a forest of tamarisk. "Creeping along in the gloom, we stumbled over fallen trunks, and started all kinds of wild animals from our paths. Some I knew, by their grunting, to be boars, which abound here in incredible numbers. Others, by their pattering trot, I recognised to be jackals; and a few that bounded away lightly were either lynxes or leopards. We halted several times, and took our bearings from the few visible stars. Often we were completely at fault; but these Turcomans, like North-American savages, possess an unerring instinct which invariably sets them right in the end.

"We had been riding pretty briskly, generally at a trot when the nature of the ground allowed, and frequently at a canter. I calculate that, on the whole, we made six and a half miles an hour during our entire journey. After midnight dense blackness came on, and the atmosphere became stifling. Once or twice I suggested a halt, but in whispered tones was informed that there was no knowing when robbers might appear. This I thought rather good, considering that I was in the company of as select a party of thieves as could be found hidden in any desert bush or crumbling ruin. In the end, even the horses seemed incapable of going any farther. The men seemed made of iron. We reined in for a consultation. It was decided to turn aside a hundred yards, so as to be away from the accustomed track, and thus lessen the risk of being attacked by any passing brigands. Amidst the dense growth of tamarisk and other bushes we found a comparatively open space, where we determined to make a brief halt. As we dismounted, a bright flash of sheet lightning lit up the ground, and some heavy raindrops fell splashing. It was clear that a heavy shower was coming on. Still, I was so fatigued that I did not pause to think of this. I only asked somewhere to stretch my wearied limbs. A horse-cloth, a leopard skin, and an old ulster which had seen a great deal of service, constituted bed and bedding. With a saddle for a pillow did I prop my weary head, and in half a minute I slept as only the wayworn traveller can sleep.

"It was still dark when voices around me told that a fresh move was about to be made. I found myself half afloat. A torrent of rain was falling, and I was thoroughly saturated, leopard skin and all. My limbs were stiff with rheumatism ; and many specimens of the divers species of insects which haunt these bush-grown solitudes had fled to me for refuge against the downpour. I was for the moment a peripatetic museum of entomology. There were juvenile tarantulas, stag beetles, lizard-like mantis, and every imaginable variety of *colœopteræ*. As may readily be imagined, I did not spend much time in examining them, but, brushing them out of my hair and ears, and shaking them from the sleeves of my coat and the legs of my trousers, I endeavoured to put myself in marching order. The Turcomans were busying themselves with their horses, and looking ineffably cross, for notwithstanding their power of endurance they were also very much knocked up. Our horses were standing round, with drooping ears and tails, piteously grazing upon the wet mud. As I mounted, my animal fell to his knees with sheer weakness and wretchedness. Then we were off again, not at a very rapid rate, for the horses were scarcely able to put one leg before another."

After riding a while the jungle died away and they entered upon open country, first broken and marshy, then cultivated, until in course of time they reached a village—one of the outlying ones of the oasis. "The number of houses was about one hundred and fifty. A few jujube, apple, and willow trees grew here and there around them, and some patches of vine and melon cultivation were to be seen. A number of bales of silk, with some tobacco, tea, and other merchandise from Bokhara, lay around, for a caravan which had come from the latter place was on the point of re-starting for

Meshed. A crowd of wild-looking people of both sexes, who were busying themselves with packing the bales upon camels, left their work to stare at myself and my cavalcade as I rode up—the women, with their draggled locks and rain-sodden, witch-like garments, perhaps the most weird of all. There was wonderment on all sides as to what kind of person I might be, and all seemed to take it for granted that I was a prisoner. So far as my personal appearance went, I might have passed for anything. I wore an enormous tiara of greyish-black sheep skin, eighteen inches in height. Over my shoulders was a drenched leopard skin, beneath which could be seen my travel-stained, much-worn ulster overcoat. My legs were caparisoned in long black boots, armed with great steel spurs, appendages utterly unknown in Turkestan. A sabre and revolving carbine completed my outfit."

Dismounting at the door of a hut, to which his horse was peremptorily led by the people, O'Donovan entered, and stripping off his dripping garments, drank a bowl of green tea presented to him. While doing this the people outside discussed who he was. Some believed him to be a great envoy from England, others maintained him to be a Russian spy. At last "a great fat man, with a mingled expression of ruffianism and humour, came in," and asked him plainly "who he was and what he was." O'Donovan tried to explain to him the functions of a "special," and said he would forward by the starting caravan a letter to Abbas Khan, the British native agent at Meshed. This proposition was met by a general shout of warning not to attempt to write a single word, or his throat would be cut immediately. The people were so startled and frightened by Skobeleff's success at Geok Tepé, and entertained such dire apprehensions that Skobeleff might be on the point of repeating his performance at Merv, that O'Donovan's appearance as a stranger and possible Russian put them in such a temper that it was not by any means safe to trifle with them. Venturing to take out his note-book to put down a few hurried items, an excited Turcoman darted from the hut with the news that the Frenghi was writing, and provoked the recommendation from many a lip that he should be finished off at once

Although forbidden to write and placed under arrest, O'Donovan did not otherwise experience any unpleasant treatment. They gave him a good dinner, they let him have a fire to dry his clothes, and when he fell asleep they left him undisturbed till sunset. He was then awakened by the entrance of a chief, Tekmé Sardar, who had shared with Mahdum Kuli the dual command of the defence of Geok Tepé. Tekmé Sardar knew the Russians well. He had given in his submission and accompanied Lomakin to Geok Tepé in 1879. When the Russian commander commenced to bombard the place, he had offered to go and persuade his countrymen to surrender. Afterwards, when the Turcomans, maddened by the massacre of their women and little ones, had repelled the Russian attack with crushing slaughter, he had fled the retreating army and made his way to the fortress, where he had been entrusted with the defence of it. It was largely due to his sagacity and skill that Geok Tepé had withstood Skobeleff so long, and if his advice had been acted on, the Tekkés would have abandoned the fortress towards the end of the siege and retreated to the Tejend, leaving simply the shell in the hands of the exhausted Russians. Recognising his military worth, Skobeleff had done all in his power to induce him to return and become a Russian subject, and he was just on the point of doing this when O'Donovan arrived at Merv. The advantages and disadvantages of surrender he discussed freely with the English correspondent. Subsequently he submitted, proceeded to St. Petersburg, and returned to take part in the administration of Akhal; but, by a curious coincidence, died almost about the same time as his great opponent Skobeleff.

The presence of this chief improved matters. He not only passed the evening with the correspondent talking politics, but slept in his tent at night. The next morning O'Donovan was escorted to the settlement of the Ichthyar, or supreme chief of Merv, situated close to the great earth fortress of Kaushid Khan Kala, and serving as the central point of the oasis. Here he was installed in a tent, and kept in a sort of honourable durance for twenty days. During this period his position was altogether anomalous. Every precaution was taken to prevent his evasion, for fear of his proving a Russian spy, while at the same time he was treated with a good deal of personal consideration, in view of the possibility of his being a person of importance who had come on a friendly mission.

The morning after his arrival was market day, when thousands of people assemble outside the fortress to trade. Hearing of the arrival of a mysterious stranger, they swarmed round his tent to have a peep at him. "Long before the sun was well above the horizon a surging crowd had gathered round my tent, the interior of which was also crammed with members of Merv society, all eager to interview the mysterious stranger who had fallen among them, as it were, from the clouds. They were the same sort of dressing-gown-robed, sheep-skin-clad, gigantic-hatted beings as those of the Caspian shore. They sat upon their heels in a sitting position, their folded arms resting upon the fronts of their thighs, and gazed at me with the ludicrous eagerness which may be observed in baboons and apes when some unfamiliar object meets their eyes. I had been fast asleep, my head resting upon a heap of baggage, and my body covered over with a large sheep-skin mantle; but these people waited patiently until it might suit me to let myself be seen, for it is an inviolable piece of etiquette among them never to disturb a sleeper.

"I was somewhat bewildered by the events of the past few days. I sat up, rubbed my eyes, and looked around me, quite unable to understand the sudden and numerous audience who had favoured me with their presence. Words cannot describe their astonishment on beholding my unwonted costume. My short, black, closely-buttoned tunic and cord riding-breeches seemed to fill them with amazement. They gazed and gazed as though they could never stop looking at the external appearance of the Frenghi. It was the gaze of the operator while endeavouring to mesmerise his subject. Simultaneously, from without, scores of eyes peeped through every nook and cranny of the tent walls; and I could hear remarks upon my personal appearance and costume, winding up with a statement of the conviction of the observers that I was most unmistakably an 'Oroos' (Russian). Let it not be imagined that, after the first eagerness of curiosity was satisfied, this sort of thing came to an end—quite the reverse. As the tidings of my arrival spread, relays upon relays of fresh sightseers thronged to the capital and besieged my abode. Instead of attending to their business in the bazaar, they abandoned everything for the chance of getting a glimpse at me. Sometimes the throng was so terrific that the tent reeled and swayed around me, and I thought it was coming down upon my head—a thing which ultimately happened, when the spectators, utterly impatient at not being able to get within reach of the peep-hole, or in line with the doorway, tried to lift up the edges of the tent and introduce their heads. This being done simultaneously, and all the tent-pegs becoming removed, the thing actually subsided upon me, nearly smothering myself and the more select party inside. Then came a rush of *yassouls*, or local police, striking right and left with sticks, and shouting reproaches against the sightseers for their violent breach of decorum in thus inconveniencing a stranger guest.

"All night long, even when I slept, the same state of things continued, both inside and outside my tent. The people seemed never to go to sleep, or to have any desire to do so. The strange cut of my tunic and riding breeches appeared to create an unquenchable thirst on the part of those who had once seen them to see them again. During the first month of my residence at Merv I might be said to have lived in the interior of a much patronized peepshow, in which I was the central—and, indeed, the only—object of attraction. At first the effect was maddening, but I afterwards fell into a kind of comatic stupor, and began to feel under mesmeric influences. One could not make a move but it was commented upon. The manner of washing my hands and face called forth loud exclamations; and the operation of combing my hair seemed greatly to tickle their fancies. More than once I asked the old moullah whether there were no means of getting rid of the persecution under which I suffered. He shook his head gravely, and said surely I was not harmed by being looked at. When the horribly irritating effect at first produced passed away, I began to look upon my ever-present, passive, human tormentors as so many caryatidic appendages of the architecture of my residence."

This state of things lasted without intermission a whole fortnight, during which O'Donovan had not a single moment of privacy or undisturbed repose. It was wearisome work, sitting in the hot tent all day to be stared at, with absolutely nothing to do. If he attempted to read a page of one of the few books with him, he was tormented with demands for explanations as to its nature, what it contained, etc. He could not even think, on account of the incessant questionings; and he says that he really believes that unless relief had arrived in one form or another, he should have become demented.

At the end of a week after his arrival, a council was held at Merv to decide what should be done with him. At this he was closely questioned by the chiefs, and a decision was arrived at to keep him in confinement until they had ascertained from the English agent at Meshed, Abbas Khan, whether he really was what he represented himself to be. If the reply was satisfactory he might hope for better treatment. Otherwise he would either be killed, or treated as a slave-captive, like the Russian gunner Kidaeff, who had been a prisoner seven years, or like many Persian officers of rank of the defeated army of 1860, who had toiled in chains over twenty years, without hope of release.

A few days after the council meeting, a regular felt house was built for him, and imagining that the curiosity of the Turcomans was mainly provoked by his European garments, he procured himself a native costume. Equipped in this, although far from getting rid of the troublesome curiosity of his neighbours, he obtained much relief, and was enabled, in company with some acquaintances, to stroll about the village, "generally with a following of not more than two hundred persons." Shortly afterwards a letter arrived from the English agent, confirming O'Donovan's nationality, and from this time he had a free run of the oasis.

His adventures during the rest of his five months' stay at Merv were of the most interesting character. From treating him with suspicion the natives went to the other extreme, and insisted on behaving towards him as if he were the wealthy envoy of a suzerain power. They feasted him until he was sick of the good things of Merv. They desired his company so much that night and day they were always visiting him, and driving him nearly mad with endless questions. Afterwards they assumed that, being a European, he must be a good medicine man, and the sick swarmed to his residence from all parts of Merv, begging for advice and physic. Then a mania possessed them to enrol themselves as British subjects, and they hoisted above his house a crimson banner, which was popularly supposed to represent the Union Jack. Finally, they elected him one of the triumvirate ruling Merv, and treated him as the president of it.

All the honours and civilities they pressed upon him would have been very pleasant if he could have felt more secure about the future, but although he could ride to Merv in a couple of days it required months of scheming for him to escape from it again. The people got into their heads that the moment he went away the Russians would rush in and occupy the place, and further that the English would lose all interest in Merv on his departure. Hence they refused to allow him to leave the oasis, and it was only after prolonged and masterly diplomacy, exercised through our minister at Teheran and the native agent at Meshed, that he at length got clear away. Early in August he quitted Merv, to represent it at a supposititious conference at Teheran, and, escorted by several hundred horsemen, rode to the Persian frontier, whence, immensely relieved at being delivered of his too ardent friends, he pushed on to Meshed. Four months had to elapse before he reached Constantinople from this point, thus extending the period of his travels to almost three years.

Geographically, his journey to Merv was of great importance. He was the first European to traverse the region lying between Askabad and Merv, and if not the first European at Merv, he was the first to survey the oasis. Politically, his presence at Merv was still more important. His letters enabled our statesmen to realise the condition of things at Merv, and the result of that realisation was a decision to leave Merv to its fate.

Up to the time of O'Donovan's arrival at Merv, one of three fates impended over the oasis—to pass under the suzerainty of England, of Persia, or of Russia. For years a large number of English writers had recommended that we should take the Merv Tekkés under our protection. It was clear that they could not by themselves permanently preserve their independence. Geographically, the Merv Oasis is part of Afghanistan. Politically, the Mervis were willing to become the subjects of the Ameer. All that was wanted after the fall of Khiva was for England to have pressed the Ameer on the one hand and encouraged the Mervis on the other, and the fate of the oasis would have been settled in a manner advantageous to our interests.

Instead of doing this, successive administrations, Conservative and Liberal, shirked all responsibility, and anything approaching decisive action. They meddled with the Turcomans just sufficiently to accentuate the resistance of the latter to the Russians, and to damage our own prestige; but beyond drifting with this dog-in-the-manger and undignified policy they did nothing. Merv might have been easily saved by diplomatic means up to the time of the fall of Geok Tepé in 1881. General Sir Charles MacGregor, Baker, and Napier's advice and practical suggestions covered the whole situation. Still more simple was it to provide for its safety after the conquest of Akhal, for the Merv Tekkés were so cowed that they were ready to suspend all their raids and accept any suzerainty, no matter how severe, that would have effectually shielded them from the Russians. Our army was located at Candahar; the remnants of the Russian force at Askabad. Stronger than the Russians on the spot, we had it in our power to support our policy with a display of military strength, and settle the fate of Merv before allowing things to subside in Central Asia. Had a masterly policy been followed by the Gladstone cabinet, O'Donovan's presence at Merv would have been invaluable in carrying it out. Merv could have been placed under Anglo-Afghan control with the greatest ease. Its possession and a subsidy would have reconciled Abdurrahman to our retention of Candahar. But the Gladstone cabinet decided to throw away the fruits of our victories in Afghanistan, and with those fruits all our old claims to protect Merv. The evacuation of Candahar sealed the fate of English influence at Merv, and if the same cabinet, recognising practically its unwisdom in 1881, has sought since to repair its errors in Afghanistan by developing Quetta and granting a subsidy to the Ameer, it has completely failed to secure the oasis of Merv from seizure and occupation by Russia.

Conscious that he could not accept on behalf of England the proffered obedience of the Mervis—had he done so the act would have inevitably been disavowed—Edmond O'Donovan did his best to put off a Russian occupation, by persuading the people to refrain from all outrages upon their neighbours and release the prisoner Kidaeff. In this he was very successful, and his influence was equally efficacious in settling once for all Persia's attempts to become mistress of Merv. For years our diplomacy in the East—which in Persia as in Turkey might have been fitly compared to attempting to invigorate decaying oaks with a farthing squirt,—had been directed to seeking to keep Russia out of Merv, by getting the warlike Turcomans to accept the feeble and imbecile rule of Persia. While O'Donovan was at Merv a Persian envoy arrived from Teheran to strive once more to induce the Tekkés to pass under the sway of the Shah, but acting on the Irishman's sound advice, they brusquely sent him back to the border.

When he himself left, there was an end to English and Persian influence at Merv. Directly afterwards the English evacuated Candahar, and the Tekkés were left face to face with the restless Russians. By degrees their hostility wore off, as we shall see directly in the case of Alikhanoff the explorer; and finally, after prolonged negotiations, Merv accepted early in 1883 the suzerainty of Khiva. By a *coup de main*, Russia, a year later, transferred this allegiance to herself, and made Merv the vassal of Tiflis. But if at different times the oasis had been governed by Khiva, Bokhara, and Teheran, it could surely have been controlled from Quetta or Candahar. A spark of Imperial statesmanship would have shrivelled up Russian pretensions long before they had assumed dangerous dimensions in Turkmenia.

To sum up. As an achievement, O'Donovan's ride to Merv altogether transcends Burnaby's ride to Khiva. Compared with it the latter is but an everyday Asiatic exploit. Two undertakings alone surpass it—MacGahan's ride to Khiva, and Vámbéry's journey to Khiva and Bokhara in disguise. MacGahan knew before he started that he would have to pass through a ring of Turcomans before reaching Kaufmann, and, if caught, would be assuredly murdered by them. Vámbéry also was aware that if his disguise were anywhere penetrated he would undoubtedly be tortured to death. But O'Donovan knew he had friends at Merv—Mahdum Kuli, the defender of Geok Tepé, for instance—and he could reckon with a certain amount of confidence that the Tekkés, in their desire to secure the alliance of the English at Candahar against the Russians, would treat him with consideration. More than once the Tekkés had invited English explorers to visit them at Merv, MacGregor for instance; and it was hardly possible that they would sacrifice him to their resentment against Russia. But if O'Donovan's two days' ride to Merv was less remarkable as an exploit than MacGahan's thirty days' chase after Kaufmann, it was attended with greater results. MacGahan's ride to Khiva was followed by no particular benefit to Europe. Khiva had been described half-a-dozen times over long before he arrived there; but in the case of Merv, O'Donovan's splendid letters filled in a great geographical blank, and enabled English statesmen to decide upon the policy to pursue in that region. As with the Atak so with Merv, O'Donovan did what England wanted to do, but could not do officially. When Skobeleff began his mysterious movements after the fall of Geok Tepé, which everybody believed would terminate in an occupation of Merv, England regretted her Government had prevented previous pioneers penetrating thither, and longed for some one on the spot to inform her of the military and political condition of the oasis. No agent could have been sent thither in time to be of use, and further, such an act would have provoked the anger of Russia. O'Donovan's ride to Merv at this juncture relieved this country of a great embarrassment, and we are persuaded that no English citizen rendered a greater service to the Empire in 1881 than this Irish ex-conspirator.

From the State, as has been said, he received neither reward nor recognition of any kind. He was not even cheaply complimented by any of Her Majesty's Ministers, which might have been easily done inside or outside Parliament. From his employers of the *Daily News* he received, it is said, a present of 1,000 guineas, in excess of his salary, and Messrs. Smith, Elder, & Co. gave him a handsomesum for the copyright of his book of travels. In parting with his rights in this he was luckier than many authors, for it is no secret that his "Merv Oasis" has failed to be a success to his publishers—this arising not from any fault of the book itself, which, to go no further in criticism, is far fuller of adventures graphically written than that amazingly popular work, Burnaby's "Ride to Khiva," but because it did not appear until public interest in Merv and his exploits had subsided, and could not be awakened again. Now-a-days, when such an immense number of new works are published, a book that does not appear at the nick of time runs the risk of losing a sale altogether. Burnaby's "Ride to Khiva" came out when there was a general demand for anything fresh about Russia; had it been published at the close of the Russo-Turkish war instead of at the beginning, it would probably have not gone beyond one or two editions. Further, it has been obtainable for some time past at sixpence, whereas the price of O'Donovan's book is fixed at the costly sum of thirty-six shillings, which of itself is sufficient to deprive it of popularity. But the sale of a book is no criterion of the value of an explorer's writings. Among geographers and politicians "The Merv Oasis" was at once accepted as a standard work of Central Asian travel, and the wish was general that when war again broke out in that region, O'Donovan might be present with his powerful, poetic, and patriotic pen.

But that, alas! can never be. The gallant Irishman, who had escaped so many dangers in Asia, was fated to perish three years later with Hicks Pasha's army in the Soudan, a victim, indirectly, to the same incapacity to govern an Empire in an Imperial manner, which had rendered his dash to Merv fruitless of political benefit to this country.

CHAPTER XIII.

COLONEL STEWART'S WATCH OVER SKOBELEFF'S ARMY.

England can always rely upon a supply of Burnabys to rectify the carelessness of her statesmen—English officers "haunting" the Perso-Turcoman border in 1880—Stewart proceeds to the spot disguised as a horse-dealer—How he elaborated his plans at Ispahan—Success attending his disguise—A good hard ride, with no "comforts"—Beluchi robbers—Their mode of operations—Arrival at Deregez—Lives alongside Mr. O'Donovan for three weeks without his disguise being penetrated—Russia complains, and he is ordered home—Appointed English agent to watch over Herat—Of vital importance to a traveller that he should be able to give a graphic account of his explorations—Inability of Marsh to do this—O'Donovan spoils his book of travels by keeping it back too long—Stewart the only military traveller rewarded by the state.

"Among the last three books presented to Parliament there is a very interesting despatch from the Russian Foreign Office that contains a remarkable phrase, in which blame is imputed to certain English officers, who, it is said, have been 'haunting' the desert, as if that were a discreditable proceeding. Now, in Colonel Stewart's paper the Royal Geographical Society can see the results of such 'haunting,' and I only wish that other inaccessible parts of Asia were haunted in the same manner. So far from its being a discreditable proceeding, it seems to me to be deserving of the highest commendation."

SIR HENRY RAWLINSON, 1881.

"It may be well asked what induces so many travellers to go into Central Asia and haunt those inhospitable deserts. Of course, the whole interest of the thing is centred in the district of Merv and its strategic and geographical position, for it cannot be concealed that not only is the place interesting from its geographical position as having been the cradle of the Parthian race, but it is also interesting from its strategic position as connecting the line of Russian advance by the Oxus with that by Kizil Arvat and north-eastern Persia."

CAPTAIN GILL, 1881.

IF it be true that a British general can always rely upon British soldiers extricating him from the difficulties his blundering may have involved him in, it is still more true that England can always rely upon her sons pushing themselves forward in the hour of danger to protect interests which appear imperilled through the supineness or stupidity of her Ministers. A remarkable instance of this is to be found in the case of Colonel Stewart, whose service to the country in 1880 has never, so far as I am aware, been properly recognized in any public form. In 1880, as stated in the previous chapter, Skobeleff spent nine months in preparing an army to attack Geok Tepé, and afterwards, according to general belief, to march on Merv. These preparations were known to Her Majesty's Government, but from a fanatic determination to reverse the policy of the previous Ministry, they would not take any steps on the spot to acquaint themselves with the nature of them, To keep watch over the Russian operations on the Atrek, the Beaconsfield Government had appointed Mr. Churchill, one of the defenders of Kars and an old resident in Persia, to the post of Consul at Astrabad. This gentleman was removed directly after Mr. Gladstone accepted office, and the consulate was left vacant throughout the rest of 1880. But for the enterprise of the *Daily News*, there would have been no guardian of English interests east of the Caspian. The tone of that paper, however, was so directly favourable to Russian aggression and Ministerial supineness, that it was impossible to rely upon it exclusively. Prompted by party feeling, editors of London dailies had been known to expurgate from their special correspondence passages which brought facts to bear dangerously against their opinions ; and many thought it not improbable, though there seems to have been no basis for the belief, that O'Donovan's letters were subjected to this reprehensible censorship. Hence a strong desire grew up to dispel by other means the cloud that had gathered over the Russian movements towards Merv, and in response to this feeling a number of persons voluntarily made their way to the theatre of war. Lieut.-Colonel Bateman Champain, R. E., paid a visit to Skobeleff at Tchikishlar; Major Thompson availed himself of his furlough to ride from Quetta through Beluchistan to Astrabad; Captain Gill—who had accompanied Colonel Baker to the Persian frontier in 1873, and was murdered ten years later by the Bedouins—suddenly turned up at Meshed; and Colonel Stewart, disguised as an Armenian horse-dealer, ensconced himself in Deregez, a portion of Persia jutting into the Akhal Oasis, in such a manner that Skobeleff could not possibly move beyond Askabad in the direction of Merv without that officer being aware of it.

The thoroughgoing manner that Colonel Stewart set about adapting himself for the *rôle* of English agent in disguise in proximity to Skobeleff's army, and the precautions he took to render that disguise beyond danger of discovery, can hardly fail to awaken admiration; all the more so since Stewart was travelling entirely on his own account, and was under no special obligation to make his enterprise successful. An officer of the 5th Punjaub Infantry, and one who had several times travelled in Persia and the Caucasus in the course of his career, he knew beforehand the class of people he would meet and the conditions that would encompass him while keeping watch in Deregez. The disguise he considered best to assume was that of an Armenian horse-dealer from Calcutta, and to elaborate this character he spent two months and a half in the Armenian suburb of Ispahan.

This place was well adapted for the starting-point of his expedition. It was the furthest spot east where Armenians were to be found in considerable numbers, and from it branched two roads in the direction of Deregez: one going round one side of the Great Desert of Persia *viâ* Teheran, and the second round the other, *viâ* Yezd and the country bordering upon Herat. To have gone *viâ* Teheran would have been to have exposed himself to the risk of discovery at the hands of Europeans or regular Armenian traders. Further, the English embassy might have checked him, as it had sought to impede Marsh, or blighted his enterprise completely, as it had succeeded in doing in the case of MacGregor. The eastern route, on the other hand—which was almost identical with that followed by MacGregor in his ride from the Persian Gulf to Herat—offered the almost absolute certainty of his finding no Europeans at all on the road, and only a few mongrel Armenians, such as he himself professed to be. To divert suspicion, he quitted Ispahan in the dress of an Englishman when he left it on the 30th September, 1880, and rode for a march and a half along the Teheran highway. Having then reached a desert spot, he exchanged his clothes for the robes and black lambskin hat of an Armenian, and threw his helmet down a *kareez*, or underground canal. Afterwards, turning east, he steered himself by compass to Nain, and joined the second road leading to Deregez.

Stewart now felt himself safe from discovery. The English traveller had disappeared in the desert on the way to Teheran, and there was nothing in the appearance of the Armenian horse-dealer at Nain to connect him with the former. Most of the Calcutta Armenians come from Julfa, the Armenian suburb of Ispahan, and of late several of them had been travelling about Persia in quest of horses—one party having penetrated even to Deregez, which smoothed matters considerably for Stewart. The pioneer dressed just as a well-to-do Armenian would have done, and had with him two other Armenians, hired for the journey, one serving as a sort of partner or clerk, and the other as a servant. Both of them had visited India and could speak Hindustani. Ordinarily all three spoke Persian, but if Stewart wanted to say anything private he spoke to them in Hindustani; the bystanders then imagining that they were speaking Armenian. If by chance anyone who had visited India had understood what was passing, which was very unlikely, there would have been nothing curious in an Armenian horse-dealer from India speaking the language of that country. Further, by posing as a Calcutta Armenian, any peculiarity of accent in speaking Persian was set down to his having learnt it in India. Believing the best way to keep the secret of his destination was to tell nobody about it, Stewart refrained from even enlightening his companions on that point. All they knew was that he meant to go to Khorassan to purchase horses; and to keep up his *rôle* he bought several when the wanderings of the party eventually terminated in Deregez.

Stewart's ride was a real ride, in the literal sense of the term. The party had no camels to convey tents and "comforts," as in the case of Burnaby's ride to Khiva; all that the three Armenians took with them was contained in the saddle bags of their three horses. The ride from Ispahan to Turbat-i-Hyderi, round the Great Desert, lasted a fortnight, during which the party traversed a considerable amount of little known ground, and were exposed for days to the peril of being captured by Beluchis, who raid against this part of Persia. On the way Stewart met two men, who with their wives had been carried off and plundered by the Beluchis. "They said they and their wives with two other men were on the road from Kirman to Tabbas, and when eighty miles to the southward of Robat-i-Khan they were pounced upon by a band of thirty-seven men, most of them mounted on the swift

Seistan camels, so celebrated for their speed. They and their wives were stripped of everything but the most necessary clothing, and were carried about on camels for three days. One of their party, who knew the country, gave offence to the Beluchis by refusing to act as guide, and was hacked to pieces by swords; another of their party was killed by the Beluchis, and they heard that a traveller had been murdered previous to their own capture. At the end of three days the two men whom I met with their wives were released near Chesma Shuturan, the lonely spring in the desert where I filled my water-bottle. They came on to Robat-i-Khan, and were anxious to proceed on their journey."

"I here heard," continues Stewart, "of the mode of procedure of these Beluchi marauders. The camels they ride travel very fast. They can go seventy or even eighty miles a day, carrying one and sometimes two men and a little food. The longest distance I have ever myself known a good trained camel to cover in a day was ninety-two measured miles on a road. This was accomplished between early dawn and evening, but the camel performing this feat would not have been able to go on the next day for any great distance. This was, however, not a Beluchi camel. The Beluchis, with their trained camels, which only require water every other day, and which can on a push last three days without water, scour the country for incredible distances, lying hidden in some ravine in the desert, pouncing upon unwary travellers, and driving off camels and cattle wherever found. Sometimes a rich caravan falls into their hands. Their camels can find enough grazing in the less arid spots of the desert to support life, assisted by a little food supplied by their owners in the form of barley meal mixed with just enough water to make a paste. A camel can exist in this way for a few weeks only while the foray lasts. The Beluchis approach some lonely spring in the desert every other day, water their camels, fill their waterskins, and go back to hide in some new spot."

A fortnight's ride brought Stewart to Turbat-i-Hyderi, on the Herat-Meshed road, and journeying past Meshed the party reached Mahomedabad, the chief town of Deregez, on the 25th of November, having been twenty-six days in the saddle. Deregez is a border district of Khorassan, sixty-five miles long by forty broad. The Governor is appointed by the Shah, though the appointment is hereditary in one family. He bears the title of Begler Begi, and is of Turkish descent. Kurds abound in the district, but a large portion of the people and the most influential are Turks. At Mahomedabad Stewart rented a house, and was given a shop in the bazaar, which although he accepted he never opened. Every day he used to resort to the bazaar, where he mixed freely with the Tekkés from Geok Tepé, Askabad, and Merv. Askabad, where the Russians are now settled down in force, is only two marches from Mahomedabad; and Lutfabad, in the Atak Oasis, through which they must pass to get to Merv, is only fourteen miles, or a couple of hours' ride. Geok Tepé, which at that moment Skobeleff was about to march from Bami to besiege, is not more than three days' distance from Mahomedabad. Russian agents were already located at the latter place, purchasing supplies to send on to Geok Tepé as soon as it should fall.

Among other persons encountered by Colonel Stewart in the bazaar at Mahomedabad was

Mr. O'Donovan. Considering that for nearly six months the Colonel had not cast eyes on a countryman, except perhaps at Ispahan, one would have thought he would have taken an early opportunity of making himself known to him; but, with true Caledonian coldness, he displayed no warmth of feeling at the *rencontre*, and for three weeks saw him constantly without disclosing his secret. One day O'Donovan said to him, "Really, Khwaja Ibrahim" (the name Stewart had adopted), "you speak English wonderfully well for an Armenian." "Yes," replied the horse-dealer, keeping his countenance, "we Armenians of Calcutta receive a very fair education!"

Stewart did not much fear detection by Mr. O'Donovan, but he was afraid of his servant. This man was a Persian, who made it a business to travel about with Englishmen new to the country, in which capacity he had served many, and even spoke a little English. Stewart had no cause, however, to fear this man's penetration, for one day he came to his servant and said, "How is it that your master, Khwaja Ibrahim, knows the price of things in Persia so well? He has told my master, and now I cannot make any profit out of him. I hear there is an English colonel coming from Ispahan to Meshed; I shall go and serve him." The English colonel was Stewart himself. Mr. O'Donovan's servant, who was afterwards in Captain Gill's employ, told the latter he never suspected the horse-dealer.

Stewart remained in Deregez till January 14th, ten days before the fall of Geok Tepé, when he was summoned home by the British Government. Somehow or other, the Russian authorities had got to hear of the presence of him and Captain Gill on the border, and complained of "English officers haunting Central Asia" while Russia was at war with the natives. With the amazing meekness in such matters that has been the characteristic of Conservative as well as of Liberal Administrations, Earl Granville listened to the Russian complaints, and, forgetting that Grodekoff had haunted Herat and Stolietoff Cabul while we were quarrelling with the Afghans, peremptorily ordered Stewart home. Shortly after his arrival, the reliance of the English Cabinet on Russia began to cool, and it sent him back again to Khorassan, to watch Herat and the

Russians from Khaf, the nearest Persian town to Herat. There he remained until a few months ago, when he was summoned home to report upon the condition of the country While he was on the spot, things remained so quiet that on his arrival in England there was a talk of abolishing his post; but early in 1883 Russian restlessness developed itself afresh, and a short time ago he was again despatched to Khaf, to stay there another year.

Beyond delivering a brief lecture before the Royal Geographical Society, Stewart has done nothing to make known his travels to the public, and hence he has missed public applause. It is often forgotten by explorers that it is not sufficient for them to penetrate a new country; they must be able to describe their experiences well, and thrust them red hot, so to say, upon the public if they desire to gain general renown. Of the two rides, Colonel Stewart's contained greater materials for an interesting and exciting story than Burnaby's ride to Khiva, and if Burnaby had done what Stewart did we entertain little doubt that he would have made a brilliant reputation out of the exploit. How seriously a man is handicapped who cannot humorously and graphically describe his experiences, may be estimated by a comparison of those two works, Grodekoff's "Ride to Herat" and Burnaby's "Ride to Khiva." Grodekoff underwent far more exciting experiences than Burnaby, yet while every page of Burnaby's book is full of interest, and he makes capital out of the most trifling incidents *en route*, Grodekoff's narrative is more or less bald from beginning to end. Yet Grodekoff's bald narrative is better than none at all. His ride is at least remembered, while Stewart's exploit lies buried in a single lecture in the archives of the Royal Geographical Society.

It is by no means necessary that a traveller should colour and exaggerate his experiences in order to write an interesting book. The truth can be described brilliantly as well as baldly. Skobeleff's reputation was largely made in England by MacGahan's magnificent accounts of the battles before Plevna. We have read many exaggerated accounts of those conflicts, many exhaustive and elaborate ones, many written by able Russian officers who took part in the struggle,—but there are none that provoke the effect produced by the brilliant simplicity of MacGahan. He does not exaggerate what he saw, he merely describes better than anybody else could possibly do what caught his eye before Plevna. Captain Marsh rode from the Caspian to India in 1872 without scarcely noticing anything of particular interest the whole way. Yet a few years later O Donovan, riding along the same road as far as Meshed, was exciting the keenest interest by his graphic and humorous descriptions of men and things *en route.*

But it is not sufficient even to describe one's adventures well. For a book of travels to be a success, the explorer must hasten home and hurry out his book directly after he arrives. Had Burnaby lagged with his "Ride to Khiva," as O'Donovan subsequently did with his "Merv Oasis," his work would not have had anything like the successful sale it did. Instead of posting straight home from Merv, O'Donovan spent four months in leisurely proceeding from Meshed to Constantinople, and it was not until a year afterwards that his book of travels appeared. By that time public interest in his exploit had subsided.

Stewart never sought to excite public interest

in his explorations by newspaper letters or a book of travel, and consequently his exploit is only known to a few. If through his reticence he has never been publicly applauded, he has some consolation in the fact that he is the only English pioneer in Central Asia who has been rewarded with any official recognition of his services. In common with other travellers, the cost of his expedition to Deregez came out of his own pocket; but while Baker, Burnaby, Marsh, and MacGregor got nothing in return for their outlay, Colonel Stewart obtained a special appointment, with an excellent salary accompanying it. A brave man, clear-headed and full of common-sense, he is just the guardian England requires to keep a watch over such a great strategical point as Herat—the key of India. If the Government ever fails in its duty to protect the place from Russian seizure, the country may rest assured that no portion of the blame will be due to the gallant officer who charged himself in the hour of danger with the guardianship of our interests on the Perso-Turcoman frontier, and displayed qualities which the most famous traveller and dashing scout might envy.

CHAPTER XIV.

LIEUTENANT ALIKHANOFF'S JOURNEY WITH A RUSSIAN CARAVAN TO MERV.

Desire of Russia for a survey of her own of the Merv Oasis—Visit of Merv Tekkés to Askabad—Invitation to the Russian traders to visit Merv—Baron Aminoff takes advantage of General Röhrberg's absence to indulge in a little frontier intrigue on his own account—Alikhanoff's previous career—How Caucasians become Russianized—Injustice to the natives of India—March of the Russian caravan along the Atak Oasis—Alikhanoff's survey of the Tejend region—Exciting incidents of the secret night ride into Merv—Fears of treachery—The people awake to find the Russians settled in their midst—Disguised as a Tekké Alikhanoff takes plans of the fortress—Plots of the Tekkés against the Russians—Exploit of Naziroff in riding from the Caspian through Merv to the Oxus at Tchardjui—Merv now completely explored.

"Here stand, my lords! and send discoverers forth
To know the numbers of our enemies."

SHAKESPEARE: *Henry V.*

"Alikhanoff's venturesome visit to Merv almost rivals in exciting incident Mr. O'Donovan's late expedition to that oasis."—PROFESSOR A. H. KEANE (*Academy*, June 16th, 1883).

MR. O'DONOVAN having secured for England a survey of the oasis of Merv, Russia began to think it high time that she obtained one also. How to do this was not a difficult matter for her frontier officials to solve. Russia could not send thither a military surveying party openly, for that would have offended England and probably provoked attack by the Merv Tekkés; but she could despatch topographical officers in disguise, and by mixing them with a caravan, thrust them upon the people without seriously exciting their distrust. Although for a few months the Tekkés of Merv had held aloof from the conquerors of Geok Tepé, they began to open up relations with them when they found no immediate advance was being made towards their oasis. The good treatment accorded by Russia to the refugees from Akhal who accepted the proffered amnesty and returned to their homes, served to lessen the distrust of the Tekkés. Some of them began to appear in the bazaar at Askabad. Finding there a ready market for their produce, and European wares exposed for sale of a cheap and novel character, suited to their needs, they became regular visitors at the Russian settlement. At last some of them began to say to the Russian traders—"Why don't you come to Merv with your wares, and sell them in the market there?" and one of the chiefs, Baba Khan,—he who had once pressed upon Captain Napier the scheme for placing Merv under an Afghan protectorate,—actually offered them guides and a residence, if they would only pay him a visit.

Such language was very tempting to Colonel Baron Aminoff, the chief of the staff of the Transcaspian district. Being an ardent geographer, he was eager to know the character of the country lying between Askabad and Merv. From the hills at the back of Askabad he could gaze for twenty miles across the level steppe in the direction of the oasis. What lay beyond that twenty miles was only known to him by hearsay. Sooner or later he was conscious that the Russians would advance across the plain to the oasis; and on military as well as on geographical grounds, it seemed to him desirable to obtain a regular survey of the intervening region. Everything favoured such an enterprise. The Governor, General Röhrberg, had just gone to St. Petersburg and left him in charge of the Transcaspian territory; a Russian caravan was at Askabad, the owner of which was desirous of finding a brisker market for his goods; and there were officers attached to his staff who could be safely trusted to mix with the Tekkés in disguise. Accordingly, in February, 1882, he made arrangements for the Russian caravan to proceed to Merv; and, there is every reason to believe, sent it off without the cognisance of his own Government—at any rate, neither the Minister of War nor the Minister for Foreign Affairs received any intimation of the intended journey, nor any report of it afterwards.

The officer chosen to conduct the survey was Lieutenant Alikhanoff, one of the many officers of broken fortunes who are to be met with everywhere along the Russian frontier in Asia. In England, when an officer misbehaves himself, he is cashiered or forced to resign. In Russia, he is simply reduced to the ranks, stripped of his titles, and sent to Siberia or Central Asia to serve as a private soldier. Such a man naturally becomes a desperado, and forms capital fighting material for generals of the stamp of Skobeleff. In many cases they retrieve their reputation, and it is the custom, if they display extraordinary courage, or render any particular service, to restore them to their former position. When the expedition against Khiva took place in 1873, Alikhanoff served under Skobeleff with the rank of captain. For his bravery during the war he was advanced to the position of major, and made aide-de-camp to the Grand Duke Michael, Viceroy of the Caucasus. Not long after this, for quarrelling and fighting a duel with a brother officer, he was reduced to the ranks, and sent beyond the Caspian to Lazareff's army. Mr. O'Donovan knew him well, and tells us that he was a "capital fellow, a brave and capable soldier, and much liked in the camp.' During the war of 1879 he acted as correspondent of the *Moscow Gazette*, and wrote the graphic letters which appear in the "Disastrous Russian Campaign against the Turcomans," under the *nom de plume* of "Arsky." How clever he is with his pencil any one can see who cares to look at the admirable sketches he furnished for the recent work, "The Russians at Merv and Herat."

By race Alikhanoff was a Caucasian—a convenient term used by Russians to designate an individual of any of the varied races dwelling in the Caucasus. The natives of the newly conquered provinces of Russia have a happy way of identifying themselves with their masters, which our language renders impossible in the case of our Eastern subjects—they turn their names into Russian ones by placing an "off" (son) at the end of them. Alikhanoff is simply Ali Khan with an "off" added to it. This transformation is possible in English with a few oriental names—for instance, Shere Ali might be Anglicised into Shere Alison, or Mr. Alison, and if Ali Khan were turned into Alikhanson, or softened into Alihanson, English euphony might not be offended; but what could we do with Tiruvarur Muttirswami Aiyar, or Vembankum Ramiergar, or Rao Sahib Urshwanath Narayen Mandlik, even though the latter two be knight commanders of the most exalted order of the Star of India? The Russian language swallows such granite blocks of speech as easily as a shark jerks a lump of pork into its capacious stomach.

We do not have, unluckily, the power of assimilating Eastern races possessed by the Russians. What a Russian conquers becomes part of his fatherland; the conquered become his fellow-citizens. We, on the other hand, still look on our Eastern conquests as foreign possessions, having nothing in common with our own country ; and regard the people of India as a race to be kept under, and forbidden to share the privileges enjoyed by the citizen of London or Liverpool. An Indian has no career in England. On the other hand, every avenue in Russia is open to the Caucasian. The Armenian Loris Melikoff rises there to a position next to that of the Tsar; Generals Tergoukasoff and Lazareff, two other Caucasians, share with him the conquest of the Turks in Armenia during the war of 1877-78. Skobeleff selects Gaidaroff (Hyder-off) to command one of the four Russian columns storming Geok Tepé, and when Alikhanoff penetrates to Merv, and later on brings about its submission, his exploit is acclaimed as a Russian exploit, and not as the achievement of a mere native.*

Merv is reckoned to be about six marches distant from Askabad, and the intervening desert is broken by the Tejend Oasis, a fertile

* Daoud Khan, an educated native of India and an English citizen, penetrated to Merv ten years before O'Donovan ; yet, as we have pointed out, his achievement has only been incidentally mentioned in a chance discussion at the Royal Geographical Society. In Russia, dubbed Daoudoff, he would have been applauded by the press as a regular Russian traveller, occupying a place with foremost Russian explorers, and conferring honour upon Russia by his exploit.

tract larger than the oasis of Merv itself. To prepare the way for Alikhanoff's expedition, a Russianised Khivan, Fazil Beg by name, who had been to Merv before, was sent ahead to secretly arrange for the reception of the caravan at the Tejend and Merv, and obtain guides for conducting it by the safest route. The caravan party comprised Kosikh, a trader, representing the firm of Konshin and Co., of Moscow, who had brought the caravan to Askabad, and still had charge of it; Lieutenant Alikhanoff, disguised as his clerk and interpreter; Ensign Sokoleff, of the Cossacks, disguised as another clerk; and a force of half a dozen *djigits*, or native horse, well armed with Berdans and revolvers, and commanded by an experienced and capable chief, Ak Murad Sardar. At various points on the way the caravan was further accompanied by parties of Turcomans, hired for the stage to render the Russians still more secure against any party of Tekké marauders that might be prowling about.

At the very outset, the party encountered difficulties. The Merv Tekké camel-drivers, on reaching the Russian frontier—two marches from Askabad—refused to accompany it any further, and had to be threatened with imprisonment before they would give in. The next march brought them to Lutfabad, in the Atak Oasis, fourteen miles from that town of Mahomedabad in which Colonel Stewart had settled down in disguise in 1880, to watch the Russians in the event of their endeavouring to make a move upon Merv. On approaching Lutfabad the caravan was stopped by a Persian official from Mahomedabad, to whom Alikhanoff said that they were on their way to Meshed with wares, and would give him a call at Mahomedabad the next day or so—a piece of deception adopted to prevent the Persians interfering in any way with their undertaking.

The following day was spent at Kahka, eighteen and a half miles from Lutfabad and eighty from Askabad, which Alikhanoff had decided to adopt as the starting-point of the steppe journey from the Persian border to Merv. O'Donovan, it will be remembered, started fifty-three miles, or two caravan journeys, further east, from the Atak settlement of Mehna. In both instances, however, the distance of the steppe journey to Merv was about the same.

The people of Kahka are Persian subjects, but they frankly expressed to Alikhanoff their hatred of the imbecile rule of the Shah, and drew up a request to become Russian subjects for him to send to his Government. From the Atak to the Tejend river O'Donovan had traversed the fifty miles of steppe in a night; the Russian caravan, however, travelled more slowly, and spent two days in crossing the expanse. Kari Bent, the dam across the Tejend where they passed the night, is famous for mosquitoes of such a poisonous character, that they even sting camels to death.

In going and returning, Alikhanoff made a more thorough survey of the Tejend Oasis than O'Donovan had been able to do during his hurried halt there. Instead of being an insignificant tract of marsh land, he found it a fertile oasis considerably larger than that of Merv. Formerly it contained 20,000 Tekké families, but the Persians harried them so much that they migrated either to Akhal or Merv, and left the place a wilderness. After the fall of Geok Tepé many thousand fugitives fled thither, and when O'Donovan secretly slipped across the oasis they were negotiating with the

Russians to be allowed to return. This was in February 1881. Alikhanoff crossed the oasis a year later, and there were then 3,600 tents, or 18,000 souls, scattered about the oasis, consisting of the remnants of the fugitives and new-comers from Merv. These were digging out new canals and establishing thriving settlements. In course of time, the skill of the Russian irrigation engineer will convert the district into another Merv, and a warlike population of a quarter of a million or so will grow up within handy hitting distance of Herat.

The Tejend Oasis is now completely under Russian control, but even when Alikhanoff visited the district Russian influence was predominant. This was not surprising, as Kari Bent is only three days' ride from Askabad, and the Russian Governor had already sent Cossack squadrons thither several times to reconnoitre the oasis and punish chance marauders. Thanks to the general fear of the Cossack the caravan was properly treated at Kari Bent, and its march facilitated to Merv.

The stretch of briar-covered wilderness between the Tejend and Merv took O'Donovan a day and a night to traverse. The slower

Russian caravan required three days for the journey, camping twice on the way. On the afternoon of the third day they met the five guides Fazil Beg, the Khivan emissary, had sent from Merv. Having marched twenty-four miles since the morning, the caravan meant to have passed the night at some wells twenty-six miles from Merv, but the guides insisted that they should either go on and pass through the settlements of the Otamish at night, or else make a *détour* of several days' duration so as to arrive on the opposite side of Merv, where the second clan of the Merv Tekkés—the Tokhtamish—resided. The Otamish, they said, were so hostile to the Russians that they would immediately kill them; whereas a good reception might be expected from the Tokhtamish. Ultimately it was discovered that these guides, not wishing to draw down on their heads the anger of the people for conducting the caravan to Merv, had resorted to this story in order to induce the Russians to enter at night. In this manner it happened that the people of Merv knew nothing of the approach or advent of the Russians, until they woke up one morning to find them comfortably ensconced in their midst.

This night ride was the most sensational part of the expedition. The first Merv settlement was reached at 11 o'clock—Topaz, a little more than twenty miles from the fortress. The moon shone so brightly that the travellers could easily count the number of tents.

"Our fellow-travellers grew silent. They hardly allowed themselves to whisper. They hurried on to get clear as quickly as possible of the robbers' nest, the watch dogs of which loudly barked a warning on our approach. We traversed it, however, in safety, and also another. The tents seemed to rise at every step like black mushrooms.

"The *aouls* consist of two or three hundred tightly packed tents, without any clay dwellings among them, and are situate a mile or two from one another. The entire country between them is covered with crops. There is no road whatever, only paths. Such are the characteristics of the environs of Merv.

"The nearer we got to the centre, the more numerous the clay structures became. Low walls enclosing gardens, melon-beds, and fields, formed, together with the canals, quite a network. Amidst such surroundings we had already ridden for more than an hour, penetrating one *aoul* after another, when the Mervis and Ovez Sardar requested us to separate ourselves from the caravan and proceed with them ahead.

"'The Otamish,' said they, 'will not fall upon the caravan, because the people accompanying it are the same as themselves—Turcomans of the Tekké tribe. The case will be quite different, however, if they chance to see you.'

"Thoroughly worn out with fatigue, we were allured by the prospect of an early rest—they said it was only half-an-hour's ride to Merv—and the three of us set off with one of the Mervis, of whom the number had increased to eight on the way. Our Kirghiz escort were in despair at our departure. They had the gravest fears for our safety.

"The *aouls* stretched along one after another as before. We traversed a complete labyrinth of irregular canals, muddy roads, and inundated fields. Tents and walls, and fields and canals, succeeded each other in rapid succession. After a while the moon disappeared, and we pushed on in the darkness, while watch-dogs bayed on every side.

"We rode for an hour, for another, for a third, amidst this environment. To all our questions as to when we should reach our destination we only received a laconic 'Quickly, quickly,' from the Mervis. In the meanwhile, it seemed to us we were being led over and over again through the same localities. This circumstance excited our suspicions, and these were further strengthened by the conduct of the Mervis. They whispered to each other; they disappeared in the *aouls* and summoned people, to whom they whispered something in secret, after which there was a stir in the *aoul*.

"'These scoundrels are up to some game or other,' said one of us, drawing his revolver; 'get ready for any emergency. Remain cool and keep your pluck up. I, for one, will answer that that Goliath, Ovez Sardar, falls before my fire.'

"'The sooner we know what the game is, the better,' said another. 'I shall empty my revolver among the blackguards, and then put an end to myself.'

"A third heard all this, and rode on in silence.

"Suddenly we saw opening before our feet

a broad silver band—this was the Murghab, the river of Merv. Still as alarmed as before, we traversed a narrow rickety bridge, sixty paces long, and emerged on the north-east side, amidst gardens and clay structures, reminding us of the Khivan Oasis.

" After a while we came to the interminably long and wonderful walls of the fortress of Merv. This is a gigantic structure, compared with which the fortress of Geok Tepé is but a mere bagatelle. Traversing this, we found ourselves riding on the other side amidst the same surroundings as before. It was half-past three in the morning when our fellow-travellers, with ourselves behind them, turned off the road and entered a spacious yard, with several clay cabins at the side. In the darkness the massive structure had an ugly appearance, and seemed to us to be a sort of trap.

" ' We have arrived. Dismount,' said Ovez Sardar, in a low tone, stopping alongside me. His eyes had an ominous look in them, and his voice excited suspicion.

" ' What place is this ? ' I demanded.

" ' Mekhman-jai Komek Beg—The guest house of Komek Beg,' he replied.

"'Where is Fazil Beg, then? Summon him hither.'

"'He is probably asleep,' replied Ovez, ordering some one to bring our Khivan to us.

"In a few minutes several dark figures made their appearance.

"'Fazil Beg, is that you?'

"'It is I,' he replied in Russian, but in a tone of voice that still further alarmed me.

"'Are you a prisoner?'

"'Prisoner? No. Why should I be a prisoner?'

"In the course of a few minutes we were led into one of the kibitkas, in the centre of which a wood fire was smouldering. Around this the master and several Tekkés were laying down carpets and felts. Ovez and several of his associates entered with us, and disposed themselves around the fire as fresh and as vigorous as if they had only ridden a verst or two. These Merv Tekkés are wonderfully strong.

"They began to make tea for us, but we were beyond anything of that kind. The moment we threw ourselves down on the soft carpets we fell asleep there and then like dead men, and slept in the dark kibitka till late in the morning, when we were awakened by the arrival of the caravan."

Quite a sensation prevailed at Merv in the morning when it was known that a number of Russians were located in the oasis. A council of chiefs was held, at which Alikhanoff declared the mission of the caravan to be purely a commercial one, and by mingled threats and persuasion—assisted by gifts previously distributed among the more influential chiefs—induced them to give permission for the caravan to remain for a few weeks in the oasis. During this period the Russian officers, while daily acting the part of traders' factotums, availed themselves of every occasion to examine the country. Disguised as a Tekké, Alikhanoff used to slip out early in the morning, before the people were awake, and survey the fortress. Perhaps the people knew more about this than he imagined. At any rate, they never ceased expressing their suspicions the whole time the Russians were there. The Tekkés were always laying a trap to catch them in conversation. Thus, on one occasion, having got Alikhanoff to dilate on the blessings of civilisation as an excuse for the Russian advance, one of the chiefs suddenly said, with a suspicious sneer, "If you are a mere trader, how does it come to pass that you know all these things?" "Oh, we pick them up at school, and in Russia the schools are open to everybody," replied Alikhanoff, readily.

Still the Tekkés were not satisfied, and the reports of their plots to murder the Russians grew so alarming at last that Gospodin Kosikh, the trader, would stop no longer, and hurried away in a state of panic, leaving his goods behind with the Tekkés on credit. But Alikhanoff, more courageous, insisted on a new road being taken for the return journey, and by proceeding first in the direction of Khiva for two marches, completed his survey of the northern part of this oasis. On his arrival at Askabad, the secret of his journey was kept so well that nothing was known about it in Russia for more than six months, and the public would not have been enlightened then had he not published an account of his adventures in the *Moscow Gazette*.

This consisted of some of his letters to Baron Aminoff, but a book is promised of his five weeks' adventures, and Alikhanoff being as graphic with his pencil as with his pen, his work should be a good one. Hardly so great an achievement as O'Donovan's ride to Merv, Alikhanoff's journey thither was none the less an exploit of which any officer might be proud. If O'Donovan had to bear the brunt of being the first European in Merv in modern times, Alikhanoff had to face Tekké hostility as the first Russian penetrating thither. He could not tell what reception would be given to him as a trader; had it been known he was an officer in disguise, he would assuredly have been sacrificed to popular fury. But there is this very great difference between the exploits of the English and the Russian explorer. O'Donovan went to Merv alone, unannounced, and, considering the worthless character of his escort, absolutely unprotected. Alikhanoff, on the contrary, sent in front a Khivan to bribe the chiefs and prepare for his reception, and the members of the caravan and escort numbered thirteen men, well armed with breechloaders and revolvers, a force insufficient to prevent a massacre, but powerful enough to inspire respect.

Since Alikhanoff returned from Merv, Lessar has been there, riding thence to Khiva and back across the desert to Kizil Arvat. More recently Lieutenant Naziroff has ridden from the Caspian through Merv, *viâ* Meshed, to Tchardjui, Bokhara, and Tashkent. Both these exploits cast into the shade Burnaby's ride to Khiva, Naziroff's ride being 1,500 miles long, or four times the length of Burnaby's.

Naziroff's adventures would make a very interesting book. He is a good specimen of the secret Russian emissary in Central Asia —of the class of men who glide hither and thither in the East, unsuspected by our authorities in England and India. His father was a native gentleman of the Caucasian province of Baku. He himself was born Nazir Beg, which he Russianised into Naziroff when he grew up. Educated at the public school at Baku, he became a cadet in 1873, and two years later was appointed an officer in the Turkestan army. The following year, 1876, he served under Skobeleff in the Alai expedition. In 1878 he went to Cabul with Stolietoff as topographer to the Russian mission. In 1880 he served on the Kuldja frontier, where a

Chinese invasion was expected. In 1882 he was sent by Russia to ride from Askabad to Tchardjui, to survey the sole remaining route unexplored by Russia running to Merv.

Speaking fluently all the languages and dialects of Central Asia, Naziroff had no difficulty in assuming a disguise. To accompany him he selected a native of Baku, Ali Hussein Kerbeli Askar Ogli, and a Persian, Meshedi Mahmed Ali Meshedi Rzi Ogli. With these he rode from Astrabad to Meshed, traversing a road thus far frequently travelled over by Russian and English explorers; then pushed from Meshed to Merv, over ground traversed by Lessar; and finally, from Merv made his way to Tchardjui on the Oxus, the survey of this section being the main object of his journey. Fifty years earlier Lieutenant, afterwards Sir Alexander, Burnes had journeyed with a caravan from Tchardjui to Merv, but he had left behind him only a brief description of the route, and there was reason to believe he had pursued a bad one. Naziroff successfully secured a thorough topographical survey of the country, and from Tchardjui rode on *viâ* Bokhara to Tashkent.

LIEUTENANT NAZIROFF AND HIS FELLOW EXPLORERS OF MERV.

[*To face page* 382.

In this manner, Russia within a twelvemonth obtained a survey of all the routes leading to Merv. Alikhanoff explored the road from Askabad to Merv, which an army advancing from the Caspian would pursue; Lessar from Khiva to Merv, which would be taken by a detachment from the Russian garrison of Petro-Alexandrovsk; and Naziroff from Tchardjui to Merv, which would be followed by a force operating from Samarcand. These surveys were instigated by the belief that sooner or later Russia would have to march an army upon Merv. But the necessity for this has now passed away. Early this year, when the Tekkés were at peace with the Russians, and were giving them no provocation, the latter treacherously sent a force to the Tejend, and a detachment of it, headed by Alikhanoff, swooped down upon the oasis. There Alikhanoff summoned the chiefs, and mendaciously representing the Tejend force to be the advanced guard of a great army, induced them to proceed to ASKABAD and submit. In return for his success in accomplishing this *coup de main* he was restored to the rank of major, and made the first Russian Governor of Merv.

CHAPTER XV.

LESSAR'S DISCOVERY OF THE EASY ROAD TO INDIA.

The Transcaspian railway—Explorers sent to report upon its extension to India—Why General Annenkoff chose Lessar as surveyor—Exploration of the country between Askabad and Sarakhs—Skobeleff's reference to Lessar in his Geok Tepé banquet speech—Effect of Central Asian travel upon explorers—The country between Sarakhs and Herat—Lessar's ride across it and discoveries *en route*—The Sarik Turcomans—Arrives in Afghanistan—The strategical importance of Kusan—Russia and the emancipation of the 40,000 slaves in Khiva—Lessar proceeds to Ghurian—Conversation with the Khan—Lessar's journey to Meshed—His survey of the Oxus—Momentous character of his explorations—Their effect upon the relations of England and Russia in Central Asia.

"Lessar's report of his journey to Herat is very interesting, and the unpretentious way it is drawn up enhances its value in the eyes of geographers. If he had done nothing more than explode the Paropamisus bugbear, which assumed that the mountains north of Cabul were prolonged at the same elevation to the westward, he would have rendered us an important national service; but he has done much more. He has traced with the eye of an engineering geographer the line of the Russian advance, in the past and in the future, from the Caspian to Askabad, from Askabad to Sarakhs, and from Sarakhs to Herat, and he has shown that, as far as physical difficulties are concerned, there is no reason why, at any time and within the limitation of a few months, a continuous railway should not be built from the Caspian to the Western Afghan capital; to which I may add that if that work were once executed, a week would suffice for the transport of troops and stores from the Caucasus head-quarters to Herat."

SIR HENRY RAWLINSON, 1882.

WHEN the Transcaspian railway was completed in 1881, the controller of the undertaking, Prince Khilkoff, had at his disposal a number of engineers, whose services he thought might be opportunely utilised in making surveys before returning home to Russia. Already the original designer of the railway, General Annenkoff, had conceived the idea of extending the line to India, and it was to test the practicability of the project that these engineers were sent forward by Khilkoff to survey the country from the terminal point of the railway, Kizil Arvat, to the new Russian fortress of Askabad. The distance between the two points, one hundred and thirty-five miles, was found to be almost perfectly level, and well adapted for the construction of a cheap railway. This being demonstrated to the satisfaction of Annenkoff, it was decided to survey the next section of the projected line, from Askabad to Sarakhs, which lay through a country that had never been entirely traversed by any European, although Baker and Gill, Butler and MacGregor, had gazed down upon the Atak Oasis from the Persian highlands overlooking it, and had penetrated to various points of the region; while O'Donovan had ridden along it to within fifty miles of Sarakhs. It is along this Atak, or "skirt" of the Khorassan highlands, that Russian troops must march to get to Merv, so that the survey projected was of a military as well as of an engineering character. The person chosen to conduct the survey was Gospodin Lessar, a courageous, enterprising, and unassuming young man. "I chose him," said General Annenkoff to the writer a year ago, "because he was a young man, and young men are mostly honest." The enterprise was an onerous one for a young and unknown engineer to have charge of. The party comprised nine Russian labourers, with two overseers to assist in the levelling and topographical work, two interpreters and a guide, and an escort of twenty-one Cossacks under the command of an officer. The transport consisted of five camels and a waggon and a cart, the party having a number of cumbrous and heavy surveying appliances with them in excess of their ordinary baggage.

From Askabad to Sarakhs is a distance of one hundred and eighty-five and a half miles, and if one can imagine the sands at the foot of the southern cliffs of England intersected with fields and canals, and the English Channel the Turcoman desert, he can form some idea of the character of a journey along such a "skirt" from Plymouth to Spithead. The principal danger attending the survey was the possibility of a body of Turcomans from Merv falling upon their flank, but had they been attacked the Russians could have easily retired to the hills, or to one of the numerous settlements of mongrel Turcomans and Persians lying along the route. The field-work of a surveyor is never very interesting, and in this case the monotony of Lessar's levelling operations, extending over a period of several weeks, was unmarked by any incident of an exciting character. The Tekkés of Merv refrained from troubling the Russians at all, and the people of the country traversed gave them every assistance in their power. On reaching

Sarakhs, Lessar returned to Askabad *viâ* Meshed, where his arrival provoked great talk in England, and drew from General Skobeleff the allusion in his famous Geok Tepé banquet speech—" Never since the time of Mahomed Shah's march to Herat, coupled with the memorable services of Count Simonitch, has the influence of the Russian Minister at Teheran been more predominant than it is to-day ; in one word, the spell of the Russian standard is powerful far away to the east, even beyond the conquered region, and this will be doubtless confirmed by the engineers who have just returned from Sarakhs.'

Proceeding from Askabad to Europe, Lessar equipped himself with the latest maps of Persia and Afghanistan, and then returned to perform the achievement by which he is best known—his journey from Sarakhs to Herat. Before he started, there was an impression abroad that he would not confine his explorations to Persia only, but would make his way into Afghanistan, which was subsequently confirmed. Said a Russian gentleman to the writer in the presence of General Annenkoff two years ago—" It is curious how nomadized people become who visit

Central Asia. They want to be always pushing onwards. Lessar, for instance, is infected with it, and is eager to renew his explorations beyond Sarakhs." The feeling is not confined to Russians. General Sir Charles MacGregor has recorded that he never comes across a blank space on a map, without feeling a burning desire to go and find out what exists undiscovered there.

Sarakhs and Herat are situated on one and the same river, the Hari Rud, which flows from Herat about ninety miles due west, then turning off at right angles runs for 120 miles or so in a straight northerly direction to Sarakhs. Beyond Sarakhs it is known as the Tejend, and gives birth to the oasis lying between Persia and Merv. One side of the Hari Rud is Afghan territory, the other side Persian. MacGregor, as we have seen, had surveyed the whole of the country from Herat to Sarakhs along the Persian side, and portions of this route had been so frequently examined by others that there was very little left to investigate—not enough, at any rate, to make a reputation by. But the Afghan side of the river was almost completely *terra incognita.* Exposed to the raids of the Turcomans of Merv and the upper

Murghab, no single traveller had ever dared to cross the river to explore it, and the Persian officials were too pusillanimous and lazy to attempt the task with the powerful escorts they always journeyed with in proceeding from Meshed to Sarakhs. In this manner, the country had remained almost a myth. But professional map-makers hate as much as MacGregor to see blank places on their productions, and hence, to fill up the gap, had extended the huge ridge, existing at the back of Cabul, right up to the Hari Rud, midway between Herat and Sarakhs. Thus, in excess of the Turcomans, there was a mountain range 15,000 or 20,000 feet high, with spurs as big as English mountains, to terrify the would-be explorer of the country.

On this occasion Lessar took no Cossacks, and was accompanied only by a few Alieli Turcomans from the Atak, and a Tekké Turcoman guide. His first journey had been performed shortly after the fall of Geok Tepé; his second took place early in 1882, after Alikhanoff's return from Merv and the opening up of friendly relations between Russia and the Merv Tekkés. From the latter, therefore, he had little to fear, and his only danger lay in a possible attack by the Sarik Turcomans, a tribe living on the Murghab between Merv and Herat, which had never come in contact with the Russians, and could not be relied upon to treat an explorer of that nation with respect. The Alielis who accompanied Lessar were dreadfully frightened of these Sariks, and candidly confessed that their only hope of safety lay in the fear they trusted the latter would experience of attacking the representative of a people, which had recently gained such a terrible victory at Geok Tepé.

Luckily no Sariks were met at all during the journey, and only a few friendly Merv Tekkés. As far as the great mountain range on the map, the country was found to be an uninhabited wilderness, in which the Afghans and Persians could not live for fear of the Turcomans, and the Turcomans for fear of the Afghans and Persians. But the principal discovery of the journey was associated with the mountain range, which, on attainment, melted away to a miserable row of hills, with an easy pass fit for vehicular traffic, 900 feet above the surrounding locality. If it be remembered that this imaginary mountain range, 20,000 feet high, had been relied upon by English statesmen and generals to serve as an impassable barrier between Sarakhs and Herat, it will be seen how important this discovery was. But Lessar was more an engineer than a politician. Ignoring the strategical aspect, he was delighted to find that the mountain range had proved to be a bit of geographical humbug, and that General Annenkoff had hit upon the easiest and best route for a railway from Europe to India.

Having effected this discovery, he says he had originally intended turning back home across the Hari Rud *viâ* Meshed, but none of his party knew the fords, and he had, therefore, only two alternatives; either to retrace his steps, which no explorer ever willingly does or push on thirty miles to the Afghan post of Kusan, where he would find himself on the main highway running from Herat to Meshed. He decided upon the latter course, and although he violated Afghan territory, one can hardly condemn his conduct, as he afterwards frankly published a full report of his explorations, and disclosed to England, in due time for her to take precautions, the character of a country which must, sooner or later, have become thoroughly known.

Owing to Turcoman raids no Afghans live near the Barkhut Hills, or ever attempt to cross them to the north, while the Turcomans on their part never pass over to the south except secretly on a foray. On this account, when the Afghan garrison saw the European and his escort advancing upon Kusan from a direction never openly used, they prepared for a conflict. But Lessar rode ahead with his two interpreters to explain matters, and before long he was comfortably seated inside the fort, having breakfast with the Khan, who had seen plenty of Frenghis at Cabul, and was not displeased to see a fresh one.

Kusan, or Khosan, is an important strategical point, of which much will be heard in the future. In journeying from Meshed to Herat it is the first Afghan settlement met with after crossing the Persian border. North of it there is no permanent settlement as far as Sarakhs. Thus a Russian army marching east upon Herat from the Caspian at Astrabad, or from the new position at Askabad *viâ* Sarakhs, would first encounter the Afghans at Kusan, from which Herat is only sixty-eight miles distant. The Afghans have a dilapidated fort at Kusan, but a handful of Cossacks could capture it with ease at any time.

Lessar was rather surprised to find one of the Afghan soldiers at the fort addressing him in Russian. On enquiry the man proved to be one of the slaves set free by Kaufmann after the capture of Khiva in 1873. Before returning to his native home in the Herat valley, he had served a short while with the Russian force.

All travellers agree that Russia gained enormous prestige by her emancipation of the 40,000 slaves of Khiva, although many of them, through the bureaucratic stupidity of her officials, perished on their way home. MacGregor, in his journey through Khorassan, constantly came across natives fervently blessing the White Tsar for having liberated them from slavery. Grodekoff was gratefully thanked by emancipated Persians and Afghans when they heard he had participated in the Khivan campaign. Colonel Stewart, while riding along the Khorassan border, "met in almost every village liberated slaves, who spoke of the kindness of the Russians in freeing them." Altogether, Russia has emancipated during her conquest of Central Asia nearly 150,000 slaves. If she had listened to the clamour of England not to step beyond her Orenburg and Caspian borders, these unfortunates would have died in chains.

While profoundly impressed with the necessity for securing a scientific frontier for India, we cannot sympathise with Sir Henry Rawlinson and those of his followers who would have kept Central Asia in its old barbarous condition, in order to add to our security. If we were Sir Henry it would be appalling for us to remember how much misery we had indirectly occasioned and prolonged, by setting England to resist the destruction of slavery in Central Asia. Our policy a quarter of a century ago ought to have been to select what we needed of Central Asia to defend India, and to have left all the territory outside the border to be dealt with by Russia. But England seems incapable of a common-sense policy.

Although the Afghan chief at Kusan treated Lessar hospitably, he would not let him proceed along the Meshed road to Persia until he had informed the Governor-General of Herat of his arrival. To shift the responsibility off his own shoulders, however, he did not object to Lessar going on to Ghurian, the chief town of the district. In this manner, the Russian explorer was able to get within thirty miles of Herat.

Lessar stopped at Ghurian a couple of days. "The Khan," he says, "did all he could to please me, but I expressed the whole time my dissatisfaction at being detained for the sake of a mere formality—for permission not to journey in Afghanistan, but merely to cross a river close to an Afghan fort. I asked him jokingly how the Afghan traders in Samarcand would get on if, whenever any one arrived fresh from Afghanistan, we were to send to ask permission of the Governor-General? The stories I told him of how the Russians freely journeyed in Persia, and the Persians in Russia, were not at all to the taste of the Afghans. The Khan endeavoured to explain the necessity for the existing state of things. 'Russia,' said he, 'is a big country, and has nothing to fear, but with us a single man may do us injury; hence our law is such that the higher authorities have to know who is journeying about. And, besides, fate having led hither a man from such a distant state as Russia, we are bound to receive him and dispense hospitality. Are we not men,' he asked, in an offended tone, 'that we may not dispense hospitality? What have we done that you should have wished to pass our door without resting a bit? You are not our prisoner, but our guest. The whole land is at your disposal—ask for what you wish.'"

The Khan refused to allow the people to sell the Russians anything, and ordered the money to be refunded which they had given to an Afghan on the road for bread for the party. The whole time they were at Ghurian he sent Lessar and his Alielis everything they wanted, and kept despatching messengers to ask if there was anything they desired.

The second day the Nizam Eddin Khan, principal councillor of the Governor-General of Herat, came with an imposing suite, and, taking Lessar aside, asked him privately if he had any secret communications to make to his Government. The Afghans took Lessar for one of those secret agents Kaufmann was continually sending to the courts of the potentates dwelling outside the Turkestan territory, and seemed surprised that his errand should have been of a casual and pointless character. However, he ordered every attention to be paid the explorer, and assigned a large escort to accompany him the next day to the frontier, on his way to Meshed.

From Herat to Meshed the country has been so often described, that Lessar found little fresh to relate. The valley of Herat charmed him, as it had done all previous travellers. Once established there, Russia would be able to dominate Central Asia, Afghanistan, and Persia. It would become a second Tiflis in point of administrative importance and industrial prosperity, and in due course Candahar would experience the fate of Kars.

After a short stay at Meshed, Lessar made his way to Sarakhs, to see if the road was suitable for a railway, and thence along the Atak back to Askabad. Everywhere he found the Turcoman raids diminishing, and the power of Persia being extended up to Afghanistan. In the course of a few years the country is likely to become quite pacified, and trade communications will then be opened up through it between Russia and India.

On his arrival at Askabad the energetic

traveller did not settle down to inactivity. Equipping himself afresh, he proceeded to Merv, then to Khiva, and finally back to Askabad across the desert. This itself was a ride sufficiently remarkable to have made anyone's reputation, for it was equal in point of distance and difficulty to three of Burnaby's rides to Khiva; but no account of it has been published, and all the notice it has received has been in the shape of a few newspaper paragraphs. The result of this journey was to prove, in Lessar's opinion, that the Oxus could not be diverted from the Aral to the Caspian along the dried-up ancient channel called the Uzboi, without an immense outlay; while, for a small sum, he thought that a body of water could be turned into another channel near Tchardjui, by means of which the desert up to Askabad might be irrigated and converted into fertile country. To test this latter theory, he set out in the spring with some companions at his own cost for the Merv Oasis, and effected an excellent survey—his fourth in three years, without any hitch, although the results are as yet unknown.

Far from being so brilliant as the explorations of many previous travellers, Lessar's journeys promise to be more momentous. It is he who has discovered the easiest and shortest road for a railway from Europe to India--and as the railway will inevitably be constructed some day, his name will be imperishably associated with it. He may further claim to have completely upset the "masterly inactivity" policy of the Gladstone Government, for when he proved that the Key of India was more within the keeping of Russia than of England,—that, in a word, Herat, by his newly discovered road, was completely at the mercy of the Cossack, the Gladstone Government had no other alternative than to meet the altered circumstances by developing Quetta, and giving an enormous subsidy to the Ameer to strengthen his hold upon Herat. Besides this, he upset elaborate English and Russian military calculations, by proving that the best road to India from the Caspian for a Russian army did not lay along the ancient highway of invasion *viâ* Astrabad and Meshed, but through Askabad and Sarakhs.

It is interesting to note that while the journey which made his name—the ride from Sarakhs to Herat—was the most insignificant in point of length, hardship, danger, and difficulty, recorded in this book, it has had, and is likely to continue to have, a more important effect on the relations between Russia and England in Central Asia than all the achievements of the other explorers put together.

CHAPTER XVI.

THE PAST AND FUTURE OF PIONEERING IN CENTRAL ASIA.

Changes in Central Asia since Vámbéry visited the region in 1863—Nothing now left of importance to explore—Unjust accusation against Russia of keeping the results of her explorations to herself—English and Russian maps of Central Asia—The region quite easy to traverse to-day—Results of its conquest by Russia—Comparison of the exploits of the various pioneers—Special features distinguishing Vámbéry's, MacGahan's, and O'Donovan's achievements above all others—Impossible for Vámbéry's exploit to be repeated—Merits of military explorers—The rivalry of Russia and England in Central Asia a trade rivalry as well as a political one—Want of patriotism on the part of English manufacturers—Obligations of Anglo-Indian capitalists to the army—Who may and who may not be relied upon in the hour of danger—A greater reward than all.

"We sailed wherever ship could sail,
We founded many a mighty State;
Pray God our greatness may not fail
Through craven fears of being great."

TENNYSON.

IN 1863, when Arminius Vámbéry set out in rags from Teheran to investigate the condition of Central Asia, an extensive expanse of territory, nearly as large as Europe without Russia, existed unconquered and to a considerable extent unexplored, between Russia and India. This expanse, comprising Independent Tartary, Turkestan, and Turkmenia, has been conquered and annexed within a period of twenty years, and to-day there is hardly a district left to provoke the ardour of the explorer. With the exception of a few spots in and about the Pamir, and in the steppes between the Hari Rud and Murghab, the region of Central Asia has been completely overrun, and the exceptions are too insignificant to interfere with geographical or political generalisations, or to afford a satisfactory field for the energies of any new traveller. It is no longer possible, in short, for anyone to make a reputation by travelling in Central Asia, and all that is really left to be done is for Russian surveying parties to go thoroughly over the ground, and complete the researches of the early pioneers. Such work, if not brilliant, is at least useful, and there is nothing that has provoked the admiration of European geographers more than the splendid liberality Russia has displayed in promoting the scientific investigation of Central Asia. In a recent work on Russia, by Mr. Geddie, of the Royal Geographical Society, that author accuses Russia of keeping the results of her researches to herself. Never was there a grosser and more unjustifiable libel. It would have been a truer accusation if it had been levied against our own country. There is not, I believe, a single State-aided Russian traveller whose researches and maps are not accessible in a cheap and elaborate form at St. Petersburg. Every year, all the maps prepared in every part of the Russian Empire by explorers and topographers are laid before the Emperor, and the majority of them are subsequently exposed on sale in the publishing department attached to the General Staff Office. We have no such institution in this country. Our War Office hoards its maps till they grow musty, in order to keep them "secret and confidential"; and then when explorers like Colonel Baker take them to Central Asia, they are contemptuously thrown away as useless. Daoud Khan, for instance, explored Merv ten years before O'Donovan, but his map was never published. Napier's researches, again, were kept secret at the India Office until their publication had been anticipated by Russian explorers, and were no longer of any use. Numerous other similar instances might be mentioned. On the other hand, Russia has invariably made known her explorations immediately after their accomplishment, and has published maps at prices compared with which those current in London are exorbitant. Whenever I have wanted good maps of Central Asia, I have always found it cheaper and better to obtain them from the Russian General Staff Office than from the London map makers. Even in regard to Afghanistan, which is a sort of English dependency, I have always obtained the cheapest maps of the latest explorations from Russia. Hence, to charge Russia with hoarding her geographical researches is to award blame where the warmest praise should rather be accorded.

It is, really, thanks to this elaborate mapping of Central Asia by Russia, that that region has become as easy to traverse to-day as any English county. Wherever Russian authority exists, the country is seamed with postal roads, and along these the traveller can journey with facilities for rapid locomotion, and with an immunity from danger, that contrast wonderfully with the condition of things twenty years ago. At that period Central Asia was the scene of anarchy and bloodshed; its markets were full of slaves; the Khanates were ruled over by cruel and treacherous despots; and all the avenues leading to them were terrorised by nomad marauders. Orenburg, which is now a busy manufacturing town, united by railway with the rest of Europe, was then as remote from Russia proper as Tashkent is to-day; the army that is now located in Turkestan was posted then in the districts of Orenburg and Uralsk; and to proceed openly in those days to Khiva and Bokhara was, in the opinion of experts, to invite the martyrdom of Stoddart and Conolly, who had been murdered with every species of indignity and torture at Bokhara in 1842. It was into this Central Asia—not the quiet and pacified province of Turkestan we know it to-day—that Vámbéry tramped his way in rags; and if his sufferings, his dangers, and the distance he traversed on foot be taken into account, it will be admitted, we think, that his journey not only surpasses all the succeeding pioneering exploits we have recorded, but nearly the whole of them put together. Marsh scudded rapidly and pleasantly on horseback through Persia and Afghanistan to India; Valentine Baker's journey was but little more than a hunting trip; Burnaby's ride to Khiva was a bit of every-day travel; Butler, MacGregor, and Grodekoff never lacked food or water, or were at any time exposed to such terrifying danger as, for instance, when Vámbéry stood in front of the Khan of Khiva, while that despot scanned his features to test suspicions which, if confirmed, would have consigned the false dervish to a cruel and agonising death. The only exploit which approaches at all Vámbéry's is MacGahan's thirty days' chase of Kaufmann across the Kirghiz deserts, after which follows O'Donovan's achievement at Merv.

As we have before stated, travellers cannot help it if their exploits are not so dangerous as their admirers would have them be. Every day the world is becoming more and more known, and more and more placed under civilised control. Another twenty years, and the term "explorer" will begin to pass into the category of obsolete words in our language. There will be nothing left for people to explore. Yet a little while, and the "traveller" will become as extinct as the dodo, and tales of adventure will have to be taken from the books of the past instead of those "new books of travel" which the publishers have been sending forth in such a stream the last ten years. Whoever wishes to make his mark as an explorer must set to work at once; if he waits, he will lose his chance for ever.

It is quite possible that there may be a score of other Burnabys, Grodekoffs, and Marshes in Central Asia, but there can never be another Vámbéry, nor yet another O'Donovan. If anyone cared to do it, he could proceed to the shores of the Aral next winter and repeat under similar circumstances what Burnaby did in 1875. But the possibility of repeating or in any way approaching the exploit of Arminius Vámbéry has disappeared from Central Asia altogether. There are no pirates and man-stealers existing now at the south-east corner of the Caspian; there are no Yomood and Tekké marauders left to despoil caravans or bands of pilgrims journeying from the Atrek to Khiva; the unknown desert stretching up to the Oxus has been mapped, and the traveller need have no fear of losing the road and perishing of thirst; half of the desert is traversed by the locomotive, and a month of tramping amidst robber bands is thus avoided; Khiva and Bokhara have become as safe to dwell in as any European city—there are no gougings out of eyes, no skinnings alive, no imprisonment in dank wells with toads and lizards and other nauseous companions, no perpetual slavery in chains to appal the traveller. All these conditions of travel in Vámbéry's time have disappeared, and the man who goes through Central Asia to-day, like the Rev. Mr. Lansdell has recently done, gains no notoriety by it. In the same manner, now that O'Donovan has dispelled the cloud that had hung for more than thirty years over Merv, and the country leading up to the oasis has been surveyed on all sides by the Russians, no reputation is to be made by riding to Merv as O'Donovan did. Really speaking, the only sensational achievement possible at the present moment in Central Asia is for an Englishman to penetrate in disguise to Herat, Cabul, and Balkh. The exploit would be of a highly dangerous character; but the achiever of it could hope for no particular reputation as an explorer, as the geographical features of the country are already well known.

If the exploits of Vámbéry, O'Donovan, and MacGahan transcend those of the other pioneers, most of whom are English military men, there is a feature in connection with the explorations of the latter which we hope will never be lost sight of by our readers. English military men are often spoken of by persons immersed in trade as an encumbrance and burden to the nation, and there are certain manufacturing M.P.'s who are never tired of inveighing against them. Now, the conflict in Central Asia is quite as much a trade conflict as a political one—if not, indeed, more so. The seizure of new markets has been a leading feature in every Russian annexation. We have by us a collection of Russian newspaper cuttings dealing with Central Asia, extending over many years, such as we believe nobody possesses, not even in Russia; and the most frequent argument in these in favour of aggression is, the commercial advantages to be derived by swallowing up the markets lying outside the Russian border. Once a market is annexed, Russia, as is well known, imposes immediately prohibitive duties to keep English produce out of it. Only a year ago a decree was published in Turkestan prohibiting the entry of our goods; the decree not specifying European wares generally, but declaring open war upon our commerce apart from that of other nations, by applying the order exclusively to "English" manufactures. When Captain Terentyieff published a famous book on the Central Asian Question ten years ago, he gave prominence to the feature of trade rivalry by entitling his work "England and Russia and the Conflict for Markets in Central Asia." Thanks to her military successes, Russia has swallowed up all the markets of Central Asia, and is beginning to encroach upon our lucrative and extensive trade with Persia and Afghanistan.

Yet throughout this twenty years' war against our trade in the East, no English manufacturer or merchant has ever spent a penny or sacrificed a moment of his ease on behalf of the interests of his class. If we were to lose India, or were to be temporarily expelled from it, there are thousands of wealthy manufacturers and merchants who would be reduced to beggary. Yet not one of these has ever generously co-operated to fix a limit to Russian aggression, or to obtain a secure outer defence for the interests they personally possess in India. It has been left for the Army, whose interests are relatively insignificant in the East, to send out pioneer after pioneer into Central Asia; and those pioneers have braved danger, exposed themselves to hardships, and spent their money freely to stem the Russian advance and cover trade interests which the traders themselves would not protect. Burnaby and MacGregor; Baker, Marsh, and Gill have performed services to the State unrewarded, which in any other country would have been publicly recognised and recompensed. Nor is the list exhausted with the names of these five officers. Scores might easily and rapidly be enumerated, who have penetrated beyond the Himalayas and the mountain ranges to the east and the west of India, displaying wherever they travelled in unknown Asia the same characteristics, which have rendered the name of Burnaby so dear to every true English heart. If, judging from the past, it would appear to be hopeless to look in the future for patriotism from manufacturers and merchants to protect

England's trading interests in the East, it must be a consolation to reflect that there are plenty of military men keeping vigilant watch over those interests, and plenty ready to sacrifice themselves in their defence in the hour of danger. "From rich men and politicians," said the foremost pioneer mentioned in these articles to the writer three years ago, "I have never received any generous assistance. The help that has sustained me has ever come from the body of the English people." And the truth of this will be admitted by all who know anything of English political life. "I should have given up agitating long ago," once observed an eminent politician to the writer, "if I relied upon the wealthy classes. It has been the letter from the admirer in the masses, with maybe a small donation, representing more to him than thousands to the millionaire, that has been my best support throughout my struggle." And it may be truly said that, after all, there is no reward that can be sweeter to the pioneers who have opened up the wilds of Central Asia, than the consciousness that their achievements are treasured in the memory of many generous minds.

All cannot be Burnabys ; some must stay at home. But the stay-at-homes are in the majority ; and, as votes go, the keeping of the Empire is in their hands. To be proud of that Empire, to insist upon its being Imperially governed, is to minister as much to its glory as to go scouting the enemy on its menaced Eastern borders. Let, then, the patriotic spirit which carried Burnaby to Khiva, and MacGregor to Herat, distinguish us on all occasions when the foreign policy of the Empire appeals for firm, decisive action. Let us exact Imperial rule from a so-called "Imperial" Parliament. Our greatest foes are not the Russians, but the shallowness, ignorance, stupidity, and indifference of our statesmen—those clay idols you and I have worshipped so long, in spite of their muddling and misrule.

By the annexation of Merv, Russia has virtually wiped out Central Asia. Nothing is left now between Russia and India but the two weak states of Persia and Afghanistan, each with a broken, scattered, disunited population very little greater than that of the Metropolis. The Kirghiz steppes, the Khanates of Bokhara, Khiva, and Khokand, the oases of the Turcomans—all have been absorbed, and now the Cossack is face to face with the Afghan. To the Russian the conquest of Central Asia is a glorious page in his history: to the Englishman, the diplomatic campaign against his advance, waged by successive cabinets, excites no other feeling than that of disgust and mortification. If the course of the Central Asian Question affords any criterion of the powers of English statesmen, then there is no other deduction possible than that the imagined wisdom of Parliamentary politicians is a myth, and constitutes no adequate safeguard for the honour of the Empire. We have the largest empire in the world; we have the richest. All the resources the most ambitious sovereign ever sighed for are at the beck of Britannia's sceptre. Possessing all these things, we lack one essential. Our statesmen do not rule our Empire greatly.

The remedy for this rests in our own hands. It is because we ourselves have been indifferent, apathetic, unpatriotic, that we have allowed our honour and our interests to be trifled with by men, capable of talking themselves into office, and fooling themselves out of it, but utterly unfit to sway the destinies of three hundred million people. The English are giants ruled by babies. For their Empire to be governed *as* an Empire, and not as a parish, St. Stephen's must be filled no longer with mere Liberal and Conservative hacks, the frothy scum of successful trade or family influence, but by men who know the Empire well, who love it more than their riches and their life, and who possess the courage and consistency to make it respected throughout the world.

THE END.

3. Colonel Valentine Baker. Left London April 20th, 1873. Returned end of Dec., 1873.

Clouds in the East. Travels and Adventures on the Perso-Turcoman frontier. London, Chatto & Windus, 1876.

4. J. A. MacGahan. Left St. Petersburg March 23rd, 1873. Returned Sept. 1873.

Campaigning on the Oxus and the Fall of Khiva. London, Sampson Low, 1874.

5. Eugene Schuyler. Left St. Petersburg March 23rd, 1873. Returned November 15th, 1873.

Turkistan. Notes of a Journey in Russian Turkistan, Khokand, Bukhara, and Kuldja. London, Sampson Low, 1876

6. David Ker. Left London March 8th, 1873. Date of return not stated.

On the Road to Khiva. London, Henry S. King & Co., 1874.

7. Captain the Hon. G. C. Napier. Left Teheran June 4th, 1874. Returned Dec. 21st, 1874.

LIST OF WORKS

BY OR ABOUT THE CENTRAL ASIAN PIONEERS MENTIONED IN THIS VOLUME.

1. Arminius Vámbéry. Left Teheran March 28th, 1863. Returned to Teheran Jan. 20th, 1864.

Travels in Central Asia. Being the Account of a Journey from Teheran across the Turcoman Desert on the Eastern Shore of the Caspian to Khiva, Bokhara, and Samarcand, performed in the year 1863. London, John Murray, 1864.

Sketches of Central Asia. Additional Chapters on My Travels and Adventures and on the Ethnology of Central Asia. London, W. H. Allen & Co., 1863.

2. Captain Marsh. Left Enzeli, on the Caspian, Sept. 20th, 1872. Arrived at Sukhur, on the Indus, Jan. 10th, 1873.

A Ride through Islam. Being a Journey through Persia and Afghanistan to India *viâ* Meshed, Herat, and Candahar. London, Tinsley Brothers, 1877.